VICTORY

1945

DESMOND MORTON AND J.L. GRANATSTEIN

VICTORY

1945

CANADIANS FROM WAR TO PEACE

A Phyllis Bruce Book
HarperCollins*Publishers*Ltd

For Stanley and Nancy Colbert,
Linda McKnight and Arnold Gosewich,
with thanks

VICTORY 1945: Canadians from War to Peace. Copyright © 1995 by Desmond Morton and J. L. Granatstein. All rights reserved. No part of this book may be used or reproduced in any manner whatsoever without prior written permission except in the case of brief quotations embodied in reviews. For information address HarperCollins Publishers Ltd, Suite 2900, Hazelton Lanes, 55 Avenue Road, Toronto, Canada M5R 3L2.

First Edition

Canadian Cataloguing in Publication Data

Morton, Desmond, 1937-
      Victory 1945 : canadians from war to peace

"A Phyllis Bruce book".
Includes bibliographical references
ISBN 0-00-255069-5

1. Canada – History – 1939-1945.* 2. Canada – History – 1945-1963.* I. Granatstein, J. L., 1939- . II. Title.

FC582.C26 1995   971.063'2   C94-932374-8
F1034.C26 1995

95 96 97 98 99 ❖ RRD 10 9 8 7 6 5 4 3 2 1

Printed and bound in the United States
Photo research: Gena Gorrell
Designed by Andrew Smith
Page composition by Andrew Smith Graphics Inc.

ENDPAPERS: Anxious relatives wait at Montreal's Bonaventure Station for returning servicemen and servicewomen. Despite the signs and sentries, chaos would descend as soon as they spotted their loved ones.

HALF TITLE: Though much of Canada relaxed after VE Day, for people on the west coast there was no peace until Japan surrendered. This was an edition of the Vancouver Sun that was sure to sell out.

OPPOSITE TITLE PAGE: Officers (including the regimental padre on the right) and men of the Royal Regiment of Canada pose at Toronto's Union Station when the regiment finally returned home in November 1945.

TITLE PAGE: Women workers moved into many non-traditional areas of employment during the war. These two technicians, can of oil at the ready, helped service aircraft.

CONTENTS PAGE: A crowd at Toronto's Canadian National Exhibition grounds in the first days of peace watch each other and the camera as a lance-corporal dances with his girlfriend.

CONTENTS

ACKNOWLEDGEMENTS

As always, we have many debts to those who helped us. Cheryl Smith, Dean Oliver, Ernesto Ialongo, and Patrick Nugent helped mightily with the research, while Dr. Jeffrey Keshen allowed us to make use of his pioneering work on wartime black marketeering. Professor Terry Copp, the country's leading expert on the First Canadian Army's role in North-West Europe, kindly read and corrected our drafts. Kathie Hill at Erindale College and Marie-Louise Moreau and Michelle Bess at the McGill Institute for the Study of Canada worked hard to permit Des Morton to make time for writing. Many others provided ideas and memories: Don Matthews, Jocelyn Smith, Susan Glover, Peter Neary, William Kaplan, Chuck Krause, and Norman Hillmer deserve special mention, as do Denis and Shelagh Whitaker, who made the period live for us with their books and conversation. At HarperCollins, Phyllis Bruce was yet again the best of editors. Camilla Jenkins and Raymond Blake did fine photographic research in British Columbia and New Brunswick, while Gena Gorrell, in addition to copy-editing the manuscript most thoroughly, gave yeoman service in finding most of the remaining photographs and illustrations in these pages.

D.P.M. & J.L.G.
December 1994

(Opposite)War production was vital, and propaganda posters spurred workers by equating them with fighting soldiers. Who could dally on a lunch break when the enemy called?

CHAPTER ONE

VE DAY 1945

It was the day that Canadians had awaited for almost six years. It was a day of breathless joy and breath-stopping anxiety as the country escaped from the predictable horrors of war into a peace that, for some, might be even worse. In one Canadian city, it brought a crescendo of destruction that reflected both the passions of war and the fears of peace.

(Above) Schoolchildren showing the flag on VE Day in Whitby, Ont.

(Right) May 8, 1945, came as a great release from the tension of war. The discipline that had kept people going blew away in a wave of riotous emotion.

As usual, the victory was proclaimed first in other capitals—by Prime Minister Winston Churchill in London, and in the flat Missouri accent of President Harry S Truman in Washington. As at the end of the previous war, in 1918, there had been a premature flurry of rejoicing caused by an excitable American correspondent. The rumour had faded fast, but the signs of imminent peace had been unmistakable. German forces in Italy gave up on May 2. On May 3, General Harry Crerar's First Canadian Army was told to hold off on assaults on the German towns of Aurich and Jever. Next day, at the headquarters of Field Marshal Bernard Montgomery's 21st Army Group, German troops from Denmark to Holland capitulated. For Canadians in the region the ceasefire came at 8:00 A.M., May 5.

Negotiations for the formal German surrender began on Sunday night, May 6, at General Dwight D. Eisenhower's headquarters in a school at Rheims in northern France. By 2:41 A.M. on Monday the 7th (or 8:41 P.M. on Sunday, in Montreal and Toronto), grim-faced German commanders, headed by Colonel-General Alfred Jodl, had settled the details and signed the papers.

Ross Parry, reporter for *The Maple Leaf*, the Canadian army newspaper, described the scene. Peace was signed at a

These four officers in the RCAF's Women's Division, delighted at Germany's capitulation, would soon be civilians again; the air force had no use for women once the war was over.

plain wooden table with a cracked top. The pens were Parker's; "What an advertisement," Parry noted. German-made china ashtrays were provided but, for once, no one smoked. The mood was solemn. The people and armed forces of Germany, announced Jodl, "for better or worse were delivered into the victor's hands". (Within a year, Jodl himself would be hanged as a war criminal.) Churchill and Truman were kept informed separately by their officers. The Russians ratified the surrender at Berlin on May 9.

Long before dawn on the 7th, radio flashed the news to North America. Editors and printers had plenty of time to fetch their long-prepared Victory editions.

"UNCONDITIONAL SURRENDER" was the double-decker headline in the *Toronto Daily Star*. Montreal's *La Presse* proclaimed, "FIN DE LA GUERRE". Farther west, the *Calgary Herald* announced, "END COMES TO WAR IN EUROPE". Like other papers, the *Herald* ran a supplement with stock photos of the history of the war. Most papers reminded readers that it had lasted 2,076 days and left 40 million people dead, wounded, or prisoners. Many Canadian papers printed the army's 861st and 862nd official casualty lists, adding 76 killed and 169 wounded to Canada's toll.

In St. John's, Newfoundland, not yet part of Canada, housewife Beatrice Giovanetti

remembered to note the historic moment as 10:30 A.M. She recalled "Lots of amusement, dances at all the clubs. For a time the noise was deafening." A city with church bells, ships' whistles, and plenty of amateur bands could make a lot of noise.

People across Canada got the good news at different hours, because of time zone differences. Many did not hear of the victory until they arrived for work. In Ottawa, government offices stayed closed on May 7 as downtown streets filled with civil servants. Much the same happened in Toronto. It was a grey day with a few thundershowers, but temperatures were in the fifties Fahrenheit (the low teens Centigrade) and there was no pressing reason to go home. Crowds, reported the *Star*'s James Nicol, shouted out versions of "Roll Out the Barrel", "Anchors Away", and "Hail, Hail, the Gang's All Here". "Eight abreast some very pretty women are parading down to the Adelaide corner. One grabs the white-gloved hand of the traffic cop and kisses it as five motorcycles snake by him. . . . Three sailors, their cheeks streaked with lipstick, and two girls on each arm, ankle along like Chief Wahoos." Bell's Toronto office reluctantly confessed that even 800 operators, 250 of them for long-distance calls, could not keep its lines from jamming during the day. True to newspaper convention, reporters checked with local maternity wards. A boy born to Mrs. George O'Brien at Toronto's St. Michael's Hospital, fifty-eight minutes after the announcement, would be christened Victor.

The national celebration of VE Day took place in front of the Parliament Buildings in Ottawa, with bands, parading units of all three services, and thousands of celebrating Canadians. With an election looming, it was a handy reminder of who had led the country to victory.

This Toronto mother (below), with pictures of George VI and her sons in the flag-bedecked windows and a dummy of Hitlerism hanging from her tree, epitomized the mixture of relief and desire for vengeance that moved many.

VE Day in Winnipeg (opposite), at Portage and Main. But if the crowds thought their pocket money would now be their own, they were mistaken; the fund-raising drives continued for the war against Japan.

A girl born elsewhere in the city would be named Victoria.

In Quebec City, Rodrigue Cardinal Villeneuve sang a Te Deum in the basilica for a huge throng. Corporations and department stores respected the feelings of Canada's most devout province by thanking God for the outcome. More cosmopolitan Montreal mixed politics, prayer, joy, and *nationaliste* disapproval. *Le Devoir*'s André Langevin reported that roistering crowds, many of them in khaki, had gathered in passers-by whether they wanted to join or not, and had draped an innocent two-year-old in a British flag. By nightfall, crowds had damaged thirty streetcars and invaded a government liquor store, though they left without stealing the contents.

Vancouver got official word when its sixty-three air-raid sirens issued three long blasts at 7:04 A.M. A constable of the Provincial Police was portrayed awaiting the precise moment as signalled from Ottawa.

In Vancouver, VE Day was celebrated with parades, and these children, with Union Jacks, Red Ensigns, and Chinese flags, seem slightly puzzled by the fuss.

Everywhere, jubilant crowds quit work, spilled into city streets, blocked traffic, and celebrated. For a few hours, Canadians acted like cheerful children, unleashed from all adult conventions. They jumped on the backs of trucks and took lifts on the running-boards of cars. Men and women hugged, kissed, and danced with strangers. The *Vancouver Sun* reported that throngs had packed Hastings, Granville, George, and Main streets, and added, a little caustically, "The bobby sox brigade jitter-bugged with strangers and friends alike and formed snake parades to march from the street and through office buildings." Reporters who visited veterans' hospitals found the patients there more subdued. "The war was over for

"Our Day of Triumph!", as the New Brunswick Telephone Co. termed it, had to be tempered with humility and reverence.

me when I got hit," confessed a wounded trooper at Vancouver's Shaughnessy Hospital. For him and for others, of course, VE Day brought no end to the pain or the disability. Nor, for people on the Pacific coast, was it as easy to imagine that the hostilities were over. Japan was still at war. Vancouver's three Boeing factories did not stop for any holidays. Since the autumn of 1944, they had been helping to build Superfortress bombers to flatten Japanese cities.

In Winnipeg, a throng congregated at Portage and Main. The *Free Press* proclaimed, "WINNIPEG GOES MAD AS GREAT NEWS ANNOUNCED". Prior planning ensured that local public schools performed their custodial role. Students met in assembly, sang approved hymns and the national anthem, and were then set to colouring outline flags of countries in the new United Nations.

This is our day of Victory
OUR DAY OF TRIUMPH!

Waited for so long . . . prayed for so earnestly. Purchased at such frightful cost against overwhelming odds . . . and paid for with the blood of our bravest sons.

TODAY NAZI GERMANY LIES IN RUINS—TOMORROW JAPAN

With deep humility, therefore, let us remember to offer reverent thanks to Almighty God and—

to seek His blessing and guidance in our places of worship and in our homes that we may be enabled to complete the immense tasks that still lie ahead.

THE NEW BRUNSWICK TELEPHONE CO. LIMITED

Canada in 1945 was an overtly Christian country, and Quebec was not the only province where devout thanks were offered. Calgary Power offered a full-page tribute to women and children. "We must keep the faith," it instructed, as had Bernadette of Lourdes. In a nation-wide advertisement, Eaton's urged prayers of thanksgiving on a victorious but humble nation.

———— •••• ————

Overseas, Canadians on leave in London joined the frenzied rejoicing, but there was no repetition of November 11, 1918, when Canadians had built a bonfire next to Nelson's column in Trafalgar Square; the flame-blackened vestiges were still visible. At a Canadian detention barracks in Headley, prisoners rioted when refused a celebratory issue of cigarettes. A hundred of them rushed the guards, threw blankets over the barbed wire, and scattered into the Hampshire and

These Canadian infantrymen gamely muster a VE Day cheer for the official camera, but front-line troops of all nations, exhausted by the struggle, felt only relief that the killing had ceased.

17

Surrey countryside. Armed troops hunted them down and took them to Reading prison.

Although the end of the war in Europe had caught almost no one by surprise, there was less celebrating close to the fighting and dying, and none at all near the front lines. For almost a year, the Germans had been forced back on every front. A German army plot in the summer of 1944 had come close to toppling the Nazi regime. But the Germans had fought with unexpected determination to defend a hopeless cause. The Allied insistence on unconditional surrender had steeled doubters to new resistance. So had the fear of vengeance from a rampaging and ruthless Red Army. "Being on German soil at the time," Joseph Dane, a Canadian infantry soldier, remembered, "orders were no fraternizing with German troops or people. It made sense. Our only thought was that our enemy in front of us knew it was the end for them." Most soldiers recalled an intense relief that their lives had been restored to them. A few even managed to get drunk. Most, sleep-starved, looked forward to a long, uninterrupted rest. The sense of relief took time to sink in. "It was like getting a million-dollar cheque," one soldier recalled, "shoving it in your pocket, and forgetting about it." Some soldiers wondered whether their tough, resilient enemy would continue the fighting beyond the official ceasefire.

Later, armchair strategists argued that VE Day should have come six months earlier, in November, as it had in the previous war. Hundreds of thousands of men and women, among them many Canadians, would have lived, instead of dying in battle or in Hitler's hideous concentration camps. But history is full of meaningless might-have-beens. Victory in Europe had come as the Allied leaders had promised at the Casablanca conference in 1942—unconditionally, with American, British, and Soviet armies meeting on German soil, and Nazi resistance utterly crushed.

In the absence of William Lyon Mackenzie King, who was representing Canada at the founding conference of the United Nations in San Francisco, J.L. Ilsley, the Nova Scotia–born Minister of Finance, was acting prime minister. True to the new wartime practice of governments regulating just about anything, he and his Cabinet colleagues had already planned what Canada would do when victory was announced. No one could tell when the actual news might arrive, but the next day would be proclaimed an official holiday for Victory in Europe, or "VE" Day. The following Sunday would be observed as a national day of prayer. From the U.N. meeting, CBC recording equipment helped Mackenzie King urge his fellow Canadians to show their gratitude for victory by subscribing even more generously to the Eighth Victory Loan.

Under these orders from Ottawa, provincial and municipal authorities made their plans for May 8. Toronto's new mayor, Robert Saunders, announced that the city's taverns could decide whether or not to stay open on the day when the news arrived, but on VE Day they must certainly be closed. So would businesses and municipal offices, though city parks would be available for dignified rejoicing. Across Canada, most officials echoed Saunders' example. Winnipeg's Mayor Garnet Coulter announced a VE Day ceremony at the Legislature with himself, Premier Stuart Garson, and the lieutenant-governor, the Honourable R.F. McWilliams, delivering speeches, the Anglican archbishop

Enlistments and Losses

I. Enrolment in the Canadian Armed Forces during the Second World War

Service	Men	Women	TOTAL
Royal Canadian Navy	99,396	7,126	**106,522**
Canadian Army			
General Service	609,128		
NRMA	99,407		
Canadian Women's Army Corps		21,624	**730,159**
Royal Canadian Air Force	232,195	17,467	**249,662**
Nursing Services		4,439	**4,439**
TOTAL	**1,040,126**	**50,656**	**1,090,782**

Male population, 18-45	2,474,000
Percentage of intake to male population 18–45	42.04

Source: Directorate of History, Department of National Defence and C.P. Stacey, *Arms, Men and Governments*, Appendix "R", p. 590

II. Canadian Military Casualties, 1939-1945

Service	Battle Fatalities	Non-Battle Dead	TOTAL	Wounded or Injured	Prisoners of war
RCN	1,533	491	**2,024**	319	87
Army	17,682	5,235	**22,917**	52,679	6,433
RCAF	13,498	3,603	**17,101**	1,416	2,475
TOTAL	**32,713**	**9,329**	**42,042**	**54,414**	**8,995**

Source: Directorate of History, Department of National Defence

V-E Day — Drumheller Alta
— Vogue Studio —

Small towns across the land celebrated too. In Drumheller, Alta., Great War vets marched at the head of the VE Day parade while the townsfolk lined up to cheer.

and a United Church minister limited to prayers, and Rabbi Solomon Frank reading scripture. War-weary Canadians, exhausted from years of overtime labour and constant patriotic appeals to do more for the war effort, had surely earned a day off. Daily horse-drawn deliveries of milk, bread, and ice of course continued. Employees in those services could hope for a holiday at some other time.

In cities such as Halifax, Kingston, Brandon, or Calgary, with a share of Canada's hugely expanded army, navy, and air force, part of the plan for VE Day was a municipal parade. It was the instinctive response of

service commanders and municipal officials alike to any celebration. In peace or war, reservists and militia—and their bands in dress uniforms—were a normal part of the entertainment. The day of victory was no exception. For a boy in Saint John, New Brunswick, May 8, 1945 meant standing at an upstairs window of the leading local department store, Manchester, Robertson, Alison, trying to get to the railing through the close-pressed bodies of adults for a glimpse of the sights below. He failed, but it was almost certainly better than being in school. Most Canadians slept in; many went to the movies. *National Velvet*, with Elizabeth Taylor and Mickey Rooney, opened that week across Canada. So did Humphrey Bogart and Lauren Bacall in *To Have and Have Not*, and Edward G. Robinson and Joan Bennett in *The Woman in the Window*, "so suspenseful that no one is allowed in during the last five minutes—and please don't discuss the ending." Others went to the big dance halls, a feature of most cities, large towns, and resorts. "Sentimental Journey" was a hit that spring, as was a nonsense song, "Mairsy d'oats and doasy d'oats/ And little lambs eat ivy". Farm families—and 28 per cent of Canadians still lived on the land—could have reminded city-dwellers that feeding mares, lambs, and other animals took hard work, and VE Day was no holiday for them, either.

Like any holiday, celebrations were marred by accidents. In Charlottetown, a truck in the victory procession caught a nine-year-old boy's clothing and crushed him to death under its wheels. Norman Madsen, a 14-year-old in Nanaimo, tried to open a mortar bomb with a pair of pliers and demolished himself and his home. His parents were out at the time. Tom Donaldson, a former Toronto policeman, lost a thumb and finger when he picked up a firecracker that had not gone off—and it did. Hyman Caplan suffered a fractured skull after an argument with three sailors.

Some Canadians ignored the holiday and behaved as usual. Confident of imminent gains in the 1945 federal election, the British Columbia Co-operative Commonwealth Federation celebrated VE Day by expelling H. W. Herridge, the angular and wilful "Squire of the Kootenays", for ignoring party policy once again. In Nelson, thirteen Doukhobors paraded naked to protest enforced schooling, and the provincial attorney-general ordered them arrested. In Toronto, thieves took advantage of the holiday to steal a safe from the Hertz Driv-Ur-Self—after years of rationing, the gasoline coupons were more valuable than the day's cash. In nearby Hamilton, a near riot was averted when police asked a restaurant owner to open his premises to hungry celebrants; a thief promptly stole $10 from the till.

In Calgary, VE Day was overshadowed by memories of the wild dust-storm that had disrupted a Victory Bond show on May 5. Twelve thousand people had gone scurrying for safety as winds smashed sets and sent planks whirling into the air, and singer-dancer George Murphy had been drowned out by screams of panic. Another tragedy followed on May 11, when *F for Freddie*, a British Mosquito fighter-bomber, crashed midway through another Victory Bond show. Its RAF crew, Flight Lieutenant Maurice Briggs and Flying Officer John Baker, had survived 107 missions over Europe in the powerful plywood aircraft, and they had come to Canada as part of the Victory Bond drive. In Montreal, Toronto, and Winnipeg, they had been interviewed and photographed as befitted unassuming celebrities. Baker dreamed of a little farm in Kent; Briggs announced, "I'd like to meet a real nice Irish girl in Canada and settle down to a life of quiet." Briggs had trained at Calgary, one of thousands in the British Commonwealth Air Training Plan. There he and Baker died, flying low at 400 miles an hour when a wingtip caught a weathervane on top of a hangar. No one ever needed to die that way.

Some people had little to celebrate. In fifteen camps across Canada, 33,843 German prisoners of war were paraded and presented the news. So were 421 Japanese Canadians, the presumed hard core of the 21,000 British Columbians "evacuated for their own safety" in 1942. Urged on by editorials and letters from across Canada demanding expulsion of the "Japs", Ottawa planned to pressure Japanese Canadian evacuees to return to a devastated country some of them had never seen. Ottawa forgot to mention that, with victory secure, German prisoners of war would not be fed quite as well—they would receive more liver, kidney, and heart in their meat ration, fewer oranges, and 300 calories less a day. With the war over, neither the Geneva Convention nor fears of reprisals against the 7,500 Canadian prisoners still in German hands deterred authorities from showing a little home-front toughness.

Some Canadians had more philosophical reasons to spurn the collective rejoicing. In Quebec, unlike Cardinal Villeneuve, conservative *nationalistes* had never been very keen on the war. Their favourite organ, Montreal's *Le Devoir,* viewed the victory demonstrations with disdain and reminded its readers of that enigmatic ancient statue, the Victory of Samothrace. Was there any reason to celebrate victory, asked editorialist Pierre Vigeant. Hadn't the war begun in 1939 to defend Poland? And wasn't that country now in ruins, robbed of half its territory by the Soviet Union, with the other half ruled by a Soviet-nominated government? The United Nations, as the Allies had called themselves, had made war against a totalitarian regime that threatened to impose its hegemony on all of Europe. What else could be said of Stalin's regime? If anything, the situation in 1945 was infinitely worse:

> *Le nazisme est mort avec Hitler, l'impérialisme allemand est réduit à l'impuissance; le communisme sort du conflit plus fort que jamais; l'impérialisme russe soutenue par l'armée rouge victorieuse, est en train de s'entourer de toute une couronne d'états vassaux et ménacer même l'indépendance des grandes nations européennes.*

(Nazism has died with Hitler, German imperialism is reduced to impotence; Communism emerges from the conflict stronger than ever; Russian imperialism, sustained by the victorious Red Army, is about to surround itself with a ring of vassal states and even to menace the independence of the great European nations.)

All that could be done, Vigeant concluded, was to pray for the special intervention of Providence to grant an era of peace.

———•·•———

VE Day in one Canadian city was different.

As peace in Europe approached, Halifax made its plans as did other communities. Mayor Allan G. Butler's proclamation, like Mayor Saunders', closed the city's businesses and summoned citizens to share the excitement of a military parade and a modest fireworks display. As elsewhere, as news of peace spread, offices, stores, and restaurants closed. Wary storekeepers hammered sheets of plywood over their plate-glass windows. City police, gathered in their cramped underground station, hoped there would be no trouble; a few score of ageing men were not prepared to take on the navy.

Meanwhile, throngs of servicemen and servicewomen joined the celebrants on downtown streets. As a release from cramped messdecks and spartan barracks, naval officers announced "open gangways"; seamen off duty were free to come and go—but to what? When the big canteen at the naval dockyard HMCS *Stadacona* closed at 9:00 P.M. on Monday night, celebrating sailors poured south towards downtown Halifax. They found the city closed down; even the usual bootleggers were out of sight. A liquor store on the way to town was an easy mark, and two others soon followed. So

THE PROVINCES

Newfoundland

Newfoundland was "the province that got away". Its delegates had been present in Quebec in 1864 when Confederation was born, but once back on the island they hadn't been able to sell the idea to St. John's merchants and their outport dependents. In 1894, with the island finances in a desperate state, Newfoundland had been ready to join, but its price had been too high for a depression-ridden Canada. The same thing happened in 1934: Ottawa looked at a government that took in only $8 million and spent $11 million, half of it in interest on a $100 million debt. Then it shut its eyes and left the British to take over, with a six-member, unelected Commission of Government, ruthless belt-tightening, and near-starvation in the outports.

But by 1945 Newfoundland's economy was riding high. Even in the late 1930s, markets had been growing eager for its fish, lumber, and pulp. Wartime made all these even more valuable, and added demand for iron ore from the rich Wabana deposits. Canadian sailors, American airmen, and troops from both countries arrived with lots of spending money, creating a huge market for barracks, supplies, and every kind of recreation. The island treasury boasted a $22 million surplus.

Newfoundlanders had never known such wealth.

Would it last? British experts thought not. A.P. Herbert, an MP, called Newfoundland "about the most complicated puzzle in the whole imperial scene". Lord Ammon, a Labour peer, proposed a big British grant, letting Newfoundlanders elect three members of the Commission of Government, and a ten-year plan to build schools, social services, and resources; in return, Britain would get the resources of Labrador and the strategic wartime bases at Gander, Goose Bay, and Stephenville.

But Canada had not forgotten Newfoundland. Nor had Quebec. In 1926 that province had lost a long court battle for Labrador, which was judged to belong to Newfoundland. In June 1945, Maurice Duplessis demanded the territory as a reward for Quebec's war effort. The vast expanses of Labrador were a tempting prize; during the war, Ottawa had felt it necessary to send in troops and a major-general to Newfoundland, less to fend off a German invasion than to match the U.S. presence there. Americans might be friends, but Mackenzie King suspected that they had larcenous tendencies towards other people's territory.

At the end of 1945, Newfoundlanders learned the good news: Britain's postwar Labour government would let them vote on their future through a fifty-member national convention. "Best guess," *Time* magazine assured its readers: "a start on the long road back to full self-governing Dominion status...." History would turn out differently.

---

was one of the city's undersized trams, a standard target for naval scorn. Commandeered by a few adventurous sailors, it raced tipsily along the tracks, avoiding mayhem by inches until it crashed into a shop front.

Monday night's destructive rampage was the worst Halifax had experienced during the war, but at least it was comparable to previous pay-night celebrations. What happened the next day was not. While naval, military, and air force detachments formed up for the city's victory parade, and service chiefs gathered with municipal leaders at the Garrison Grounds to receive the appropriate salutes, the gangways remained open. Three thousand sailors, and smaller contingents from the other services, headed for the city centre. This time, revelry swiftly turned to destruction and looting. Fuelled by stocks from shattered government liquor stores and Keith's Brewery, cheered on by civilians eager to share in the spoils, a uniformed mob poured down Barrington Street, demolishing stores and restaurants. Alec Lomas, son of the manager of the Birks store, worked feverishly with his father and staff to move valuables to the safe. Then, as the display window shattered and the crowd tore the big brass Bs from the front door, Major Lomas sent his family fleeing for safety. Within minutes, the shop was ransacked.

Having done nothing to give their men alternative entertainment, the service chiefs seemed stunned by the disorder. Outnumbered and frightened, the navy's shore patrols had been as ineffective as the city police, and worse armed. Policy forbade issuing them even truncheons, and word-of-mouth instructions ordered them to ignore what they could not handle. Rear-Admiral Leonard W. Murray, Commander-in-Chief, Canadian Northwest Atlantic, shrugged off warnings and early reports; police matters were not his business. When he grasped the reality of a widespread riot, he ordered that the seamen summoned for the parade be marched into the affected area to restore discipline. Their ranks simply dissolved into the mob. When the beer supply ran out in the *Stadacona* wet canteen, angry sailors smashed the place and headed out to join the riot.

In the afternoon, Murray and Mayor Butler were reduced to cruising city streets in a

Soon Keith's Brewery was looted, and the liquor began to flow.

sound truck, pleading with the crowds to go home. Army and air force commanders got better marks from civic officials. Brigadier R.G. White of Military District No. 6 summoned troops from Debert and Aldershot. Air Vice-Marshal A.L. Morfee ordered airmen confined to their stations. Though 41 soldiers, 19 airmen, and 34 sailors were among the 211 indicted for riot offences, the navy took most of the blame for $5 million in devastation. Admiral Murray added to the fire by insisting that local civilians had done most of the looting. Official Halifax never forgave him, or the critics from "Upper Canada" who blamed Haligonians for inspiring the riot by their wartime greed and VE Day indifference.

"Why?" a Halifax optician scrawled in let-

CWACs did their own "liberating"; these two carry a case of port along with the celebratory Stars and Stripes.

ters a foot high on his wrecked storefront.

Halifax had been closer to the war than any other Canadian town. From 1939, it had been the anonymous "East Coast port" where hundreds of convoys had formed up and sailed for Britain. Its magnificent harbour had been home to most of Canada's hugely expanded wartime navy, now the third largest in the world. Nowhere had the war brought more social dislocation. A cramped, impoverished city of 65,000 had had to find room for 55,000 more people. Thousands of sailors, soldiers, and airmen had crowded into forts, barracks, an air base, and a dozen different naval establishments. When they could, servicemen brought their families to Halifax, but rental accommodation, scarce and miserable in quality, was beyond the means of even destroyer captains earning $5 a day. Even the city's prostitutes, with their informal local trademark of white rubber boots, had to do most of their work in darkened alleys.

Seamen found wartime Halifax a grim, prim exile, although local people did their best to be hospitable to the influx of homesick outsiders. Many women performed war work as volunteers at canteens and opened their homes to lonely sailors. The YMCA, the Salvation Army, the Knights of Columbus, and the Merchant Seamen's Club all did what they could, but for a sailor earning less than a dollar a day and spending his service crammed into a fetid messdeck, a clean bed in a private room was a luxury beyond financial reach. At the Ajax Club, sailors could relax over a magazine and beer. Then a neighbouring church insisted that the club be closed, and the only place a serviceman could get a legal drink was the barnlike, men-only wet canteen at the dockyard. Government liquor stores shut down at noon on

The result of resentment at the city's lack of amenities, too much alcohol, and mob rule was the looting and destruction of much of downtown Halifax. "Is Justice Wasted on Germans?" the placard asked on this looted store, but shopkeepers wondered if justice would ever see them recompensed for their wrecked businesses.

Saturday. Haligonians might see their city as "The Warden of the North"; sailors complained that it was a cold, snobbish place, eager only for their money.

With plenty of other problems to preoccupy them, officials far away in Ottawa had never considered a crash program to expand the local housing stock. In the first four years of the war, only 776 new houses were built in Halifax. Local business prudently refused to expand to serve thousands of customers who would vanish as soon as peace broke out. Nothing in the navy's British traditions said that it had much responsibility for its men's recreation and welfare. Even the famous "Navy Show", with its variety acts, was an afterthought; its best song, John Pratt's doleful lament "You'll Get Used to It", was not entirely true.

The VE Day riot got a faster response than all these wartime miseries. With a federal election in progress, the acting prime minister was on the scene in hours with the promise of an immediate inquiry and prompt low-interest loans for wrecked businesses. Mr. Justice Roy Kellock of the Supreme Court of Canada arrived to investigate. So did Admiral Murray's

THE PROVINCES

Nova Scotia

For Nova Scotia 1945 was an election year, but no one doubted the outcome. Since Confederation, Nova Scotians had only given power to the Tories in 1878, 1925, and 1930, and it would not happen again in 1945. Summoned to Ottawa for a wartime stint as navy minister and regional voice in the Cabinet, Angus L. Macdonald had now returned; his ancient caretaker, A.S. MacMillan, could retire with confidence. Whether it was the Gaelic or the immense dignity he brought to the small change of patronage politics, Angus L. was unbeatable. Before the word was debased, he gave "charisma" a rare significance.

Nova Scotians faced the peace with great anxiety. Halifax's huge grain elevator, with its capacity of 2.25 million bushels, had sat mostly empty since its construction in 1925. The war had filled it, but who could now afford Canada's grain—or Nova Scotia's apples? And would there even be apples to sell? Winter frosts had cut the crop to a quarter of the normal, 50,000 barrels,

and Japanese beetles—caricatured with buck teeth and a Rising Sun flag—threatened the rest.

Of course, Nova Scotians had a scapegoat for their plight: Confederation. They also had a solution: secession. Alone among the provinces, its legislature had once voted to split with Canada—in 1886—and in March of 1945 industry minister Harold J. Connolly revived the cry. "We have tried the constitutional method of sending representatives to the Federal Parliament. It has not been a striking success," explained Connolly. "So let us say to Canadians, after the peace bells have rung, something like this: We are just as good Canadians as you are; we have just as much concern for the welfare of Canada [but] from now on, unless the tariff policies of Canada are so arranged as to give Nova Scotia an even break, we intend to keep more of our money in Nova Scotia. From now on we intend to work out for Nova Scotia the destiny for which she was intended."

As usual, the election ended the talk. Angus L. took 53 per cent of the votes and 28 of 30 seats. The CCFers, who doubled their vote from 7 to 13 per cent, got both the opposition seats, and the luckless Conservatives, with 34 per cent of the vote, got no seats at all. And, for lack of overseas buyers, Nova Scotia's once-thriving apple industry died.

---

old enemy, Vice-Admiral George "Jetty" Jones, the Chief of Naval Staff. Murray, the uncharismatic commander of Canada's share of the Battle of the Atlantic, was quietly relieved of his command and discreetly loaded with responsibility for the riot. Wartime commanders could take note: gratitude for the brass was not high on Canada's postwar agenda.

Nova Scotia's VE Day riots were not limited to Halifax. In Kentville, soldiers from nearby Aldershot smashed the windows in the local liquor store. At Sydney on Cape Breton Island, celebrants battled police and firemen

until 4:00 A.M. on Tuesday morning. At New Waterford, troops and RCMP arrived to help local police after mobs of youngsters looted the main street. Afterwards, the disturbances were blamed on pent-up spirits and understaffed, overaged police forces. They were also the result of social tensions in a province where the extremes of wealth and poverty were painfully visible. They were a symptom of anger at what had happened during the war years, and of fear of what might follow.

For over a million men and women from a population of 12 million Canadians, the war had meant service in the navy, the army, or the air force; for 105,451 of them, it had also brought death, wounds, or captivity. For their families, the war had meant anxiety and sometimes heartbreak. For some, army pay and allowances had provided unusual economic security; for most it had meant a shrunken standard of living, the burden of single parenthood, living under the same roof as in-laws or parents. Canadians faced regulations, rationing, new taxes, and an endless barrage of directives, appeals, and invitations to sacrifice for the national war effort.

Yet, for an unmeasured majority of Canadians, the war years had been the best time they had known. Instead of the dwindling wages and the hopeless prospects of the Depression years, there had been work and wages for all. Some had held two or even three jobs, with all the overtime hours they could wish. Even with soaring taxes and compulsory savings directed into the endless series of Victory Bonds, most people found themselves with more money than they could possibly spend. Who could buy or even repair a home when any available construction materials were channelled to build camps and barracks? In the 1914–18 war, buying a car had been proof that someone was prospering: registrations tripled from 45,000 to 157,000. By 1941 the last car a civilian could buy had rolled off the line, and by 1942 new tires were simply unavailable. The factories that would have produced refrigerators, stoves, and big new cabinet radios were too busy turning out Bren guns for the army, radar sets for the navy, and wireless sets for Canada's Soviet allies.

Did VE Day mean that the time of prosperity was coming to an end? Were the civilian looters who pillaged Halifax stores seizing the last opportunity in their lives to gain something from the war? Or would postwar Canada really be different?

———·•·———

For the moment, of course, nothing much changed. News reports revelled in the humiliation of Hitler's officials and dwelt, more cautiously, on the horrors of his regime. In the Pacific, the distant and sometimes half-forgotten war with Japan continued. Officials hastened to remind Canadians that a forest of regulations remained in place. Adults, warned the Department of Labour, must still carry their registration cards. Gasoline rationing would remain in effect; people must not waste their tiny supply in hope of an imminent flood. Materials for home construction and repair seemed scarcer than ever. "The main trouble is, we can't get men to go into the foundries," explained Toronto plumbing wholesaler Roy Belyea. "In addition, copper and brass are still on the prohibited list. . . ."

What would Canadians ask of their country after the war? Had the fighting raised the country's ideals along with its national income? Had the revealed power of government to mobilize a tremendous national effort changed people's expectations? To the horror of the Canadian Chamber of Commerce, barely 45 per cent of the people it polled in 1944 still backed unfettered free enterprise. More favoured socialized ownership and a mixed economy. Other newfangled opinion polls suggested that Canadians wanted national health insurance, full employment, and a role in keeping the world at peace.

It remained to be seen if such ideas would outlive the war.

CHAPTER TWO

EARNING A VICTORY

Victory came in 1945, but it did not come at once. For Canadians in uniform, some of the worst fighting took place in that year, and almost eight thousand of them would die before the war ended.

(Left) These Canadian soldiers, moving out by train for overseas, get a taste of their new life—not quite the way Mother used to make it.

(Above) One of the toughest soldiers produced by the Canadian army was Brigadier Jean Allard, an officer who led from the front. Here he briefs two officers of the Fort Garry Horse before that famous regiment moved its tanks across the Oranje Canal in mid-April 1945.

31

From Vancouver to Brussels, 127 days earlier, bleary-eyed Canadians had greeted 1945. It was the sixth New Year's Eve of the war and it simply had to be the last. Yet buried behind the local news of municipal elections, fresh shortages of fuel, butter, and meat, and road-choking blizzards was evidence that the Germans were still fighting hard. A few days earlier, Hitler's generals had launched their offensive through the hilly, forested Ardennes, where Belgium, France, and Germany met. Censors could not hide all the bad news: American divisions had reeled back from the German armoured thrust. At a town called Bastogne, a tough U.S. airborne division had been rushed in to plug the gap. Instead, the division was virtually cut off. Its general answered a German surrender demand with one printable word: "Nuts." His bravado was about all the Allies could boast of that day.

At dawn on New Year's Day, the Germans sent another surprise. More than one sleepy Canadian soldier came to life as a German fighter flashed past the window of his Belgian billet, guns blazing. Confident of Allied hangovers and overconfidence, the *Luftwaffe* had scrambled to find 800 fighters and bombers to strafe British and Canadian airfields across Belgium. By 8:00 A.M., columns of black, oily smoke rose against the wintry sky. In an

Convoys were fat targets for U-boat wolf packs as long as Allied air cover was unable to stretch across the entire North Atlantic. At last, long-range Liberator bombers filled the gap, and by late 1943 the tide had turned in the Battle of the Atlantic.

hour and a half, the *Luftwaffe* had wiped out 144 Allied aircraft and damaged 84 more.

———◆———

For the first three years, the war news had been dreadful. From September 1939 to April 1940, the British and French armies had waited, trained, and worried while the Germans crushed Poland, built Balkan alliances, and prepared for a fresh *Blitzkrieg*, or "lightning war", in the west. In April, after the Germans struck suddenly at Denmark and Norway, British attempts to help the Norwegians were crushed by Nazi airpower. On May 10, 1940, that power spearheaded a fierce armoured advance through the same Ardennes that would ring with battle five years later. Shattered, demoralized, the Allied armies broke apart. The British rescued their survivors from the beaches at Dunkirk. In an effort to save

(Opposite, above) RCAF WDs relax in barracks at St. Hubert, Quebec, in March 1942. Military life was closed to women until wartime necessity forced all three services to open their doors. The tough work women did, in virtually all non-combat positions, would change the way they saw themselves.

(Below) Merchant seamen had to be lucky to be rescued in the cold Atlantic. These crewmen from the British ships Ashantian *and* Wanstead *made it to St. John's, Nfld., in April 1943 and soon were back at sea.*

France, Britain even sent green Canadian troops to Britanny, only to bring them back without most of their valuable equipment. Confident of Hitler's triumph, Benito Mussolini chose the moment not only to attack a beleaguered France but to claim the Mediterranean as an Italian lake. By the end of June 1940, only Britain and her dominions stood against Germany and her Axis allies.

A *Luftwaffe* blitz of London and other British cities should have been followed by an invasion. Instead, Hitler switched his forces eastward to invade the Soviet Union in June 1941. Despite easy victories and millions of Soviet prisoners, a bitter winter and the vast expanse of terrain stopped the *Blitzkrieg* into Russia. When it resumed in 1942, huge numbers, better equipment than they had lost, and stoic courage again helped the Red Army contain the Nazi assault.

Almost everywhere, the war went well for

The political and military leaders of the Anglo-American alliance—with Mackenzie King in the picture only as their host—met twice at Quebec City to plan strategy. This first important meeting, in 1943, plotted the invasion of France; the second, a year later, prepared strategy for the war against Japan.

Hitler. At sea, German u-boats hunting in packs seemed to sink Allied shipping at will. Stretched by worldwide commitments, Britain's Royal Navy needed Canadian help in the North Atlantic. Until 1943, the tiny corvettes of a hurriedly expanded Canadian navy had sunk only four enemy submarines; given their obsolescent equipment and ill-trained crews, the poor showing was no surprise. Only the Allied bomber offensive actually made Germans suffer some of the misery they had brought on the rest of Europe, and that at a brutal cost in bombers and flyers.

The best news during those dreary years

was that Japan's unheralded attack on Pearl Harbor, on December 7, 1941, had brought the enormous might of the United States into the war. Though the Americans went to war to avenge what President Roosevelt called "a day of infamy", their first objective would be to destroy Hitler. That would take time. Americans were almost as ill prepared for war as Canada had been in 1939. Throughout the first five months of 1942, American power was humiliated, from Wake Island to Bataan. Japanese planes and ships sank both the American and the British Far East fleets. That made the fall of Hong Kong inevitable, but no one expected the surrender of the British and Australian army in Malaya and Singapore, or the capture of General Douglas MacArthur's army in the Philippines. Australians, who had sent hundreds of thousands to share in Britain's wars, found that Britain had nothing left to help them as Japanese forces drove south as far as New Guinea and Melanesia and sent bombers to devastate Darwin. They would not forget that only the Americans could spare troops to defend them.

Then, almost unnoticed, the tide turned. In November 1942, at El Alamein, not far from the gates of Cairo, the much-battered British Eighth Army had broken the Italian and German line. By early 1943, Germany's Afrika Korps had abandoned its Italian allies in full flight. In General Montgomery, Britain had found a match for Germany's brilliant General Erwin Rommel. An eccentric figure with two badges in his beret and a thick woollen sweater, Monty liked to gather his citizen-soldiers around him so that they could see who was giving the orders and why.

(Left) Canada's army produced some great leaders. Bert Hoffmeister, a pre-war militiaman and the commanding officer of Vancouver's Seaforth Highlanders in mid-1943, soon became the country's best division commander. His mighty 5th Canadian Armoured Division created a proud record in Italy and the Netherlands.

(Right) Once in action, soldiers lost any sense of war's glamour. For these infantrymen in Italy in May 1944, war was sore feet, heavy packs, unrelenting tension, and moments of unspeakable terror.

The Cape Breton Highlanders baseball team of May 1944, at an Italian rest camp.
Within days, these men would be going into action against the Hitler Line south of Rome,
one of the Canadians' great victories in Italy.

Far more important than El Alamein, though few Canadians knew it in 1943, was a hard-won struggle between Hitler and the Soviet Union. At Stalingrad, on the Volga River, an entire German army—twenty-two divisions—had been surrounded in September. In December, 80,000 starving, frozen Axis survivors gave up; 850,000 Germans, Italians, Hungarians, and Romanians had died. Hitler's reputation as a master tactician, buoyed by ruthlessness and luck, collapsed. Now Nazi propagandists had to feed their people accounts of smashing Axis victories that, oddly enough, pushed ever closer to Berlin.

In the summer of 1943, Canadian soldiers joined Montgomery's Eighth Army for the invasion of Sicily and the struggle up the long, mountainous boot of Italy. The Canucks soon discovered that, in the blood and rain and mud of warfare, there was little honour and no glory. Still, like their fathers in 1914–18, they also learned that with courage, common sense, plenty of artillery, and lots of young lives, they could drive German defenders from the Hitler Line and Ortona, liberating Rome on June 4. In Russia, titanic forces of tanks, artillery, and infantry engaged in huge battles that few in the West ever understood. They ended with the *Wehrmacht*'s Central Army Group surrounded and destroyed.

On the other side of Europe, an even bigger battle began. On D-Day—June 6, 1944—thousands of Allied soldiers, among

D-Day put the Allies back into France, four years after Dunkirk. These infantrymen from the 3rd Canadian Division were crammed into their landing craft in the final moments before the assault.

them a division of Canadians, hit the Normandy beaches. By the time the first frail toe-hold had become a full-blown second front, Canada had three divisions and an armoured brigade in France, and the two infantry divisions had suffered heavier losses than any British division.

With General Eisenhower, a steady Kansan, as supreme allied commander, and General Montgomery in charge of the 21st Army Group, General Crerar's First Canadian Army fought its way along the Channel coast. British patrols found the huge Belgian port of Antwerp intact but, before Montgomery could seize the estuary, the Germans had fortified the approaches to the city. Lacking Antwerp as a port for supplies, the Allies were stalled. Without much help from tanks or other tools of war, Canadian infantry faced flooded fields, narrow dikes, and an enemy fighting for its life. It took five miserable weeks and 6,367 casualties, but the Canadians cleared the approaches; Antwerp could receive ships.

By early 1943, Allied victory was already assured. That was the year when Canadians finally contributed a serious share to the Allied war effort on land, in the air, and at sea. At the darkest moment of the Battle of the Atlantic, in the spring of 1943, Canadian escort vessels were gradually taken out of the fight. For lack of trained crews and high-quality equipment, they had been little more than a nuisance. At last they got the training and the electronic gear that would make them a threat to enemy submarines. When

Soon after H-Hour at Bernières-sur-Mer, the Canadians were ashore in force. Carrying the bicycles that some staff genius had thought would speed the advance inland, infantrymen debarked and struggled through the surf to French soil. The bicycles were instantly ditched.

SOME MEMORABLE DATES AND HEADLINES

WITH CANADIAN FORCES IN FRANCE
THE **MAPLE LEAF**

AUGUST 8th 1944 — **Canadian Army Now In Normandy**
AUG. 9 — **Large Canadian Attack Launched**
AUG. 21 — **Falaise-Argentan Gap Now Closed**
AUG. 24 — **Paris Is Liberated by the Maquis**
AUG. 26 — **British and Canucks Race to Seine**
SEPT. 2 — **CANADIANS COME BACK TO DIEPPE BATTLEGROUND**
SEPT. 4 — **British And Yanks Now In Belgium**
SEPT. 7 — **Allied Patrols Enter Germany**
SEPT. 21 — **CANADIAN TROOPS CAPTURE BOULOGNE**
SEPT. 30 — **TRUCE LETS CIVILIANS LEAVE CALAIS**
OCT. 12 — **CANADIANS CUT SCHELDT ESCAPE ROUTE**
OCT. 23 — **Canadians Put Squeeze on Breskens Pocket**
OCT. 30 — **Canadians link up on South Beveland**
NOV. 2 — **Walcheren Landings Make Good Progress**
NOV. 27 — **Nijmegen Push Makes Early Gains**
FEB. 9th 1945

The Maple Leaf *was the soldiers' newspaper, published in Italy and in France. Headlines from the French edition measured the progress of the Allied march to victory.*

the warships returned to the North Atlantic, their toll of u-boats increased dramatically; seventeen of the navy's twenty-seven confirmed u-boat sinkings occurred in the last six months of the war.

In 1939, Mackenzie King had wanted Canada to specialize in air power. Not only was such fighting romantically high-tech, it was unimaginable that enough aircrew could be lost to require conscription. In early 1943, the Royal Canadian Air Force's contribution to the bomber offensive, No. 6 Bomber Group, was formed. It too had to learn its terrifying business. In four months the Group lost a hundred bombers, a crippling

toll made even worse by the flight to Europe from bases in Yorkshire, where fog, icing, and added distance were fatal to crippled aircraft. Still, the Canadians endured, learned the value of training, discipline, and better technology: by the end of 1944, 6 Group boasted the highest accuracy and lowest casualties of any group in Bomber Command.

One might wonder why half the war was over before Canadians were seriously involved in the fighting. Perhaps there were benefits to entering a war in 1939 with only a handful of professional sailors, soldiers, and airmen, and virtually no equipment fit for fighting. There was blind luck, too: only at Hong Kong and at Dieppe eight months later did Canadians suffer the fate, common in those years, of being defeated by better armies. The price of rushing Canadian corvettes into service was paid mainly by merchant ships sunk in Canadian-escorted convoys, and by the largely foreign crews that drowned in them. If home-front Canadians heard little of their fighting air force, it was because Mackenzie King had been determined to keep the RCAF, and the money to pay for it, at home in Canada, training the Empire's aircrew. Until 1943, the British paid most of the cost of Canadian squadrons overseas and absorbed most of the Canadian flyers in their own units, while Canadians wondered what had happened to the young men they had sent overseas. Later, the value of the bomber offensive would be hotly debated; what mattered in 1943 was that, in 6 Group, Canadians were making their own identifiable contribution to the air war.

The Allied cause was in much better shape at the outset of 1945 than the usual Monday-morning quarterbacks believed.

The Bomber Offensive

The Allied bomber offensive against Germany was, for Canadians, the most costly single operation of the war, and the most controversial. For almost five years, Britain and the United States spent vast sums designing and building multi-engine bombers and training thousands of crew members to drop bombs on Germany. From 1941, it was the focus of the major Allied effort. Was it efficient? Was it moral? Was it effective?

In 1939, when Mackenzie King wanted Canada's main war effort to be in the air, he was hoping to save Canadian lives. Compared to land fighting, he believed, air-force casualties would be relatively light. In fact the RCAF lost 9,060 casualties in bomber operations; most of them died.

After the war, critics like economist John Kenneth Galbraith questioned whether the huge operation had even affected the German war effort, which grew steadily despite the rain of bombs and kept German forces equipped and supplied almost to the end. More recently, a controversial CBC television program asked whether Canadian losses were suffered attacking German military and industrial targets, or merely spreading death and terror among helpless civilians. The answers are complex and unclear.

Some pre-war air-power theorists had preached that air forces could win wars quickly and cheaply by terrorizing the civilian population. In practice the war taught that civilian populations were tougher than anyone had imagined. Despite a belief, even on the ground, that bombing was accurate, so-called "precision bombing" was impossible. Unless aircraft flew at suicidally low altitudes, few bombs came close to their intended targets. Claims that the *Luftwaffe* had targeted Buckingham Palace or that the American B-17 could drop a bomb in a barrel were absurd.

What the bomber offensive did, at great cost in aircraft and crews, was to hit back at Germany. Whatever the moral qualms—courageously expressed at the time by the Anglican Bishop of Chichester, and more safely and smugly half a century later—the goal of the bomber offensive was to hurt the Nazi war effort in any way possible.

Canadians, in the RCAF's own 6 Group and in every bomber squadron of the Royal Air Force, knew the odds of surviving an operational tour were low. They also believed that they were damaging the Nazi cause. Critics have argued that German munitions production improved in quantity and quality virtually until 1944, and that the bombing was more effective than the Nazis in forcing Germans into an all-out war effort. Advocates of the bombing strategy claim that munitions production would have increased at far higher rates without the constant toll of destruction and disruption and that the Germans had to divert large forces to anti-aircraft defences. The argument will not end soon.

The bomber offensive against Nazi Germany spent Allied resources and lives in profusion, and controversy persists about its military value. This target photo of Münster from a Halifax bomber of the RCAF's 408 Goose Squadron leaves no doubt that the raids caused enormous damage to German cities.

Allied air power and almost total air superiority was a trump card for war planners. Only bad weather could keep air support from cowing the enemy; when events went as planned, soldiers on the ground could whistle up fighter bombers from "cab ranks" circling overhead.

On the ground, American, British, Canadian, and French divisions far outmatched German strength in troops and tanks. Even if the New Year's *Luftwaffe* raid caught some Allied pilots on "the morning after the night before", the battle cost the Germans forty-seven planes, half of them at the hands of the RCAF's 126 Wing. And the Allies had so many planes and pilots that in 1944 Ottawa slowed down the British Commonwealth Air Training Plan—the program that trained over 130,000 Allied aircrew at landing strips across Canada—and officially wound it up on March 31, 1945.

A few days into 1945, the Canadian and British squadrons of the 2nd Allied Tactical Air Force were back at full strength, ready to do anything the army needed and the weather permitted. Farther south, the German bulge in the American line stopped growing and started to shrink. Montgomery

took charge of the northern flank and began squeezing. The great German offensive had failed utterly, and the tanks and crack troops destroyed by the Allies would never be replaced. The only benefit the offensive gave Hitler was a delay in Monty's advance to clear the west bank of the Rhine.

Four months earlier, in September 1944, Montgomery had planned an ambitious airborne offensive to take him over the German line and across the Rhine. His reach had exceeded his grasp: his armoured columns failed to reach Arnhem before the Germans crushed the British and Polish paratroopers guarding its bridge over the Rhine. It was, as a famous movie recorded, the "bridge too far". Next, Monty had planned a January assault. The hardships of a winter campaign would be offset by the ease of moving across frozen terrain. Operation "Veritable" would launch Allied troops against Germany's well-fortified Siegfried Line. The troops would need their tanks; moving later meant warmer weather, thaws, and flooding, and taking heavy armoured vehicles across the flat, water-logged terrain could be impossible.

While Monty planned attacks, most of the First Canadian Army dug in and waited along the Waal and Maas rivers, and Crerar sent the XXX British Corps off to help the embattled Americans. The Canadians spent most of January doing frosty guard duty in their front lines. Near Nijmegen in Holland, Lieutenant-Colonel Roger Rowley's Stormont, Dundas and Glengarry Highlanders

The combined Allied bomber forces levelled much of Germany. Huge stretches of the cities were bombed-out ruins, incapable of supporting habitation.

As in most wars, the generals won the glory and the soldiers paid in blood. Field Marshal Sir Bernard Montgomery in his trademark two-badged beret and General Harry Crerar of the First Canadian Army were not bosom friends, but they had to work together—and did.

found themselves fighting an unexpected naval battle. Spotting German midget submarines getting ready to attack a bridge, the unit lined up a couple of its anti-tank guns and blasted them out of the water. To Rowley's great annoyance, the Royal Canadian Artillery insisted on a share of the credit. At the end of January, it took Canadians four days and sixty-five dead to wrest Capelse Veer, a flooded island in the Maas River, from the tough German paratroopers who guarded it. It was a grim foretaste of fighting to come. Soldiers who had survived Normandy in the summer and the struggle to clear Germans from the Scheldt Estuary in October now faced their third campaign. They knew they would be braving reinforced concrete bunkers, thousands of buried land mines, field guns carefully ranged on the few roads above water, and—above all—men of General Alfred Schlemm's First Parachute Army, defending their own soil. Delays lengthened the odds. January turned to February; snow changed to driving rain, and low-lying polderland became a bottomless morass. If the Germans blew the Rhine dikes, the battlefield would be the bottom of a vast lake. Beyond the polders, where the ground rose, were the neat groves of a state-owned forest called the Reichswald. Beyond were the Hochwald and Balberger Wald forests. Young pines a couple of yards apart blocked the way for tanks, and forced infantry into narrow forest lanes a machine-gun could easily sweep.

Tanks with hatches closed, or "buttoned up", were sitting ducks for German bazookas or *Panzerfausts*, hand-held rocket launchers whose missiles could easily penetrate a tank turret. Being hit was awful. Powered by aviation gas, Sherman tanks were so flammable that troops called them "Ronsons" after the popular cigarette lighter. Crews had only a few seconds to bail out after a hit, and only a few made it. Most crew commanders therefore ran with the hatches open, preferring the risk of snipers, and many paid the price. Even then, the odds against tanks in close-wooded country were heavy. The Canadian Grenadier Guards began one battle with sixty-three tanks, but only ten survived the approach march. Allied planners knew the problems with the Sherman, but mass production made it easier to replace the tanks lost than to stop and design better ones.

Canadians and the Dutch

Until 1945, few Canadians had had much to do with The Netherlands. In 1941 there were almost 200,000 Canadians who claimed Dutch roots, but few noticed. They blended easily, spoke English, and some traced their ancestry back to the United Empire Loyalists.

The war changed everything. Princess Juliana, heir to The Netherlands' throne, made her wartime home in Ottawa, and a hospital room was declared Dutch territory so that her daughter Beatrix could also be a legitimate "native-born" heir to the throne.

A stronger link was forged when General Crerar's First Canadian Army liberated most of The Netherlands in the spring of 1945. The Dutch had found the war an appalling experience. The German invasion in 1940 had caught them utterly unawares, and formal resistance had collapsed in five days, though not before the modern port city of Rotterdam had been systematically devastated by German bombing. The years of occupation were made worse by extensive collaboration by Dutch Nazis, the extinction of a large and prosperous Jewish community, and brutal repression of resistance and even protest. At the end of the war, much of Holland was flooded and its population faced death by starvation.

The Canadians arrived as liberators. Fighting was fierce and casualties were high, but Canadian soldiers and their commanders did all they could to avoid civilian casualties in Europe's most densely populated country. Half a month before VE Day, fighting was stopped by an informal truce. In Operation "Faust" and Operation "Manna". Allied aircraft and Canadian trucks delivered food and medicine to people in the western Netherlands. By VE Day, two countries that had hardly known each other had become friends.

In the aftermath of war, relations could easily have been strained. Homesick Canadians were not ideal guests in a suddenly impoverished country. Communities with old-fashioned values had to live with well-paid soldiers with a taste for wine, women, and song. The war-deprived Dutch craved much that the new arrivals could offer, from cigarettes to canned fruit. Military discipline, never a Canadian strong point, sometimes faded from sight. Nonetheless, writing in 1980, Dutch-Canadian historian Michiel Horn could record the amazing fact that friendship between the two countries remained largely intact.

And when many Dutch contemplated their future in a ravaged, overcrowded, and vulnerable country, they remembered the homeland of their friendly liberators and chose to emigrate to Canada. Between 1945 and the 1961 census, Canadians with Dutch ancestry more than doubled, to 412,000 people.

The First Canadian Army liberated The Netherlands, and the Dutch, brutalized by the Nazis for five years, responded to the Canadian troops with a surge of gratitude that still persists. Here a Royal Winnipeg Rifles soldier enjoys a moment with his admirers at Deventer on April 10, 1945.

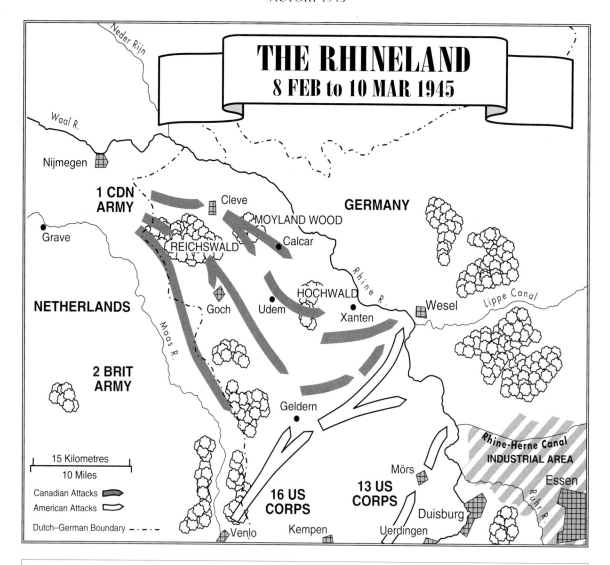

THE RHINELAND
8 FEB to 10 MAR 1945

Though few infantrymen would have traded places with the men in the "iron dungeons", they had little sympathy with the tank crews' terrors, or their regular need to refuel and get fresh ammunition. Tanks always seemed to disappear when the infantry needed them. And infantry were not so easily replaced. On paper, a battalion should have four rifle companies of about a hundred and fifty men each and a support company with heavy weapons. In fact, companies were lucky to have a hundred men in battle, and their platoons could be as small as eighteen or twenty. With three Bren machine-guns, a small two-inch calibre mor-

tar, and a radio set to carry, as well as the general issue Lee-Enfield rifles, to say nothing of ammunition, food, water, and a change of clothing, there was good reason for foot-soldiers to be weary and cautious. Who, on the eve of victory, would be the last to die?

For Operation "Veritable", the first phase of the Canadians' battle of the Rhineland, Montgomery ordered Crerar to take the First Canadian Army eastward into Germany, with the Maas on its right flank and the Rhine on the left. North of the Cleve–Calcar road, the 3rd Canadian Division would fight its way along the flood plain of the Waal and the Rhine to seize the river crossings at Emmerich. South of the road, the British XXX Corps, including the 2nd Canadian Division, faced the heavily defended Reichswald. Crerar was not a man for clever tactics. A veteran artillery officer from the First World War, he could only offer his men all the firepower a gunner could devise. What he could not control was the weather. The month's delay caused by the German offensive was nearly fatal to the Allied plan. An early thaw and driving rain sent the river Waal rising up to its banks. To help, the Germans blew gaps in the dikes.

On February 8, the day chosen for the attack, the mile-long Quer dam collapsed. By evening the 3rd Division's objective was a vast lake, deep enough to drown German minefields but leaving villages as small, fortified islands. At dusk the 3rd Division attacked. Most men crossed in Buffaloes, big, tracked, amphibious vehicles that flailed ponderously through the water, spinning in any direction when a track hit an underwater obstruction and sinking like stones when hit. After dark, drivers had no way of keeping direction or turning back to their objective. Interference made radios useless too. On the other side of the Cleve road, the XXX Corps made better progress on drier ground.

General Schlemm pleaded for help, but the German high command refused; they were waiting for the American Ninth Army to attack across the Roer River. So was Crerar. Unless the German forces faced attack on two fronts, his efforts might be doomed. But were the Americans coming? German engineers settled the matter: they jammed a sluice gate, flooded the Maas valley, and sent 100 million tons of water pouring into American-held territory. Schlemm finally got the help he needed. Would they be in time? The test was at Cleve. By a hair's breadth, the British got to Cleve first. All day on the 10th, a desperate struggle raged through and around the devastated city. By dawn on the 11th the British had won, but it was clear that the Americans had been prevented from attacking.

It was also clear that if the going was incredibly difficult for Crerar's advancing troops, it was close to impossible for the vehicles trying to deliver food and the huge stocks of ammunition his guns and rocket batteries needed. Steady rain and mist grounded Allied air support. By now Crerar's troops faced nine German divisions, four of them Schlemm's tough paratroopers. Still, Crerar would have to keep going alone. On February 19, he ordered fresh attacks. For the next phase, Lieutenant-General Guy Simonds' II Canadian Corps, with the 2nd and 3rd Divisions,

Like many other German soldiers, this young Nazi paid in full for his Führer's ambitions.

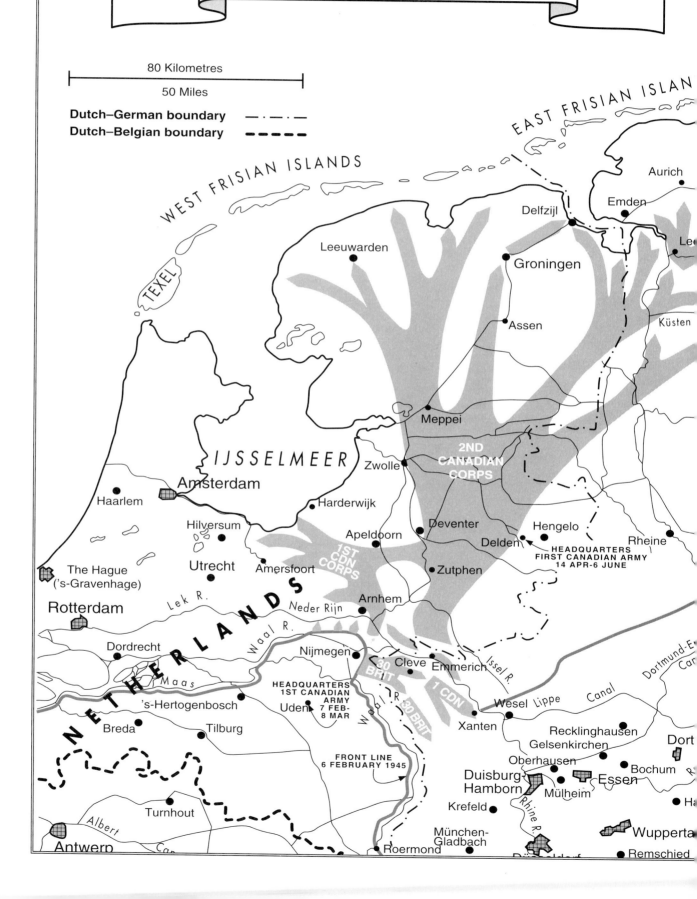

FIRST CANADIAN ARMY
FROM THE MAAS TO THE WESER
NOV 1944 — VE DAY

80 Kilometres

50 Miles

Dutch–German boundary — · — · —
Dutch–Belgian boundary — — — —

EAST FRISIAN ISLAN

WEST FRISIAN ISLANDS

TEXEL

Aurich

Emden

Delfzijl

Le

Leeuwarden

Groningen

Küsten

Assen

Meppei

2ND
CANADIAN
CORPS

IJSSELMEER

Zwolle

Amsterdam

Haarlem

Harderwijk

Hilversum

Apeldoorn

Deventer

Hengelo

Delden

Rheine

HEADQUARTERS
FIRST CANADIAN ARMY
14 APR-6 JUNE

1ST
CDN
CORPS

Utrecht

Amersfoort

Zutphen

The Hague
('s-Gravenhage)

Lek R.

Neder Rijn

Arnhem

Issel R.

Rotterdam

Waal R.

Nijmegen

Cleve

Emmerich

30
BRIT

Dortmund-E

Can

Dordrecht

1 CDN

HEADQUARTERS
1ST CANADIAN
ARMY
7 FEB-
8 MAR

Maas

Uden

Waal R.

Wesel

Lippe

Canal

30 BRIT

's-Hertogenbosch

Xanten

Recklinghausen

Dort

Breda

Tilburg

FRONT LINE
6 FEBRUARY 1945

Gelsenkirchen

Oberhausen

Bochum

Duisburg
Hamborn

Mülheim

Essen

Ha

NETHERLANDS

Krefeld

Rhine R.

Turnhout

Albert

München-
Gladbach

Wuppert

Antwer

Can

Roermond

Remscheid

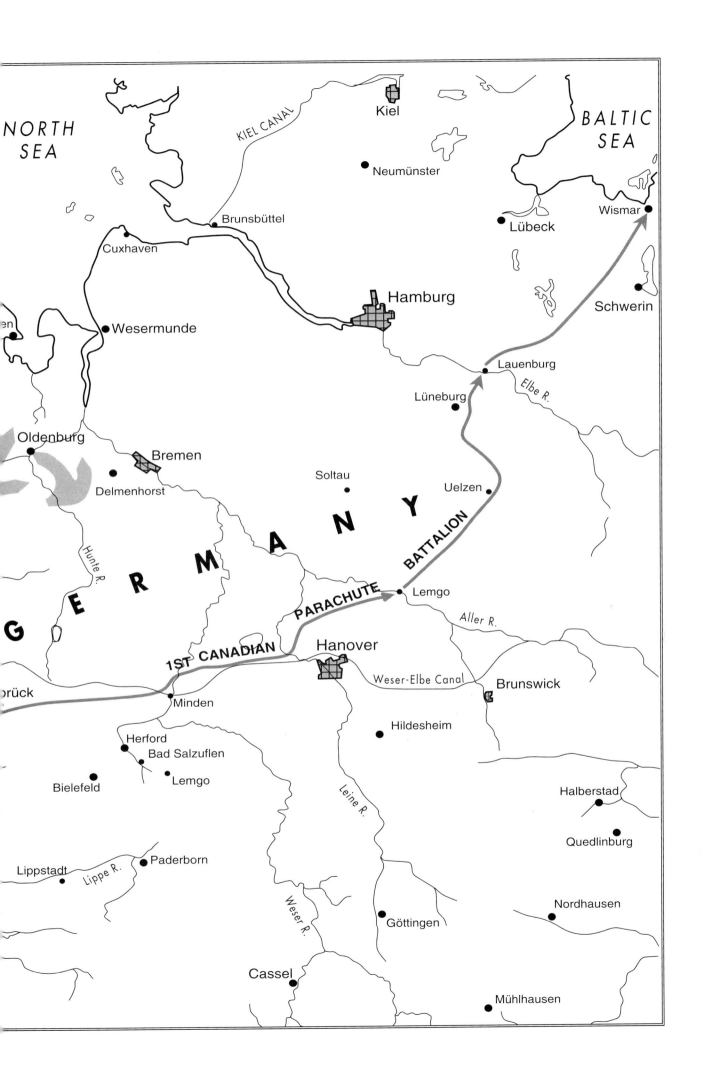

The "Zombies"

When France fell in 1940 and Britain seemed to be next, Mackenzie King's government pushed the National Resources Mobilization Act (NRMA) through Parliament. The NRMA allowed conscription, but only for home defence. Many of the men conscripted, for short periods of training and later for full-time defence duties, volunteered for General (overseas) Service. Other NRMA men refused. That these men should be fully trained for war but unwilling to fight offended patriots. Soon the reluctant warriors were dubbed "Zombies", a word borrowed from the Hollywood version of Afro-Caribbean voodoo to describe men without souls. The term of abuse soon became a badge of defiance to men who had been coaxed, bullied, and punished in attempts to persuade them to volunteer. "If the government wants us," they claimed, "let them say so."

In November 1944, when the call came for 15,600 "home defence draftees" to go overseas, many resisted. At Terrace, B.C., men of the 13th Brigade pointed an anti-tank gun down the sole railway track into their camp. At London, 600 men of the Oxford Rifles went absent and 100 men of the Dufferin and Halton Rifles scaled a six-foot fence to get away. In Quebec, 600 of the Fusiliers de Sherbrooke and 700 from the Régiment de Châteauguay vanished. "The nearest approach man's ingenuity has made to perpetual motion," commented an Ontario police official, "is the process of draftees going AWOL, being picked up by the police and put back in barracks, to go AWOL again." When RCMP and military police invaded Drummondville, Quebec, in March 1945 to hunt down deserters, 2,000 local people attacked them with bottles, brooms, and sticks while local police looked on.

In mid-January, General McNaughton, the Minister of National Defence, reported 8,300 ex-Zombies in Britain, but 2,800 were absent without leave and another 6,300 were "unreported". Military and civilian police spent the winter of 1945 rounding up absentees. Sweethearts and families were warned that sheltering deserters was a serious offence under the Defence of Canada Regulations. By the end of March, 11, 836 NRMA men had left for England, along with another 2,400 who had finally decided to volunteer. By the war's end, 4,881 NRMA men had reached Europe, 55 had been killed, 6 were missing, and 226 were wounded. The ultimate toll was 69 dead conscripts. In October 1945, the Department of National Defence confessed that 13,416 draft dodgers were still missing—9,647 of them in Quebec. A postwar amnesty allowed them to go home.

Conscripting Zombies for overseas service had hardly been worth the trouble—but then, no one had known in November 1944 that the war would end in six months.

The Blushing Bridegroom

Collins/Montreal/Gazette/1943

would seize the Goch–Calcar road, while his British corps forced a way through the Siegfried Line defences to Goch.

Many Canadians would remember Moyland Wood, near Calcar, as the heart of the Reichswald battle. Earlier, men from Britain's 15th (Scottish) Division had cleared half of it at huge cost. They could go no farther. Faced with news of failure, Simonds turned icy. Without Moyland Wood, his own spectacular battle plan, "Blockbuster", could not get started. His subordinates were suspicious of Simonds' ambition—as front line soldiers usually are—and they knew their lives were on the line. The Regina Rifles lost a hundred men just getting close to the woods. German shells bursting in the air over the open fields killed or wounded half the Canadians on "Slaughterhouse Hill", the slope in front of the wood. Colonels and generals had no idea of the Germans' strength; what they did know was that Simonds would fire them if they could not report victories. At the "sharp end", junior officers were learning how hard it is to get sodden, shivering, scared infantrymen moving. As for the troops themselves, wearily gathering up their packs and their weapons, none of it made much sense. When orders came, they took a last look at old buddies and humped forward once again.

Brigadier Jock Spragge gave the Moyland Wood job to a West Coast unit, the Canadian Scottish. It was C Company's turn to move forward. At first there was no resistance, even to the hundred men of the half-strength company. Suddenly, at the edge of the wood,

Canadians died for every inch of ground liberated in Europe. Awaiting collection by graves registration units, these infantry lie by the side of the road at Bretteville-sur-Laize, now the site of one of Canada's many war cemeteries.

German paratroopers unleashed a torrent of fire. Only five men escaped unharmed, sixteen were dead, and more than half the company remained as prisoners. For the disaster, Spragge, an exhausted Normandy veteran, was relieved of his command. Two days later, on February 21, the skies had cleared. Backed by tanks, Wasp flame-throwers, and Typhoon fighter-bombers, all four companies of the Royal Winnipeg Rifles took Moyland Wood. Six days of fighting cost the regiment 183 men, half its fighting strength.

South of Moyland Wood, battalions of the 2nd Division took up the battle at Louisendorf, short of the straight, narrow Goch–Calcar road. Getting there and staying would cost the 4th Canadian Infantry Brigade heavily; no one had told them that two German Panzer divisions had been shoved into the line to back up General Schlemm's parachute divisions. On the

19th, the Canadians attacked. Many were still largely untrained, transferred from the Service and Ordnance corps because the high command had underestimated infantry losses and politicians at home had resisted conscription. In two hours, Lieutenant-Colonel Denis Whitaker's Royal Hamilton Light Infantry (the Rileys) had advanced 2,000 yards and consolidated beyond the road. On their right the Essex Scottish kept pace, but a British flanking attack never even started. The Canadians, drawled a British staff officer, "could handle the situation."

That night, battle groups from the two newly arrived Panzer divisions smashed their way into the hurriedly improvised Canadian defences. Whitaker, a survivor of Dieppe, Normandy, and the Scheldt, counted eight separate German assaults that night. Eventually he summoned his LOBs (men "left out of battle" to rebuild a shattered unit), formed his own counterattack force, and drove out any Germans who dared invade his lines. His neighbours, the Essex Scottish, never had a chance. With an unprotected flank, they were overrun. While three German tanks and forty troops took up positions around the Essex Scottish headquarters, Lieutenant-Colonel John Pangman stayed in touch with his men from the basement. The Royal Regiment of Canada, sent forward to replace the vanished regiment, found Major Ken McIntyre and Able Company still holding out, with thirty-five men and the wounded. Pangman was rescued from his basement. On the 21st, skies cleared and Typhoon dive-bombers blasted the Germans from the air. By then, the Canadians had won. The battle had cost them 400 men, half of them from the Essex Scottish, but the Germans had lost eight 88mm self-propelled guns and eleven new Panthers, the best tank of the war. Seven had been knocked out by the 17-pounders of Lieutenant David Heaps' troop from the 18th Anti-Tank battery.

It took Crerar's army two weeks, from February 8 to February 21, to get through fifteen to twenty miles of the Siegfried Line to Calcar and Goch, and finish Operation "Veritable". By then, Schlemm was waiting for him with the best of the remaining German divisions in the west, and masses of artillery. The next phase of the attack, Operation "Blockbuster", would take Crerar's divisions through the Hochwald to the Rhine between Xanten and Wesel. As architect of the battle plan, Simonds decided to shift his line of attack from the Cleve–Xanten road to the undamaged Goch–Xanten railway, lifting the track so his wheeled vehicles could use it as a road. That was a clever solution of a logistics problem, but for 65,000 Canadian and British troops on the ground the next thirteen days were a nightmare of rain, cold, confusion, and death. Simonds had dreamed of a brilliant armoured stroke. If British divisions had so far faced the heaviest fighting on Crerar's front, the Canadians in Simonds' II Corps would have their chance. Too bad the Germans were also strongest on that front. Worse, the February weather guaranteed clouds, rain, and mud—the conditions that had made Passchendaele the most evil memory of the previous war. Men on foot, not in tanks or planes, would have to win the battle.

The night of February 25–26 was long, cold, wet, and dangerous as German shells plunged into the soft, wet ground where Canadian infantry and tanks formed up. A

WRENS, CWACS, WDS

In August 1939, before the war, 638,000 Canadian women were "gainfully employed"; on October 1, 1943, with more jobs than people to fill them, the Department of Labour reported 1,075,000 women in the workforce, not counting about 750,000 women who supplemented men's work on family farms, or women in the armed services.

Though it had enlisted women as nurses since 1899, the Canadian army never seriously discussed recruiting women for general service until 1941. The British army, their mentors in much else, had done it during the First World War and again at the outbreak of war in 1939. Recruiting Canadian women seems to have been considered largely because the Royal Air Force wanted to use members of its own Women's Auxiliary Air Force (WAAF) at its RAF schools in Canada, in trades from cook to flight controller.

Originally the Department of National Defence proposed to enlist "female auxiliary personnel" through the civilian Department of National War Services, but within weeks of the decision on May 13, 1941, the services went ahead with their own organizations. On July 30, the Cabinet War Committee approved a plan by the defence minister, J.L. Ralston, for a Canadian Women's Army Corps (CWAC). A few weeks later, the RCAF's minister, Chubby Power, presented plans for a Canadian WAAF (soon renamed the Women's Division of the RCAF or "WD"). The navy only sought authority for its Women's Royal Canadian Naval Service (WRCNS, or "Wrens") in July 1942.

Recruiting women was always justified by the need to free up men for more active service. While a tiny number of women were exposed to incredible danger as agents in Nazi-occupied territory, almost all served in medical, clerical, culinary, or service roles that fitted male expectations of women's role in the workforce. The air force was the most open to expanding women's roles; the navy was the least, though its Wrens seem to have had the most positive image with the public. The CWAC suffered from a mid-war "whispering campaign" about the morality of its members that undermined recruiting and morale. Finally, a formal campaign was launched by the War Information Board to improve its image. Perhaps the rumour-mongering merely reflected the generally low status of the army in public esteem, but the army's women paid a cruel price.

In all, the WRCNS enlisted 7,126 women; the CWAC 21,624; the RCAF(WD) 17,467. There were also 4,439 commissioned nursing sisters in the three services. One nursing sister and three members of the RCAF's Women's Division were killed in action.

"The Proudest Girl in Canada" was the one who joined the Canadian Women's Army Corps, and in all more than 21,000 did—some for patriotic reasons, others for adventure. CWACs performed a variety of useful military roles and they eventually received all the veterans' benefits that men did.

German attack hit the Canadian line at 2:00 P.M. Men of the Royal Hamilton Light Infantry and tanks of the Fort Garrys drove them off. German manuals said British troops did not make night attacks; these were not British troops. At 3:45 A.M. on February 26, minutes after the German attack, the sky turned white; the entire Canadian Corps artillery had opened fire. At 4:30 A.M. the Canadian infantry divisions attacked. On the left, the 2nd Division had the 2nd Canadian Armoured Brigade in support. Suddenly Winnipeg's Queen's Own Cameron Highlanders lost Lieutenant-Colonel Tommy Thompson—at twenty-three, the youngest battalion commander in the army. There was a momentary, paralysing panic. Major David Rodgers quelled it. Single-handed, he cleared two fortified houses and took command of the battalion. He was recommended for the VC; General Montgomery said a DSO would do. Montreal's Régiment de Maisonneuve had a tough time too—running into mines, machine-guns—and booby-trapped portraits of Hitler. "I guess they thought that if we saw a picture of Hitler, we'd want to tear it off the walls," remembered Lieutenant Guy de Merlis. Late in the afternoon, Lieutenant-Colonel Julien Bibeau got his stalled unit moving again, with the help of flame-throwers. The Maisies lost ninety-three men that day, twelve of them dead.

Behind the 2nd Division followed four battle groups of the 4th Canadian Armoured Division, tanks belly-deep in churning mud as they headed up the slope. For two hours there was painfully little progress against German mines, 88mm guns, and tanks. Then months of battle experience slowly paid off. Veteran tank-infantry teams tackled German strong points and took them. By afternoon the Canadians had reached Keppeln and stopped.

On the right, the 3rd Division had a much tougher time. The 8th Brigade—the Queen's Own Rifles from Toronto, the Régiment de la Chaudière from the Beauce, and New Brunswick's North Shore Regiment—began to advance, backed by the 1st Hussars from London. On the right the fields were too soggy for tanks, and German paratroopers made progress impossible. Major Ben Dunkelman of Toronto's Queen's Own Rifles belonged to the family that owned Tip Top Tailors. As a Jew, he knew what would happen to him if he ever became a prisoner. Veterans recalled him as one of the keenest soldiers they knew. Outside the village of Mooshof, Dunkelman's company fought its way into a German position. Then German counterattacks wiped out one platoon and reduced another to only five unwounded men. Its sergeant, Aubrey Cosens, was an old man of twenty-three to his frightened teenaged soldiers. He spotted a friendly tank, ran to it with bullets tearing through his battledress, and got it to smash into a fortified German farmhouse. Then, with the few survivors behind him, Cosens raced into the German strongpoint, emerging with twenty German paratroopers as prisoners. Moments later, a German sniper shot him through the head as he walked back to report. Cosens' feat earned him a posthumous Victoria Cross. Out of 115 men who started the day in his company, only Dunkelman and 35 others survived intact. "For all my exhaustion," he recalled, "I did not sleep well that night."

The 1st Hussars had another feat to perform: helping the North Shores take Keppeln. As the New Brunswickers came over the hill, it seemed undefended; in fact it was the base of an ambush, on a bare slope swept by German fire. Two companies were pinned down and the unit's lightly armoured carriers were wiped out. Known to his men as "The Good Shepherd" for his long cane and his care for them, Lieutenant-Colonel John Rowley went to the Hussars for help; their tanks would have to draw German fire if the infantry was to advance. Major Jake Powell of C Squadron had lost six of his nineteen tanks that morning at Mooshof, but at 1:20 P.M. the thirteen survivors rumbled down the slope, with infantry clinging to the back decks. Only five tanks survived, but they led the North Shores into Keppeln.

The Chaudières' objective was the little village of Hollen, an inferno of shells and smoke. Twice the Chauds were thrown back; twice they returned. One company spotted a white flag and assumed the Germans were giving up. Instead three Panther tanks emerged and opened fire. Not until it grew dark did Lieutenant-Colonel Armand Roy's Chaudières win Hollen, and it was 9:00 P.M. before Brigadier John Rockingham could launch the 9th Brigade's attack on the next objective, Üdem. By midnight, the Highland Light Infantry from Galt and the Stormont, Dundas and Glengarry Highlanders were fighting through the town. By dawn on the 27th, the North Nova Scotia Highlanders had passed through to the outskirts, the last German counter-attacks had been beaten off, and the base for launching Operation "Blockbuster" was finally in Canadian hands.

The battle on February 26 cost 214 young Canadians' lives. Not since Normandy had there been such a toll. Winning the victory was not cheap.

To the high command this was the heavy price of success, a necessary investment for attacking the ultimate German positions in the Hochwald Forest. And there were more

instalments to pay. For "Blockbuster", Simonds planned to seize the Goch–Xanten railway line and push through the two-mile–wide Hochwald Gap, between the two forested hills of the Hochwald on the north and the Balberger Wald on the south. If Simonds failed, Crerar explained, he would give the initiative back to the British XXX Corps and Simonds' rival, Lieutenant-General Brian Horrocks. The two Canadian infantry divisions would each seize one of the wooded slopes on either side of the Gap, and the 4th Canadian Armoured Division would smash through the middle. With their masses of tanks, guns, and infantry, surely they would not fail.

For Canadians in the 2nd Infantry and 4th Armoured Divisions, the five days from February 27 to March 3 brought some of the fiercest fighting of the war. The Germans were ready, in an ideal defensive position. The assaulting tanks bogged down in the mud or sat like clay pigeons on the railway embankment. Airbursts—shells bursting over the trees—sprayed down white-hot steel rain. Schlemm had collected 717 mortars and 1,054 guns, including an extra 50 of the famous 88mm anti-tank guns. Canadians would also remember the *Nebelwerfer*s, or "Moaning Minnies", rockets that added to the pandemonium and destruction. It was small comfort to the soldiers that Canadian gunners had achieved an even more devastating efficiency.

Simonds' British and Canadian infantry divisions had a straightforward if incredibly difficult job. The impossible task assigned to the 4th Canadian Armoured Division, under Major-General Chris Vokes, would take a little longer. In a parody of the tactics dreamed up by early tank enthusiasts, tanks and infantry would thunder into the Hochwald

Gap, overwhelm the defenders, and burst into the river valley beyond. Instead, they literally rode into the valley of death. Bogged down or trapped on the narrow railway embankment, successive armoured regiments were almost destroyed. Infantry advances were countered by well-rehearsed German counterattacks, reinforced by a hurricane of artillery fire. First came the Algonquin Regiment, backed by tanks of the South Alberta Regiment. German 88mm guns and *Panzerfausts* picked off the front and rear tanks, and the rest were trapped. In all, nine tanks and eleven Bren-gun carriers were knocked out. Forty Canadian survivors watched helplessly. Simonds was anxious. Faced with the setback on his left, would Crerar shift the action to Horrocks' Corps? No, Crerar and Montgomery still wanted the Canadians to fight the battle. On the 28th, it was the turn of Lieutenant-Colonel Fred Wigle's Argyll and Sutherland Highlanders, from Hamilton. The lead company finished the day with only fifteen of its hundred men still fit to fight. The Lincoln and Welland Regiment attacked the same day. With tanks bogged down, the infantry attack got nowhere. Senior commanders seemed oblivious. The generals' main contribution, a bitter veteran remembered, was barking orders to "Get moving!" and sending junior staff officers to find out why the troops wouldn't.

After three teams of infantry and tank regiments had largely failed to break through, the Lake Superior Regiment got its orders for March 1. Backed by the tanks of Lieutenant-Colonel Ned Amy's Canadian

The battle for the Hochwald Forest in late February 1945 was as bitter as anything Canadian soldiers had faced. Mud and cold compounded the difficulty of moving over narrow forest roads defended by well-sited enemy positions.

Newfoundland at War

In 1945, Newfoundland was neither the self-governing dominion she had been in the earlier war nor the Canadian province she would become in 1949. Instead, the island had survived the humiliation of 1934 when, bankrupt and misgoverned, it had reverted to the status of a British crown colony. Like Canada, Newfoundland had been bitterly divided by the trauma of the earlier war. Twice, in 1916 and in 1917, the Newfoundland battalion had been wiped out; almost every island family mourned a brother, father, or uncle. That was why Newfoundland's Commission of Government agreed to offer troops, but only if Britain paid and if the men served in the artillery, where mass casualties were unlikely.

In 1940 Newfoundlanders formed two regiments of heavy artillery. The British provided the officers and most of the NCOS, but Newfoundlanders learned fast and by the end of the war some had qualified for commissions. At the end of 1941, one of the regiments was changed into the 166th (Newfoundland) Field Regiment. It went to Tunisia early in 1943 and fought through the long, hard Italian campaign, supporting British, Indian, New Zealand, Canadian, and American troops. The original unit, the 57th (Newfoundland) Heavy Regiment, landed in Normandy a month after D-Day. Its big 155mm guns and 7.2-inch howitzers backed British and Canadian troops in France, Holland, and Germany. In February 1945, as the Canadians advanced on the flooded ground between the Maas and the Rhine, Newfoundland gunners

"The Call Is for Men, Real Men", the flyer says, urging Newfoundlanders to enlist. Thousands did, in the British and Canadian forces, but Newfoundland's main contribution to the war was likely its geography. Its ports and airfields were essential to winning the Battle of the Atlantic, and as a staging post for the air ferry service over the ocean.

blasted the Germans holding them up. After the murderous battle in the Goch–Wesel area, the regiment backed the British crossing of the Rhine. It was still in battle when VE Day came.

A total of 2,327 Newfoundlanders served overseas with the two artillery regiments, and 72 of them lost their lives. Many more died in October 1942, when U-69 torpedoed the Sydney–Port aux Basques ferry *Caribou*. Of 237 people aboard, more than half perished, including 14 children.

Many Newfoundlanders joined the Royal Navy and Royal Air Force and others crossed to the mainland to serve with all three of the Canadian armed forces. The links they made with their future country helped make it easier to accept confederation with Canada as the island people's best alternative.

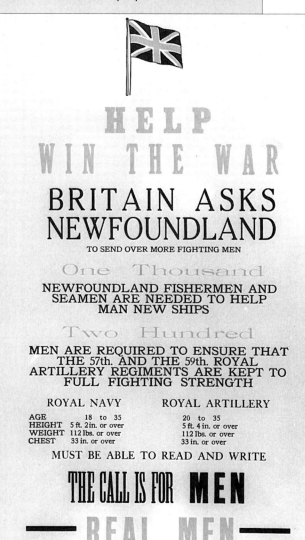

Grenadier Guards, they would push through to Xanten on the Rhine, eight miles beyond the Hochwald Gap. When Amy insisted on finding another route, legend says, Major-General Chris Vokes was so furious that he threatened to put the whole regiment under arrest. Next day Vokes cooled off, but the fighting soldiers felt a long way from their commanders. Three days into "Blockbuster", Simonds' divisions were battered, worn out, and losing confidence. His forward troops had only a weak grip on their edge of the gap and a tantalizing glimpse of the corridor on the far side that led out to the Rhine. Still, Crerar had not switched his weight to the other route.

Much later, Brigadier Denis Whitaker, a bitter critic of Simonds' generalship, found the Germans were confused too. Why would the Canadians keep sending in battalion-strength attacks or slugging away at forest defences when any sensible commander would have gone around the Hochwald? General Schlemm and his generals had a healthy respect for Canadian courage and Canadian guns, but Canadian tactics were predictable and, well, dumb.

On the flanks, the battle had not gone much better. Struggling through the forests, infantry from the 2nd and 3rd Divisions had been slaughtered by airbursts and in ambushes. Obvious routes through the forest were intensely mined: each footstep brought fear of a crippling explosion. Dense tangles of bush were wired and booby-trapped. Platoons and sections got lost in the woods, and communications soon broke down, sometimes because all of a company's radio operators were wounded or dead.

On March 1, when the Essex Scottish stormed the Hochwald, C Company on the left flank lost three-quarters of its men. Its commander, a pharmaceutical sales manager from Windsor aged thirty-four, Major Fred Tilston, had never led a company in an assault. He learned fast. Twice he was wounded, once in the head and once in the hip, but he stayed to organize his men against the German counter-attack. He felt he had to: two-thirds of them had never been in battle before. Six times Tilston dragged himself over open ground to bring back grenades and bandoliers of bullets. A third hit blew off one leg and mangled the other. Barely conscious, he passed on orders to the next-in-command and collapsed. This time, Montgomery approved the Victoria Cross. Tilston lost both his legs but he survived, barely, to collect his vc.

On March 2, the turn came for the Lake Superior Regiment, 4th Armoured Division's motor battalion and one of its best. Four days into the fighting and two days after their last hot meal, the "Lake Sups" still had spirit. Corps and division planners ordered a night attack, backed by Amy's Grenadier Guards. The Algonquin Regiment, with tanks from the Governor General's Foot Guards, would follow through. As usual, darkness and mud took their toll. Supporting tanks bogged down or "brewed up" into flames. Handfuls of Canadians fought lonely battles with German paratroopers. The Algonquins, moving through the melee, were caught in the confusion. As usual, communications broke down. At dawn the few surviving tanks pulled back, and an isolated group of almost forty Algonquins was overrun and captured.

Later, the regimental historian of the Lake Superior Regiment left an account of the area as the burial party found it:

> Pte Yanchuk, G, . . . was within a few yards of an enemy position, lying on his back with a grenade clutched in his hand,

killed as he charged. At his side, . . . Pte Middlemiss, WR, . . . was sitting in a shell-hole in a life-like position. He had been with Yanchuk when a burst of small arms fire stopped him. He crawled into a shell-hole, sat there and died. An unknown Canadian made the enemy position. With arms locked around a German he was burned to a crisp by a mound of hay which caught fire alongside the slit-trench in which he fought hand-to-hand. Sgt Lehman, TM, was lying a few yards away, struck down as he brought in the platoon.

At dawn on March 4, the Canadians felt defeated—and suddenly triumphant. The Germans had backed off. Farther south, the American crossing of the Roer had caught Schlemm between two powerful armies, and he could waste no more time or men defending the Hochwald Gap. Now he had to help the rest of the German army across the Rhine and then destroy every one of the nine bridges in his sector. Schlemm's men, drawn into what journalists soon christened "The Wesel Pocket", fought hard. Faint-hearted soldiers were told that their comrades had orders to shoot anyone trying to surrender. Deserters faced summary court martial and execution at each bridge. For the 4th Armoured Division, the struggle at the Hochwald Gap merely continued at the Wesel Pocket. At Veen a battalion of German paratroopers exacted terrible casualties from waves of Canadian attackers; the Argylls lost one of their four rifle companies, trapped in one of the villages there. Algonquins, Lincoln and Wellands, and tanks of the British Columbia Regiment finished the battle. The infantry alone lost 311 men killed and wounded.

On March 8, the 2nd Division and the British 43rd (Wessex) Division took Xanten. When it fell late that night, General Schlemm made a tough decision. Despite Hitler's orders, he would withdraw all that remained of his 1st Parachute Army. Observers from the Führer's headquarters, startled by a British attack, finally got Hitler's approval. At dawn on March 10, Schlemm stood at the Weser bridge in a thin drizzle as the last Germans crossed the Rhine. He had lost 40,000 German dead and wounded and 50,000 prisoners, but he had stemmed the Allied tide for thirty-one days. The month had cost Crerar's army 10,334 British and 5,655 Canadian casualties. However bitter and weary the Canadians might feel after "Veritable" and "Blockbuster", Crerar's First Canadian Army had fought the last major battle in the west. If the soldiers had made the difference, not their generals, that was true of most wars.

The Rhineland battle, in fact, was a superb feat of arms against the best formations of the German army. If most Canadians and their historians have ignored the battles, it is because, like the corresponding assault on Cambrai at the end of the First World War, victory already seemed inevitable. Indomitable Canadians helped make it so.

———————

In 1939, to draw a united Canada into the war, Mackenzie King had promised there would be no conscription, a pledge echoed by the Conservatives and repeated by King's ministers during a Quebec election after war was declared. In 1942, political pressure, not military need, had led King into a plebiscite to release him from his promise. Canadians but not Quebeckers had agreed. "Not necessarily conscription," King had intoned, "but conscription if necessary." Was it necessary

Political warfare reached its peak in November 1944, when King was obliged to send home defence conscripts overseas to reinforce hard-pressed units. Miraculously, his government held together—barely.

by the fall of 1944, with the war almost won but the ranks of Canadian battalions half empty for lack of trained reinforcements? For soldiers and many civilians, King's continued refusal to force conscripts to fight further justified their contempt for the fussy little prime minister. Thousands of fully trained conscripts—"NRMA men" was the official term—sat in Canadian camps, waiting for invaders who would never come. These were the men that other Canadians called "Zombies".

King's defence minister was a Nova Scotia lawyer, Colonel James Layton Ralston. His generals failed to grasp the overseas manpower problem until the late summer of 1944. Few wanted to report bad news or reveal a lack of foresight that might curtail the army's fighting role. Only when a badly wounded Major Conn Smythe, owner of Maple Leaf Gardens, returned to Toronto and decided to blow the whistle were Canadians told that the men who had been considered fit only to be cooks, clerks, and mechanics had been remustered as infantry, handed rifles, and sent in to fight. Ralston's response was to go over and see for himself. With a lawyer's prudence and the experience of a former First World War infantry battalion commander, he convinced himself by the fall of 1944 that conscription was in fact necessary. His notes from an overseas visit show that he was not fooled by solemnly repeated exaggerations and myths, but neither could he ignore the reality of understrength platoons and companies. The men who did most of the dying were also doing double duty as patrols, sentries, and carriers of heavy weapons. Severe casualties in both Italy and North-West Europe had drained reinforcement pools and left fighting units painfully weak. Slack recruiting may have allowed too many unfit men to enlist, but was it fair to the men — or their comrades — to send the unfit to fight? But King still resisted; why,

The great cartoonist Bing Coughlin pays tribute to "scrounging", an honoured if unsanctioned specialty of Canadian troops. These American MPs may find their tires if they follow the arrow to the Canadian leave centre.

THE PROVINCES

Prince Edward Island

Canada's smallest province has always had trouble getting much respect. Canadians amused themselves, in the hard winter of 1945, with reports of Charlottetown's two snowploughs. The older, used to clean off a pond for a children's skating rink, plunged through the ice. The pond would have to be drained and the plough repaired, but no problem: there was a new one. But the new plough was taken down to the harbour to clean the ice for a horse race, and it too plunged—to the bottom of the ocean.

The problems of water, and how to cross it, had to be an issue for the island province, particularly after a nearly new ferry, *Charlottetown*, was sunk by a U-boat in the summer of 1941. A tunnel or a causeway were obvious answers, but Premier Walter Jones opposed either solution. A tunnel would be full of smoke unless electric trains were used, and electricity cost more on P.E.I. than any-

where else in North America. A causeway would cost even more, $67 million. The best available brains, Jones insisted, must be put to making the ferry system work better.

Money was a big issue for a province that ran a 1945 deficit of $400,000—to be shared by only 90,000 people. Other provinces made big bucks from liquor sales; dry P.E.I. made only $100,000, all of it from vendors filling doctors' prescriptions. A much bigger industry, providing armies with dehydrated potatoes, would certainly end with the peace; no one who had suffered the dried, diced spuds would eat them voluntarily, not even the wartime workers who had made a good living at a Summerside factory. The discovery of oil under the ocean had kept islanders waiting for a gusher from a man-made island in Hillsboro Bay. Two years of drilling had left the island with the deepest hole in the world—14,696 feet down—but the war was over and the drill crews were packing up their rigs.

Islanders who came home from the war found that little had changed, on the land or in the grumbling. And that seemed to be the way most people liked it.

when the war was virtually won and hundreds of thousands of volunteers filled army units in Canada and Britain, must he enrage Quebec and anti-conscriptionists to find a few thousand soldiers?

King had a secret weapon, General A.G.L. McNaughton. An old enemy of Ralston—and of conscription—McNaughton had been King's choice in 1939 to command the Canadian army overseas. A former professor of chemical engineering with a passion for technology, McNaughton seemed like a scientific general for a scientific age. In truth his fascination with gadgets and his age (he was in his fifties) made him a question-

able field commander. He had been sent home "for health reasons" late in 1943, after British complaints that he was too old and tactically inept. Ralston had approved his recall and McNaughton never forgave him. Moreover, years of wartime adulation had persuaded McNaughton that he could put life in the Zombies' souls and make them volunteer for overseas.

By late October 1944, after weeks of Cabinet argument about army manpower, King persuaded himself that Ralston was merely power-hungry and unreasonable. On November 1, after discreet but satisfying enquiries, the prime minister popped his surprise. General McNaughton, he announced, would replace Ralston as minister of national defence, and would find the volunteers. McNaughton utterly failed. When Parliament met on November 23, the new defence minister had to plead that conscription was indeed necessary for 16,000 trained NRMA infantrymen. "Chubby" Power, a Quebecker and minister of national defence for the RCAF, had pledged opposition to conscription; he resigned. St. Laurent, justice minister and the newest Quebec minister, felt no such obligation. Neither did Ralston's erstwhile allies. King's government was saved.

Throughout the early weeks of 1945, McNaughton endured fresh humiliations. A by-election in the Ontario riding of Grey North seemed to promise him the safe Commons seat he needed as a minister. The Tories could have allowed their one-time hero an easy victory; instead the Progressive Conservative leader, John Bracken, and the local candidate, Owen Sound mayor Garfield Case, denounced "Mr. McNaughton" for quitting the army and leaving his soldiers without reinforcements, as well as his posh private railway car and his wife's Catholicism. Claims that Zombies had thrown their rifles overboard when they embarked for overseas helped Case beat McNaughton on February 5. Though the stories were exaggerations, there was no denying that many NRMA men deserted.

Was conscription necessary? The army had no doubts. With the wisdom of afterthought, historians are not so sure. As in 1918, the Canadian army could have managed without conscripts, though only barely. One reason was the new minister's insistence on reversing a decision the King government had made in 1943, to split the army between England and Italy. On February 9, 1945, the Combined Chiefs of Staff, British and American, met in Malta and approved Operation "Goldflake", transferring the two Canadian divisions in Italy to North-West Europe. For more than a month, the 1st and 5th Armoured Divisions were in transit from Leghorn to Marseilles and thence up the Rhône to be refitted with better equipment in Belgium. By mid-March, when Lieutenant-General Charles Foulkes brought his reconstituted I Canadian Corps into action in Holland, "Goldflake" had preserved close to half the Canadian army in the field from significant losses for more than a month. With the long lull in Canadian fighting between the Scheldt and Rhineland battles, the crisis that seemed likely in November never quite materialized. But the memory that survived among infantry soldiers was that distant politicians had left them to fight with half the men they should have had. For twenty or even fewer men in a platoon to do the work of forty was no mere symbolic grievance. From carrying heavy weapons to filling the sentry roster, fewer men meant more work and more danger.

———— • • ————

No one ever suggested conscription for the navy or air force. Indeed, the RCAF had such a surplus of would-be flyers that four thousand of them were released early in 1945—only to be called up by the army as conscripts. Eager aircrew trainees, among them future defence minister Paul Hellyer, found themselves rudely transformed into mere soldiers, without the luxury of shirts, ties, or sheets on their cots. When they reported, the army promptly docked them the hundred-dollar clothing allowance the RCAF had paid them on release. Twenty years

The first commander of Canadians overseas, General Andy McNaughton made a difficult transition to politics in November 1944. In his attempt to win a by-election in Grey North, Ont., the next February, the tough old soldier went down to defeat.

later, Hellyer would force unification on the Canadian Forces. Service distinctions had cost him personally.

By 1945, the RCAF had forty-seven squadrons overseas—a third of them flying Lancasters and Wellingtons with Bomber Command, others with Fighter Command, Coastal Command, and the 2nd Allied Tactical Air Force. In the Rhineland battles, British and Canadian squadrons flying Typhoons, Spitfires, and other combat aircraft had kept the skies clear of remnants of the *Luftwaffe* and blasted German defences on the rare occasions when the weather permitted ground-level flying. A Canadian fighter squadron fought in Italy, a bomber reconnaissance squadron flew out of Iceland, and two transport squadrons were part of the massive airlift that helped the British match the Japanese in Burma. Other squadrons flew anti-submarine patrols from fog-bound bases in Newfoundland and the Maritime provinces. Canadian

GET OUT THAT TANK...

...BEHIND THE BARN

FARMERS GET IN TOUCH WITH YOUR LOCAL SALVAGE COMMITTEE

PHONE

 ISSUED BY THE DIRECTOR OF PUBLIC INFORMATION FOR NATIONAL SALVAGE OFFICE, OTTAWA, UNDER AUTHORITY OF HONOURABLE J. T. THORSON, MINISTER OF NATIONAL WAR SERVICES. Printed in Canada

IF THE CAP FITS
7458
WEAR IT!
H.M.C
CANADA NEEDS YOU
somewhere ON THE WAR FRONT

Back the Invasion
JOIN THE C.W.A.C.

Not since the historic and gallant days of Madeleine de Vercheres have Canadian women been offered such opportunity to serve their country. Now, they may stand "shoulder to shoulder" with their fathers, husbands and brothers. Thousands of Canadian girls are, today, facing the *facts*. Thousands are meeting the realism of war in the same gallant manner as did our world famous Canadian heroine. Women can and must relieve "A" men for front line duty—Women of Canada your Country calls you and needs you—Back the Invasion—

For further information apply to your nearest Recruiting Office.
This does not in any way obligate you to enlist.

Get your copy of the new CWAC Digest.
Write Captain Helen Rankin—Aylmer Annex, Ottawa.

THIS IS OUR BATTLE TOO!

CANADIAN WOMEN'S ARMY CORPS

LOOK WHO'S Listening

THIS POSTER IS PUBLISHED IN THE INTERESTS OF THE
NATIONAL VICTORY EFFORT

House of
Seagram

NEWFOUNDLANDERS!

THE EMPIRE NEEDS YOUR HELP

THE FIGHT IS ON! OUR PEOPLE, CIVIL AND MILITARY··· ARE AT GRIPS WITH ALL THE BRUTALITY & TREACHERY THAT **HITLER'S GANG CAN COMMAND**

WHAT CAN WE STAY~AT~HOMES DO? THE ANSWER IS CLEAR —— *BUY* **WAR SAVINGS CERTIFICATES** *and*

FOR FREEDOM

RUTH MURDOCH.

HELP WIN THE WAR

flyers in RCAF squadrons were outnumbered by the 60 per cent of their compatriots who flew with the Royal Air Force, and who provided it with an estimated one-fifth of its flyers.

If the Canadian contribution in the air tended to fade into RAF statistics, Canadian sailors were almost equally invisible in the Royal Navy. However, in 1943, the Royal Canadian Navy gained what no other Canadian service ever gained—an operational sector of its own. With American consent, Rear-Admiral Leonard Murray moved his headquarters from St. John's to Halifax and took over a huge expanse of the north-west Atlantic, from 47° west and south to 29° north. The tide turned in the summer of 1943, when the RCN received new weapons and equipment and the British had a breakthrough in deciphering the German naval code. Unfortunately, the U-boats had improved as well. Gnat torpedoes homed in on the sound of the target's propellers, and Snorkel breathing devices allowed a U-boat to take in fresh air and charge its batteries with a device no larger than a garbage can breaking the surface rather than exposing itself by surfacing entirely.

The war at sea continued to the very end. Early in 1945, censors allowed Canadians to know that merchant ships had again been torpedoed in the St. Lawrence and the minesweeper *Guysborough* had been

German U-boat crews suffered extraordinarily high losses, but stayed in the war to the end. This message intercepted ten days after VE Day shows that the Führer, dead for more than two weeks, still exercised his hold. But "the sour apple" of defeat nonetheless had to be eaten.

sunk in the Halifax approaches on March 17. Of the crew of ninety, five officers and forty-eight ratings had died, most of them during their nineteen-hour wait for rescue. On April 16, it was the turn of the minesweeper *Esquimalt*, off Halifax's Sambro light. This was an appropriate tragedy for the base sailors called "Slackers": when the *Esquimalt* met the U-190, its radar was turned off, it was sailing straight, not in evasive sweeps, and the CAT gear, designed to ward off acoustic torpedoes, was neatly stowed on board. A Gnat from the U-190 sank the little warship in four minutes. Two of its six life rafts stuck tight. By the time anyone noticed the tragedy, the survivors had been seven hours in the icy Atlantic and forty-four of the seventy crew had perished. In many Canadian papers, the casualties from the *Esquimalt* appeared in the VE Day edition.

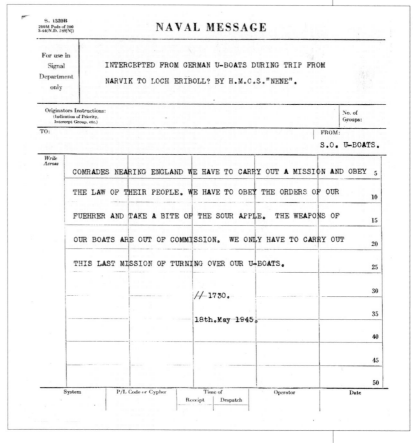

S. 1320B
200M Pads of 200
3-44(N.D. 249(N))

NAVAL MESSAGE

For use in Signal Department only

INTERCEPTED FROM GERMAN U-BOATS DURING TRIP FROM NARVIK TO LOCH ERIBOLL? BY H.M.C.S. "NENE".

Originators Instructions:
(Indication of Priority, Intercept Group, etc.)

No. of Groups:

TO:

FROM:
S.O. U-BOATS.

Write Across

COMRADES NEARING ENGLAND WE HAVE TO CARRY OUT A MISSION AND OBEY 5

THE LAW OF THEIR PEOPLE. WE HAVE TO OBEY THE ORDERS OF OUR 10

FUEHRER AND TAKE A BITE OF THE SOUR APPLE. THE WEAPONS OF 15

OUR BOATS ARE OUT OF COMMISSION. WE ONLY HAVE TO CARRY OUT 20

THIS LAST MISSION OF TURNING OVER OUR U-BOATS. 25

//-1730. 30

18th.May 1945. 35

40

45

50

System | P/L Code or Cypher | Time of Receipt | Despatch | Operator | Date

Most of the RCN's admirals had been embarrassed by little ships like the *Esquimalt* and content to leave them to peacetime amateur sailors of the Volunteer Reserve (RCNVR). (Unlike the straight gold-lace bands that marked a regular naval officer's rank, volunteer reserve officers of the "wavy navy" wore thinner, undulating gold stripes.) Admirals yearned for "real" warships, a real fleet, and the proud victories that would protect the peacetime navy against the indifference and contempt that twice had almost eliminated it. In 1944 a few destroyer battles in the Bay of Biscay had endowed the RCN with a record of *real* battles with *real* gunfire. As a satisfying offset to the loss of the powerful destroyer *Athabaskan* and its 128 dead and 83 taken prisoner on April 29, 1944, Canadian destroyers sank two German destroyers on June 8. A service trying to build its own traditions would never forget Lieutenant-Commander John Stubbs, captain of the sunken *Athabaskan*, shouting from a life raft to a sister ship, "Get away, *Haida*, get clear," before he drifted into mines. Stubbs, a peacetime regular, did not survive.

A real navy also needed naval aviation. The RCN's investment began with *Puncher* and *Nabob*, small U.S.–owned escort carriers lent to the Royal Navy and manned by Canadian sailors and British Fleet Air Arm squadrons. When *Nabob* was torpedoed off Norway, its captain and crew managed to fly off the aircrew and get the badly listing ship safely back to Scotland in a major feat of seamanship. *Puncher* spent the last two months of the war off Norway, providing air cover and launching Barracuda bombers to drop mines. The British cruiser *Uganda* was taken over by the RCN and brought to Halifax, to Scapa Flow, and eventually to Australia to join the British Pacific Fleet. The *Uganda* served off Okinawa and the Japanese home islands, protecting British aircraft carriers from kamikaze bombing attacks. These were the ships and traditions Canadian admirals strove to establish for the sake of their postwar survival.

—————

For the Canadians in Europe that postwar world was only a couple of months away, but it had not yet arrived. The Rhine River still had to be crossed. Long before the Rhineland battles, Montgomery's 21st Army Group staff had begun planning Operation "Plunder". "Veritable" and "Blockbuster" had been the overture; Wesel, just across the Rhine, would be the objective. Nothing could disrupt the plan, not even the unexpected capture by the American 9th Armoured Division of the bridge at Remagen, miles upstream. That, said Montgomery, would only be a useful

The German army continued to resist fiercely through April 1945. This Bren gunner and his mate from the South Saskatchewan Regiment, their invaluable shovel close at hand, seek shelter from enemy fire near Holland's Oranje Canal.

THE PROVINCES

New Brunswick

Poorer and less populous than Nova Scotia, New Brunswick lived on small but steady hopes. The province's economy depended on pulp, paper, and the lowly potato, but the annual salmon season attracted the wealthy and the powerful. The greatest of them, Franklin Delano Roosevelt, would never again bring his entourage to Campobello or lend his patronage to salmon-fishing on the Restigouche. New Brunswickers found solace in the news that his successor, Harry S Truman, had found nothing better than a dogfish in distant Puget Sound.

If Roosevelt was gone, peace brought his wealthy friends and enemies back to the Restigouche and the Miramichi, the Tobique and the Upsalquich. The Restigouche Riparian Society, claimed *Maclean's* magazine, was a New York *Who's Who*, with Vanderbilts, Pulitzers, and Whit-neys. Members boasted that each fish cost them $1,000. That summer, ex-president Herbert Hoover landed "a silvery battler" and the Duke and Duchess of Windsor reported five salmon in their first day at the club. Visionaries dreamed of using former war planes and their pilots to fly fresh lobster to restaurants in big American cities. For such luxuries, money was apparently no object.

If anyone threatened the fishing, it was the Liberal premier, J.B. McNair, with his talk of hydro-electricity from the Saint John River and even from the beautiful Tobique. New Brunswick's postwar development plan, revealed months before the war was over, promised $24 million for reconstruction, half of it to be spent on the forest industry and even a little on a survey of the Chignecto canal, the old dream of slicing the isthmus that linked New Brunswick and Nova Scotia. Others argued that money should be spent on schools and teachers; students could finish high school only in Saint John, Moncton, and Fredericton.

Whatever the cause, most New Brunswickers believed that the postwar world would be better. That marked them off from a lot of other Maritimers.

---

diversion. For once, Eisenhower agreed.

Simonds had his own scheme for "bouncing" the Rhine: when the German pocket broke up, the Calgary Highlanders would race for the railway bridge at Wesel, followed by the rest of the 5th Brigade. It was not to be. As dawn broke on March 10, the Canadian company commanders were peering through mist and rain, trying to choose a route, when they heard two loud thunks. The Germans had blown the bridge.

For Hitler's army the Rhine was indeed the last ditch, and the Allies expected a bitter struggle. After Xanten, Crerar's staff had two weeks to plan the next stage. Masses of material—boats, bridging material, and mountains of shells—piled up near the riverbanks. Units rested and got to know the hundreds of green reinforcements who now filled their ranks, many of them former Zombies. Few veterans ever tried to make their life miserable. The first conscript to die, at the end of March, was killed by a German booby-trap as his regiment, the Algonquins, fought to clear Veen. "They were just as good as any reinforcements we have had," claimed the Algonquin's colonel. No one argued otherwise.

In Operation "Plunder", the Canadians' task was to cross the Rhine and seize Emmerich and the Hoch Elten ridge behind it. To spearhead the crossing, General

Dempsey's Second British Army had the lead, with the 9th Brigade of the 3rd Canadian Division, temporarily attached to Britain's famed 51st Highland Division, playing a key role.

The assault began at 10:00 P.M. on March 23, with British army and Royal Marine Commandos. By midnight they were in Wesel and the ancient trading city was in ruins. Farther north, the 51st Division's objectives were Rees, Speldorp, and Beinen. The Highlanders ran into the 15th Panzer Division and brutal street fighting. When the Highland Light Infantry, a unit from south-western Ontario, crossed in Buffaloes before dawn on the 24th, their first job was to rescue a platoon of the British Black Watch. The battle turned into the toughest two-day struggle the Canadian battalions could remember. Caught in a bottleneck between the river and swamps, the North Novas lost 114 men, 44 of them dead, before the HLI could help them. Progress was slow, admitted the HLI war diary, "as the enemy fought like madmen." When the rest of 3rd Canadian Division attacked Emmerich, veterans described the destruction as worse than Monte Cassino, the notorious Italian battle. German tanks hidden in buildings swept the narrow streets. Canadian soldiers fought their way systematically, house by house. Finally, on the night of the 30th–31st, the Queen's Own Rifles and the Chaudières lined up to assault the Hoch Elten ridge. To their astonished delight, they found little resistance. Artillery and Allied airpower finally had a target they could pulverize. Lieutenant-Colonel Ross of the Chaudières exaggerated only a little when he called this objective "*peut-être le plus*

Moving through Arnhem in April 1945, these Governor-General's Horse Guards stop to get their orders from their sergeant.

69

Cold, soggy, flooded fields made fighting appallingly reminiscent of Great War battlefields, but from November 1944 until March 1945 Canadian soldiers had to live and fight in such conditions.

bombardé dans l'histoire de la guerre." By April 1, Crerar's engineers had built the first of three Rhine bridges.

With the Rhine crossed, Montgomery and the American generals again argued over the right way to invade Germany. Having created his bridgehead, Montgomery wanted the strength to force his way to Berlin. Earlier that had been Eisenhower's strategy, but he had changed his mind. If the Red Army was thirty miles from the Führer's capital, as the Soviets claimed, they should take the city and the Western allies should settle for a broader advance. Besides, Montgomery's plan would put him back in charge of major U.S. forces and, after the Ardennes, American generals and possibly Congress would be furious. The U.S. Ninth Army passed from Montgomery to his resentful U.S. counterpart, General Omar Bradley, and the 21st Army Group prepared to move forward on a broad front to the Elbe.

For much of the world, the result of the Soviet advance would be enormous. For the Canadians on the left flank of the Allied armies, there was no share in the debate and little understanding of the consequences. Reinforced by Foulkes' I Corps, with the divisions from Italy, Crerar's army finally had a majority of Canadian troops. The newcomers headed for Arnhem and Apeldoorn, sweeping around to hold the Germans in western Holland, while Simonds' II Corps headed east and north across The Netherlands and into Germany.

For front-line Canadian soldiers, the next few weeks brought a kaleidoscopic experience of cheering Dutch throngs and savage battles with Dutch SS and German paratroopers—often with the Dutch resistance fighters as valiant allies of the Canadians. Mostly, though, the Germans wanted to get away and Crerar was happy to let them, if it liberated The Netherlands and saved its starving people. Groningen, a city of 140,000, was typical. Dutch SS lurked as snipers upstairs, and with machine-guns in basements. When the 2nd Division entered the city on April 15, it took four days to crush resistance. Civilians crowded the streets, ignoring flying bullets to greet their liberators. Canadians would remember Groningen as a strange mixture of bitter fighting and wild parties, some of them fuelled by the contents of a warehouse of gin "Reserved for the *Wehrmacht*".

Near Otterloo, fleeing German units almost overran the headquarters of the 5th Armoured Division. In his pyjamas, Major-General Bert Hoffmeister led cooks, clerks, and staff officers in a six-hour battle in pitch-darkness. At a cost of 50 casualties, the Canadians left 300 Germans dead and wounded and captured 250 prisoners. Sergeant Edward

Knight of the 60th Battery, Royal Canadian Artillery, killed one German with his pistol and, when it jammed, strangled another with his bare hands. After Otterloo, another gunner complained, everything was really dull. For men of "Hoffy's Mighty Maroon Machine", it was only another of their legends.

In western Holland, Foulkes' corps faced a new problem—behind the German lines, Dutch civilians were starving. By March, even German concentration-camp inmates had bigger rations. The army's orders were clear: nothing short of unconditional surrender. Crerar and Foulkes faced decisions no Canadian had ever had to make before. Fortunately, Foulkes' Allied superiors shared his humanitarian priorities. Even if it meant negotiating with Nazis, Dutch lives mattered more. Canadians halted at the Grebbe line, an old Dutch defence system. After three meetings with nervous German generals, 360 Canadian and British army trucks began delivering a thousand tons of food a day to points inside the German lines. Meanwhile, Canadian squadrons in Bomber Command joined in Operation "Manna", dropping packs of British compo rations, dried fish, medical supplies, and Red Cross parcels near Amsterdam, Haarlem, and The Hague.

By April 6, II Corps had passed through The Netherlands and back into Germany. There were no more welcoming crowds. When German civilians were found helping their troops, Vokes ordered houses destroyed. At Friesoythe the Argyll and Sutherland Highlanders' popular colonel, Fred Wigle, was killed. Vokes heard that he had been shot in the back by civilians, and ordered the village bulldozed. Later he learned that Wigle had been killed by German soldiers trying to

escape. "I confess now to a feeling still of great loss over Wigle," Vokes recalled, "and a feeling of no great remorse over the elimination of Friesoythe."

Nowhere was the fighting easy. German sailors, marines, and students from military schools had something to prove to enemy invaders, and if their resistance was increasingly disorganized, it was always dangerous. Canadians remembered steady, soaking rain, bone-weariness, and constant danger. In three days of clearing the approaches to Oldenberg, from April 26 to April 29, the 5th Brigade lost 130 casualties, almost a tenth of its fighting strength. Le Régiment de Maisonneuve suffered most, with 54 dead and wounded.

On April 25, Canadian bombers from 6 Group attacked Hitler's Alpine retreat at

As they liberated The Netherlands, Canadians were welcomed with jubilation. At Groningen, accompanied by the ever-present small boys, the 5th Canadian Armoured Division marched through the ruins to a service of thanksgiving on May 13, 1945.

Berchtesgaden and coastal batteries on the Frisian Islands. Four of the 192 planes did not return from 6 Group's last bombing raid.

By late April there was little resistance to the British, American, and Canadian advance. Germans, civilian and military, were desperate to flee the advancing Russians, even if it meant filling the huge open-air "cages" where the Allies gathered their prisoners. Still the soldiers moved warily. No one wanted to be the last to die from a German booby-trap, a sniper, or some Nazi fanatic.

And few felt charitable to the defeated, either. Throughout the war, rumours of hideous Nazi atrocities had circulated, but most Canadians had discounted them as myths, like the "bayoneted babies" and "crucified Canadians" of the earlier war. Once the Allies were in Germany, the evidence was horribly apparent. British troops liberated Bergen-Belsen and Canadian war artist Alex Colville was sent to sketch the scenes. He would never forget the horror or the stench; nor would anyone who saw them. Pitiful survivors, skin and bones in their striped rags, stacks of dead, and the gas ovens of Hitler's "Final Solution" were all the proof soldiers needed of Hitler's near-success in ridding Europe of those he deemed "undesirable". Allied officers rounded up German civilians and marched them through the camps, certain that neither they nor anyone else would ever be able to deny the unspeakable bestiality they had witnessed.

The war in Europe was over, but who could make it stop? Soviet armies inched their way into Berlin against desperate resistance. On April 29, deep in his bunker, Hitler finally married his mistress, Eva Braun. Next day, they committed suicide. A loyal few followed suit; others joined in a wild debauch. The Nazi regime dissolved. Power fell to Grand Admiral Karl Dönitz, mastermind of the u-boat war and the man fated to hand over his shattered, despised country to its enemies. On May 3, Montgomery's staff had begun negotiations with the opposing German commanders. Soon after noon on May 4, Crerar got the news: fighting would stop at 8:00 A.M. on the 5th, London time. At 8:35 that night, the BBC reported an unconditional German surrender. On May 5, in an unheated hotel room in Wageningen, Foulkes accepted the surrender of German forces in The Netherlands from General Johannes Blaskowitz and his staff. The I Corps war diary reported: "They looked like men in a dream, dazed, stupefied and unable to realize that for them their world was utterly finished." Or perhaps they knew it too well.

Ordinary soldiers on both sides slowly realized that they had won a reprieve from death or mutilation. But there were dangers still. On May 4, the chaplain and another officer of the Canadian Grenadier Guards went forward to help some German wounded. They were killed. Major Sandy Pearson summoned his company of Calgary Highlanders to announce peace. "There were no cheers or celebration," he recalled, "just great relief." "I think we were all a bit numb," Major-General Harry Foster of the 1st Division remembered, "I think everyone was just too bloody tired to get excited." Farther back there was more energy for celebration. A Dutch teenager in The Hague remembered that a tank came down the street and he had no breath left to cheer. "There was a big hush over all the people, and it was suddenly broken by a big scream, as if it was out of the earth, and the people climbed on the tank and took the soldier out, and they were crying."

John Gray, a wartime intelligence officer and future publisher, found his euphoria dampened when he discovered German soldiers outside a big house in Holland waving, shouting, and obviously as happy as the liberated Dutch.

It wasn't just a rough hockey game we had all been playing, and even if these men had not committed the mindless bestialities of the Nazis—of which we had still to learn the full story—they could not expect us to stop thinking them loathsome just because pieces of paper had been signed saying the shooting would stop . . . .

Far away in the Pacific, the shooting and the suffering had not stopped.

CHAPTER THREE

LIVING TOTAL WAR

Rationing, shortages, controls, worries—for Canadians at home that was what the war meant. Life changed dramatically and, except for those whose husbands, sons, or brothers fought and died overseas, generally much for the better.

(Left)With sons and husbands away, some women found comfort in cooking or purchasing special treats for servicemen. These Haligonians put together party foods for the navy.

(Above) This mother working at the shipyard at Pictou, N. S. found her own solution to the daycare problem.

75

"THE TIME IS NEAR TO LAUNCH YOUR spring offensive," *Chatelaine* told its readers in March 1945. "Your enemy is that ubiquitous fellow, Dirt," and if Dirt could be attacked first in "preliminary skirmishes" then the "Big Drive" would finish him off. For five years the government, assisted by the media, mobilized Canadians' resources and mustered their full strength behind the struggle. In the process, Canadians worked together more closely than ever before. The Gross National Product more than doubled between 1939 and 1945, the greatest period of growth in the country's history. And almost 50 per cent of the GNP went to arming and supplying soldiers, sailors, and airmen and to aiding the nation's allies—a staggering statistic, especially when compared to the approximately 10 to 15 per cent of a much smaller GNP spent that way in the First World War.

What made the huge spending on war even more impressive was that the government, equipped with an able public service and economic and statistical tools that had not been at hand in 1914, simultaneously controlled inflation and managed the distribution of civilian supplies much better than in the previous war. Between 1914 and 1918, inflation had galloped out of control, producing food, fuel, and housing prices so much higher that labour unrest developed on an unparalleled scale. But not this time. The Wartime Prices and Trade Board opened its doors in September 1939, and for two years ruled with a light hand. Once inflation began to pick up steam, however, the WPTB clamped down and imposed price and wage controls in October 1941. The results, achieved through a combination of exhortatory advertising and sometimes tough prosecution of cheating butchers and bootleggers, were stunningly successful. The flow of goods to department stores and corner groceries, while reduced sub-

Despite shortages, companies tried to keep their products in the public eye, offering recipes that could stretch out rationed foods. This Heinz ad from October 1945 reflects the effort to get meat to liberated Europe.

stantially, was nonetheless maintained, and prices were tightly controlled. As a result, the overall cost of living in April 1945 was only 18 per cent higher than at the beginning of the war; after the imposition of price controls, food prices to the end of the war rose by only 6 per cent, rents by 1 per cent, and clothing by less than 2 per cent; fuel prices actually declined.

"It's legal now," *Chatelaine* told its readers just before the end of the war, "to own a new evening dress that touches the floor." Full-length skirts, provided that they were made of fabrics "not directed to the manufacture of essential garments", were allowed again. So too were dresses with more than nine buttons and hems of more than two inches, and lounging pyjamas and teddies, considered too frivolous during wartime. At the end of 1944 the federal government also lifted restrictions on the number of shades and brands of cosmetics. "The lid's off," the newspapers cheered.

The war's impact on the lives of Canadians at home was far-reaching. Every aspect of daily living was affected, from the clothes people could buy to the food they ate, the jobs they held, and the cities and towns they lived in. The ordinary freedom to choose was constrained to a degree that was simply frightening. But controls and constraints became normal and those who violated them faced severe penalties, ranging from harsh looks from neighbours and co-workers (who were encouraged to report violators) to jail terms or fines. Canada was at war, and the government demanded that everyone, man, woman, and child, play a role.

Clothing was one aspect dramatically affected. Silk stockings, common if expensive before the war, had all but disappeared, so much so that in Britain and overseas, not to mention Canada, they had literally become hard currency. "A pair of full-fashioned hose is the most prized possession in the wardrobe," *Saturday Night* told its readers. Women painted their legs, complete with "seams" down the back, or, grumbling, resorted to thicker rayon or even thicker lisle. Teenagers wore bobby sox and everyone waited for nylons, the miracle hosiery of the 1940s, to reach the stores with the coming of peace.

Homemakers also had to deal with rationing in the kitchen. Some foods almost disappeared—as late as 1945, baked beans were limited to half the 1941 production, canned soups were in short supply, and most of the country's canned salmon was still being sent overseas. Worse still, the WPTB had put coupon rationing in place for sugar, tea, coffee, and butter in 1942; in 1943, meat and preserves went on the list and polls reported that only 45 per cent of Canadians favoured tighter restrictions, a sign that the pinch was being felt. The family ration books had to be kept safe; to lose them meant going without until they were replaced. Sugar and butter initially were limited to a half-pound per person per week, though both rations

Canadians had to accept food rationing as part of wartime life from 1942 onwards. But compared to Britain or, far worse still, occupied Europe, the restrictions were never especially onerous.

Cigarettes destined for soldiers overseas were very inexpensive, and civilians and companies, like this Calgary bakery, kept the boys well supplied.

would be reduced before war's end. Tea and coffee were first limited to one ounce of tea or four ounces of coffee per person per week. The meat ration varied, depending on cut, from one to 2.5 pounds per week per person, and housewives, while trying to keep on good terms with their local butcher, kept careful track of the coin-sized blue cardboard tokens that had to be turned in for meat. There were also meatless days, laid down by Ottawa's "price czar", as Donald Gordon, the head of the WPTB, was usually called in the press.

Quickly a black market in meat took shape, as farmers, slaughterhouses, and shady meat dealers co-operated to bypass government inspectors. Early in 1943, many butcher shops and restaurants maintained that they could not get meat without paying extra under the table, and the A&P grocery chain, which refused to deal with black marketeers, had to close five Ontario stores temporarily when they could not get supplies in August 1943. The quantities of meat allowed to families by the WPTB were, in fact, far from skimpy, and the recipes in women's magazines would have sounded lavish indeed to struggling housewives in Britain or on the Continent. *Chatelaine*'s suggested dinners for a week in January 1945 were roast chicken, meat balls, lamb chops, pot roast, cold pot roast, baked cod, and meat pie. About all that was short in Canada was pork, thanks to shipments for overseas and a drop in Canadian hog production. By mid-1945, however, American officials were warning that livestock numbers were falling and that, if a hungry Europe was to be fed, the meat ration in North America might have to be cut. That included Canadians, the Americans suggested. Ottawa thought differently. The U.S. problem was home-made, Canadian officials insisted, because only federally inspected U.S. meat could be sent across state lines or shipped overseas.

As usual, Washington's pressure forced Canada to follow suit, though Canadians were assured that a renewal of meat rationing was due to European famine. From July 13, restaurants were ordered to observe meatless Tuesdays and Fridays. In September the meat ration was reduced to twenty-one ounces of unboned meat a week, and protests erupted from Charlottetown to Victoria. Some butchers in Montreal closed their shops and, backed by thousands of longshoremen, overturned meat trucks and fought baton-wielding police. Seventy-three were injured and a police sergeant was left near death with a fractured skull. More constructively, *Maclean's* interviewed Marcel Thomas, the chef at Montreal's tony Mount Royal Hotel. Meatless days, Thomas said, made life more interesting; besides, rabbit was available although hard to find. Happily for Scots, the WPTB ruled that haggis could be eaten on one meatless day, Friday November 30—St. Andrew's Day. "It was felt that an exception could be

Though people were weary of trying to make do with what they had, clever ads like this turned domestic sacrifices into vicarious war exploits.

IT WAS FLANNELLETTE Grandma was after, twelve yards for three night shirts. But when the clerk mentioned flannellette was getting scarce, she bought the whole bolt! Grandma didn't *mean* to be a saboteur. But she is . . . she's a hoarder.

You know, of course, that many products are getting scarce. That's why it's so terribly important to buy wisely. In the case of washables, for instance—

shirts, shorts, dresses, overalls, pajamas—it's important to get them Sanforized if you can to avoid waste from shrinkage. And for heaven's sake don't buy any more than you need. It's one thing you can do to help *win*.

·SANFORIZED·
Reg. trade-mark

In times of hardship, some people naturally put their own families first. It was a job to convince them that cheerful, well-meaning Granny was a traitor just because she bought a whole bolt of flannellette.

made for haggis," *Time* interpreted the board's decree, "because as many Scots contend it is a hardship to eat as maintain it is a hardship to go without." Almost as suddenly as it had been imposed, meat rationing disappeared. The United States, exporting a mere 5 per cent of its meat production compared to Canada's 30 per cent, announced that its rationing was at an end. Canada followed suit, though one official observed bitterly that "It was a hell of a Christmas present to the people of Europe."

Wartime sugar rationing interfered with candy-making and baking, and dietitians strained to produce recipes that could be made without sugar. Magic Baking Powder recommended its "luscious" Shadow cake—"It doesn't call for a grain of sugar." Clever cooks experimented with honey or maple syrup.

Cigarettes were often in short supply and, being heavily taxed, cost more than before the war (though, thanks to the co-operation of the tobacco companies and the government, a dollar could send 300 smokes to soldiers overseas; for prisoners of war in enemy hands the price was even lower). Liquor, so heavily taxed that a $3.50 bottle of rye whisky produced $2.70 for Ottawa, was scarce because alcohol was an essential ingredient in munitions production. At the end of 1942 the federal government took control, cutting off liquor advertising, controlling the hours of taverns, and limiting adult Canadians to one case of beer, forty ounces of liquor, and four bottles of wine a month, presumably an ample amount for all but the most sodden. But the allowed quantities were not always available—at one point only twelve ounces of liquor per month could be secured in Ontario—and the lineups outside provincial liquor stores were always lengthy. As a result, bootleggers thrived, charging up to five times the usual price for bathtub booze, sometimes spiked with shaving cream, shoe polish, or Gestetner machine fluid, and flavoured with lemon extract. In May 1945, de-icer killed three Winnipeg women and an airman. The next month a hundred drunken migrant farmworkers terrorized Tillsonburg, Ontario, their anger fuelled by a mixture of shaving lotion and hair tonic. "When you ration anything to grown-ups," warned the Winnipeg coroner, "that is the thing they want most of all." Controlled or not, those who sought to get drunk managed to find the alcohol, and

the alarmed Toronto police observed that wartime prosperity had produced record numbers of arrests for drunkenness. In 1944, the number of men arrested was 50 per cent higher than in 1936; the number of women arrested for public drunkenness was almost double the 1936 figure, though only one-eighth the number of men locked up.

Not that drinking was made attractive anywhere in Canada. Surly employees in government liquor stores sold whisky by the bottle, discreetly hidden in brown paper bags. In taverns there were usually separate rooms for men only and for women and their escorts. Tavern regulations banned entertainment, music, and food, leaving patrons nothing to do but sit and drink as much and as fast as possible. Still sternly prohibitionist, Toronto's *Telegram* agreed with suggestions that George Drew's Ontario government shut down women's beer parlours: "Ontario does not wish to have repetitions here of . . . the laxity of morals in the United States which has accompanied . . . saloons and cocktail bars." Some were wiser. An Anglican bishop in British Columbia, the Right Reverend Eustace Sexton, caused a brief stir by warning that compelling drinkers to resort to hotel bedrooms "leads in many cases to other abuses. . . . Every citizen ought to be able in a free country to order a mug of beer or a glass of wine with his meals." The province's Ministerial Association was properly outraged: would Sexton want his daughter to work as a barmaid? A slur on barmaids, the Vancouver Trades and Labour Council shouted, backing the bishop.

The government urged cooks to save their old kitchen fat and bones for the war effort. "Fat is ammunition," WPTB advertisements said. "Do you know: One pound of fat supplies enough glycerine to fire 150 bullets from a Bren gun. . . . Bones produce fat and aircraft glue. . . . Save and strain every drop to speed victory." Butchers bought the used fat and bones from their customers, paying four cents a pound.

At Deer Island, at the mouth of New Brunswick's Passamaquoddy Bay, everyone who could scooped up herring. Herring scales were a crucial element in the United States Navy's fire-fighting compound, and the factory that turned the scales into a foul-smelling paste paid its workers a lavish $50 a day.

Everywhere across the country, there seemed to be scarcely a family that did not

have a Victory garden to produce radishes, carrots, and tomatoes; backyards were too valuable to be allowed to grow only grass. People without yards dug up plots in communal Victory gardens, often located under power lines or in other waste space.

The government also mobilized the nation's money. A series of Victory Loans

To finance the war and control inflation, the government soaked up as much disposable income as possible in Victory bond and stamp campaigns. In 1942 Calgary, drugstores took turns sending stamp-sellers out to dun passers-by for their quarters.

extracted cash from individuals and corporations, helping to damp the fires of inflation and to finance the war's costs. The first war loan, in January 1940, raised only $200 million. The eighth, in April 1945, took in an astonishing $1,568 million, or about one-seventh of that year's GNP. The media gave Victory Loan advertisers as much space as they wanted, and newspapers in the big cities and small towns used their front pages to urge Canadians to give: "Come on Canada!" the Toronto *Globe and Mail* blared on its entire front page. "Buy the new Victory Bonds."

Taxes drew in billions more. The government's aim was to pay as much of the war's cost as possible through taxation, and to use tax policy to ensure that those able to afford it paid the most. The left-wing monthly *The Canadian Forum* noted with approval that for those with $500,000 in income, the tax bill was $433,682. There were not very many like that, however. In 1939 a single taxpayer earning $10,000—a very large amount indeed—paid only $946 in income tax. The same taxpayer in 1944 paid $4,312 plus another $400 in refundable but compulsory savings. A married taxpayer with two children and the same income saw income taxes increase from $660 to $3,346 plus $600 in compulsory savings over the same period. Farther down the income ladder, the increases were proportionate, and eight times as many Canadians paid taxes.

Corporations too were hard hit. Businesses paid a tax of 18 per cent on profits, and in addition they paid excess-profits taxes

As part of the 1945 Victory Bond drive, a naval gun and a 25-pounder took position on Regina's beflagged Scarth St. The local boys would have been happier, though, if the sentries had stayed home.

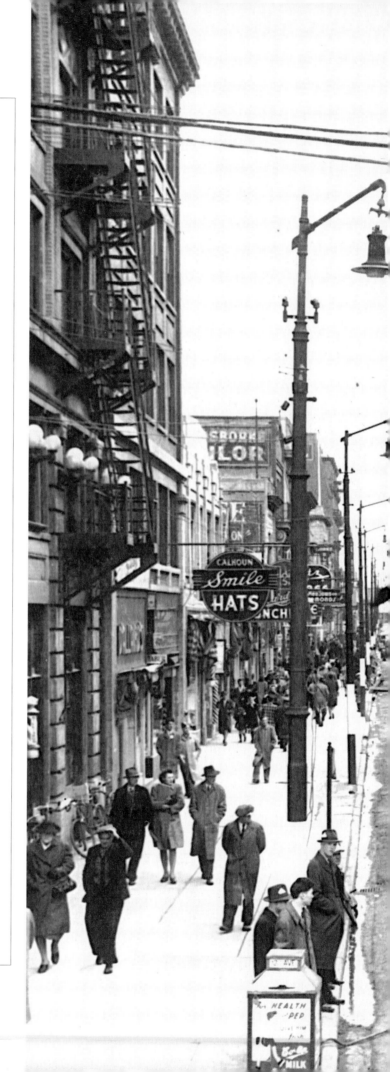

This drugstore in Crossfield, Alta., devoted its window to encouraging Victory Bond purchases—driving home its point with photos of the local men and women who were in the forces.

that ranged up to 100 per cent, the excess being everything above the "standard" of profits for the years 1936 to 1939. No matter how much money it made during the war, no company could retain more than 70 per cent of its prewar "standard". Still, the sales of such corporations as Ford, John Inglis, Canadian Pacific, and Inco were so huge, the write-offs available for plant improvements so generous, that the country's large concerns were in their best shape since the 1920s.

Perhaps that was what led stern critics to complain that Canadians had it too soft. "We in Canada are at war but not in the war," *Saturday Night* said early in 1945; "we don't know what being in the war means. But the people of France and Belgium know." That was true, as was the magazine's food writer's complaint that "If we did realize it more fully perhaps our citizens would not stage a run on the tea and coffee supplies just because of an unfounded rumour, or grab off all their ration books allow them to buy when they eat half their meals out, and so don't need all the butter and sugar." Hoarding was against the law, punishable by a $5,000 fine and up to two years' imprisonment, but it was hard to prove. The WPTB's advertising urged Canadians not to be "a cupboard Quisling. Is that too hard a name for people who selfishly lay in unnecessary stocks of clothes or food, or other goods for fear of shortages?"

In fact, even with rationing and scarcities there was still so much food in Canada that consumption was greater than it had been during the Depression. Most people had money, something they had not had a few years before, and rationing tended to equalize distribution. Food in profusion astonished and angered visiting Americans, who somehow failed to realize that a different country might have different restrictions on scarce goods. One Boston newspaper reporter, whose article caused a "flapdoodle" in the Canadian media, described Canada as a land of milk and honey—and steaks. Cross-border shoppers from Detroit poured across the river (sometimes causing delays of up to four hours in the tunnel and three hours on the bridge) to hit the shops of Windsor and get the rubbers, overshoes, canned meat, and chicken they couldn't find at home. "They are the best customers we have," one operator of a stand at the city's farmers' market said; "they really buy—don't even ask the price." In 1945, when meat rationing ended in Canada, Detroiters flooded in and, because live chickens could not be carried on their city buses, caused a municipal crisis by slaughtering the birds in Windsor's streets. Some, *Time* reported, "stamped on their heads or decapitated them by slamming doors on their heads." For their part, Windsor shoppers crossed the bridge to buy infants' clothing, towels, and women's underwear, all in short supply in Canada. Some Canadians wore their purchases home to avoid Canada Customs.

Though food was readily available, new cars were not. Ford and General Motors, the leading automobile manufacturers, directed their production to the military market, with civilian automobile production for Canada in 1941, 1942, and 1943 totalling under 12,000. Canadians made do with prewar cars, worrying over their balding tires and hunting for spare parts. "He's doing wonders keeping them rolling," the Ford Motor Company told the public, urging them to be understanding of their dealers' "valiant effort to service your car" in the face of shortages of mechanics and parts. The shortages were genuine. With Canada's prewar sources of natural rubber closed off by the war in the Pacific, tire production fell, and what there was went to the armed forces. New or used tires could not legally be bought, sold, or traded after May 1942, and the same rule applied to inner tubes. Tires were available only for "essential" users—doctors, for example, who had to make their house calls, or clergymen or farmers—and even then they were scarce. The black market in tires thrived. Tire thieves also flourished, stripping the tires off parked cars with practised speed.

Gasoline, though rationed, was readily available in under-the-table transactions. In 1941, aiming to reduce non-essential consumption by half, the government decreed that gas could not be sold between 7:00 P.M. and 7:00 A.M. on weekdays or from 7:00 P.M. Saturday to 7:00 A.M. Monday. The next year, coupon rationing limited non-essential

New automobiles were impossible to acquire in wartime Canada, but even older ones could become patriotic billboards. This "Churchill mobile" won first prize in a Hanna, Alta., parade in 1942.

Victory Loans

At the beginning of the First World War, no one believed that money for the war could be raised from ordinary Canadians; the country's borrowing had always been handled in London. But by 1916 the British economy strained under the shock of total war, and the Canadian government had no choice but to seek other sources of funds; it turned to the people. To everyone's astonishment, the money poured in, and when the Second World War began Ottawa was ready to go back to the well.

The carefully organized fund-raising campaigns began in January 1940 and continued throughout the war, backed by the full resources of advertising agencies and the willing co-operation of newspapers, magazines, and radio. Bond advertising featured superb posters and emotive phrases that implicitly suggested how easy Canadians had it at home while their men overseas risked their lives in battle. By VE Day ten public bond issues had raised a phenomenal $10.24 billion, each successive campaign generating more income from more individuals.

At the same time as it appealed to the affluent, Ottawa tapped the piggy-banks of the rest of the nation. War savings certificates were available in amounts from $5 to $500. Sold at 80 per cent of their face value, they matured in seven and a half years. These generated another $318 million. Then there were war savings stamps, priced at 25 cents each. When $4 worth of stamps had been accumulated by children, they could be turned in for a $5 war certificate. The stamps raised another $50 million. And as there was little to buy in wartime Canada, the government's bond campaigns sucked money out of the economy and helped keep inflation under control. When peace returned, the cashing in of all of these carefully hoarded bonds and certificates helped fund the civilian economy and got the postwar boom rolling.

Money was needed to fight the war, and advertising agencies and entertainment industries threw themselves into the task. In Saskatchewan, a western motif—with the requisite music and pretty girls—drew crowds to buy War Savings Stamps.

users to 120 gallons a year, enough for 2,000 miles of driving. Tourists were allowed only 20 gallons for their stay in Canada. Milk and bread delivery to homes in the cities was curtailed and truckers—except for those on long-haul routes—had their operations limited to a 35-mile radius. Such tight regulation guaranteed that the desperate would willingly pay high prices for their gas—30, 40, or even 50 cents a gallon!—and while the government calculated that rationing had reduced overall consumption by 5 per cent in 1942, at least 300 million gallons found their way onto the black market.

Rationed and restricted though they were, Canadians tried to keep up the semblance of normal life. Wherever they lived, the radio kept them informed and entertained, the movies provided escapism, and music got their blood pounding. People danced to Glenn Miller's "Moonlight Serenade" or "Slip Horn Jive" and Benny Goodman's "Bugle Call Rag", and swooned over Frank Sinatra's lush "Night and Day" and Bing Crosby's "Don't Fence Me In". The "crooners" made teenage girls go crazy, so much so that ministers preached about the collapse of moral standards and warned of the dangers of misplaced and excessive emotion. Older Canadians wept when they heard nostalgic songs like "The White Cliffs of Dover" and "When the Lights Go On Again" and old sweats laughed at "Kiss Me Goodnight, Sergeant-Major". The movie houses were packed and patriotic Hollywood films were the favourites.

Major-league baseball continued in the United States, and Canadian cities near the border followed the Detroit Tigers and Cleveland Indians very closely. At home, football proceeded with teams of servicemen playing in the professional and amateur leagues. The National Hockey League maintained its schedule, though most of the best players were in the forces. Army, navy, and air force teams played excellent hockey, depending on the whims of postings and the ability of commanding officers to cajole Ottawa headquarters for a good left-winger. But some genuine stars remained in the professional league. The fiery Maurice Richard played for the Montreal Canadiens from 1942 onward, and "The Rocket" scored fifty goals in the fifty-game season of 1944–45, the first player to accomplish that feat. English-speaking fans complained that he would never have managed fifty goals had the NHL been at full strength; others griped bitterly that the twenty-three-year-old Richard ought to be in the army. More, however, admired Richard's blinding speed and hard, accurate shot.

With their fathers, brothers, or uncles absent overseas, youngsters collected bubble-gum or cigarette cards featuring the characteristics of the 25-pounder and the Sherman tank. They built Spitfires and Lancasters out of balsa wood (if it could be found in hobby stores) and devoured comic books, though the government's War Exchange Conservation Act blocked the importation of comics from the United States. Home-produced substitutes, printed in black and white, gradually found fans after their introduction in 1941. *The Invisible Commando* and *Captain Wonder* had their readers, but the favourite was *Johnny Canuck*. "Canada's answer to Nazi oppression", Johnny Canuck battled Hitler's villains, all of whom spoke guttural English: "Ach! fools . . . you promise arrest, but dot svine Canuck goes on smashing our war machine!" Escaping yet again from Nazi captivity, Johnny Canuck boasted that "The Germans had better start making

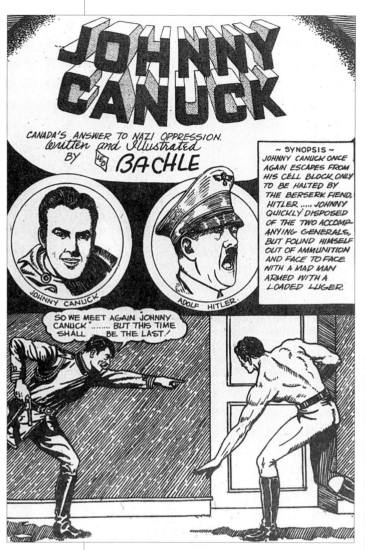

Bare-chested and bemuscled "Johnny Canuck" foiled the Nazis in "Canadian white" comic books, printed in black and white to save scarce dyes.

more bellicose Shakespearean plays than usual. Physical fitness received heavy emphasis, and school cadet corps, always commanded by teachers with Great War experience, began the process of preparing boys for service if the war lasted longer than all hoped. "Straighten up, you boys," the martinets shouted at their laggard cadets. "What kind of soldiers will you make?" The schools were short-handed too, with male and female teachers enlisting by the thousands, and the retired teachers who were rehired to fill in sometimes lacked the energy to keep up with their young pupils in increasingly crowded classrooms.

The teachers may have been less sure of the war's outcome than their students, certainly until 1943 or 1944. Everyone listened to the radio for news and each night the deep bass of Lorne Greene, dubbed "the voice of doom", read the national news over the CBC. By 1945 the reports were almost all upbeat, as the Axis, the popular term for the Berlin-Rome-Tokyo alliance, suffered defeat after defeat. (Italy's Duce, Benito Mussolini, in fact, had been toppled from power in September 1943, and Italy, though not all Italians, was nominally attached to the Allied side after that date.) On the lighter side of radio entertainment, "The Happy Gang" was heard at noon six days a week and became a beloved national institution: "Knock! Knock!" "Who's there?" "It's the Happy Gang!" "We-l-l-l come on in!" was soon the country's most popular bit of patter.

Happy patter could not hide the war's horror. Young women sometimes plunged headlong into marriage with boys who had

stronger ropes if they want to hold Canadians captive." Drawn and written by Leo Bachle, a Toronto commercial artist, Johnny Canuck had no special powers—he was simply an average Canadian, "a fine fighting Canuck" like all the servicemen fighting Hitler.

The schools, like the comics, reinforced the children's certainty that victory was inevitable. "Britons never, never, never shall be slaves," they sang in the classrooms, and all believed it to be so. Much of the school curriculum focused on the war, with history instructors inevitably tilting their classes towards the causes of the conflict, and English teachers looking harder at war poetry or the joined up. Sometimes the newlyweds were together for only a few nights before the groom was dispatched overseas; sometimes the next word came in the form of a telegram from the Department of National Defence, saying that John or Joe had been killed or wounded or was missing in action. The relatives of the missing lived in a fearful limbo, grasping at straws to hope that their son or husband was alive; all too often, definitive word never came, prolonging the agony beyond the humanly endurable. In the cities, telegraph delivery boys were the harbingers of doom, and the dreadful waiting for bad or good news became the constant companion of many. As always, there was someone to profit from unhappiness: cub reporters boasted of their skill in prying photos of soldiers or airmen from grieving families.

While they waited for their men to come home, women worked, entering the war plants at a record pace, thanks to the nation's increasingly acute need for factory workers. The Great Depression, with its unemployment rates well above 20 per cent, had been replaced by a labour shortage. A million men

War, said one officer, was 15 per cent terror and 85 per cent boredom, so magazines and books were much sought after. The Red Cross organized their collection, but shipping space was always scarce.

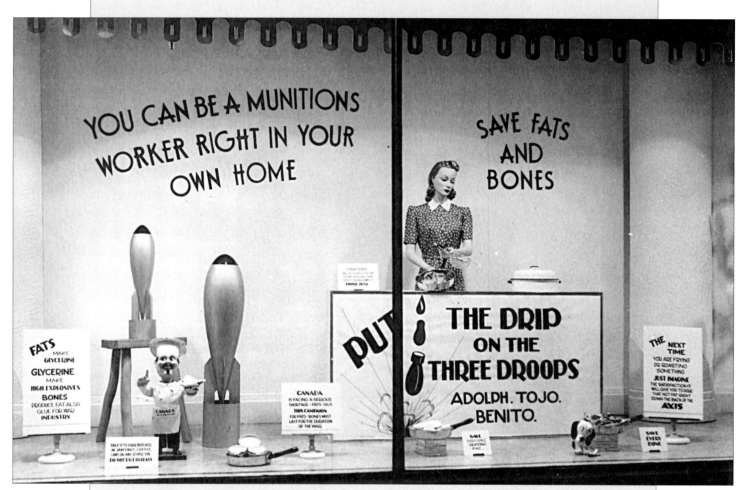

"Repair, Recycle, Reuse"

The effort devoted to wise use of resources was staggering, as this window display demonstrated.

Canadians today, carefully putting out their blue boxes full of glass, cans, and plastics, tying up their newspapers, and composting their food waste, like to think they invented recycling. But compared to the efforts during the war, today's attempts at conservation look like mere gestures.

Waste was a direct attack on the war effort. Housewives saved fat and bones so the glycerine could be extracted for war use. Toothpaste tubes, then made of aluminum, were recycled; so were rubber tires, metal saucepans, and iron fences. Old fur coats were cut down into sailors' vests. Garages were raided by scrap collectors for old Model TS, while farmers contributed ancient ploughs and tractors for conversion into minesweepers and Spitfires. To save scarce dyes, comic books lost their colour, thus creating a much-sought-after present-day collectible, "Canadian whites". To the great satisfaction of prohibitionists, liquor was rationed, freeing scarce grains for export and alcohol for the munitions plants. Boy Scouts scavenged newspapers, and collected wooden six-quart and eight-quart fruit baskets so they could be reused in the next year's harvest. Children looked for milkweed pods, said to be valuable for flotation devices but in fact employed in synthetic rubber experiments (that failed to work). What with scrap drives, paper drives, and bond drives, the home front was regimented as never before or since.

and women joined the armed forces. The war plants—Victory Aircraft in Malton, Ontario, the ammonium nitrate factory at Trail, B.C., the Canadian National Railway's Fort Rouge shops in Winnipeg, New Brunswick's Saint John Dry Dock and Shipbuilding Company, and the Dominion Arsenal in Quebec City, to name only five out of hundreds—increased their number of workers from 115,000 men and 6,000 women in October 1939 to 905,000 men and 261,000 women at the wartime peak in October 1943. Most of those women workers were single, many fleeing from the grinding labour on farms, but thousands were married, often mothers. To make things easier for them, several provinces co-operated with Ottawa on a fifty-fifty shared-cost basis in sponsoring a few daycare centres in large cities. Some of the bigger war plants established their own facilities. There were also more than a million men and almost 800,000 women working in agriculture, where net income tripled between 1939 and 1945 although rural populations declined all across the country. In Alberta, for example, the agricultural population dropped by 25 per cent while farm sizes increased. The disappearing rural population moved to the factories, where they were joined by the urban workers who came off Depression unemployment—civilian industry absorbed almost two million men and women. At the hitherto conservative Royal Bank, for example, women had made up only 21 per cent of the staff in 1939; at the end of the war they accounted for 71 per cent, and that percentage held up into the peace.

Such employment figures, coming after years of depression and despair, meant money in the bank. Wages were controlled by the omnipresent federal government, and they rose slowly during the war. But there was virtually all the overtime everyone could want, and two-income and three-income families were common. The result was that Canadians had more money than ever before—but there was almost nothing to buy except Victory Bonds.

With Dad overseas and Mom in a war plant, Junior was on the streets to all hours. Flouting the wartime clothing regulations by wearing zoot suits with wide-shouldered jackets and pants with twenty-eight-inch-wide trouser legs and twelve-inch pegged cuffs, teenage gangs frequently fought with soldiers or sailors and engaged in petty crimes. The servicemen could handle themselves well in any scuffles, but alarmed police created special squads, told the newspapers about increases in juvenile delinquency, and pressed city councils to enforce 10:00 p.m.

As teenagers developed their own culture, they found a distinctive style of dress. Maclean's noted that while home-knitted diamond socks were "hubba hubba" for him, what she needed was a Deanna Durbin hairdo and as many bangles as possible.

Never let it be said that a new hat was too frivolous for wartime.

curfews for teenagers. No one had any workable solution to the problem, for women had to work and men had to fight, and the government could not simply pass a regulation to put violent teens on short rations. But when the men came back from the war, those trouble-making kids would be brought back into line. "Just wait until your father gets home," exasperated moms said. If Father came home. . . . Probably it was frustration that motivated the teenage hoodlums. In that they were joined by all Canadians; everyone lived in fear that a loved one would be killed overseas, and that constant worry was a major drain on people's energy.

Then there was the severe shortage of living accommodation in cities big and small. Housing was so scarce, and so much of it was substandard in the large cities, that five or six or more men and women frequently shared a single room, their varying hours of shift work giving them their only chance at the bed! It was not only the large cities that had problems. Small prairie towns like Medicine Hat, the site of one of the sixteen British Commonwealth Air Training Plan bases in Alberta, had families living in unheated cellars and garages. Ottawa tried to meet the need with emergency housing construction, but it could simply not keep up. The resentment over wartime crowding—and over gouging by unscrupulous landlords who developed ways to get around the government's freeze on rents—had much to do with the violence of the VE Day riots in Halifax. Still, a military base of any kind meant business for small-town and big-city merchants, and the pages of base newspapers and magazines were crammed with advertisements from local stores, restaurants, and hotels.

Controls worked, in other words, if the public supported them and if shortages were not so extreme as to virtually compel cheating. The WPTB's orders were all-embracing: bicycles could be sold only to those with priority permits; sewing machines and parts could not be produced; the sale of office safes was restricted; the use of elastic in girdles was restricted; hockey sticks could be made only in certain styles; cardboard cake cartons were limited to fourteen styles and sewing thread to only forty-two colours; and the use of metal in luggage was curtailed. The WPTB controlled the pricing of goods, as well, and a butcher who charged more than the permitted price for hamburger risked being fined or forced out of business. Some were.

There was no end to government intrusion. The National Selective Service administration, created to direct the labour force to the places in military or civil life where the demand was greatest, effectively determined who could work and where. To take a job, a Selective Service permit was essential; to leave a job, seven days' notice was necessary; and no employer could ever advertise for workers—only Selective Service

could do that.

The regulations made necessary by war were terribly burdensome, but while people griped, they ultimately accepted the necessity for the controls. Before the war was over, in fact, Canadians had begun to enjoy the

Urban housing was in short supply throughout the war, as workers flooded from the countryside to city factories. A close reading of the garbled first paragraph suggests that Winnipeg officials were beside themselves with worry.

URGENT

AN APPEAL TO EVERY HOUSEHOLDER IN GREATER WINNIPEG

The city is facing a serious housing shortage. Many families, including servicemen returned from overseas, cannot obtain shelter. By May 1st, the crisis will be acute unless the house-will be acute unless the house-holders make their spare accom holders make their spare accommodation available NOW.

To meet the situation a **Winnipeg Emergency Housing** office has been opened at 521 McIntyre Building.

Cards have been mailed to every householder in Greater Winnipeg. If you have spare rooms which you are willing to rent in your home, please fill in your card and return immediately to

Winnipeg Emergency Housing
Office: 521 McIntyre Building   **Phone 97130**

To meet this emergency, act NOW. Your prompt and willing assistance is essential. Please help—it's urgent!

Signed:
G. F. BENTLEY,
City Clerk.

Greetings

FROM NO. 4
I.T.S.

No. 4 INITIAL TRAINING SCHOOL
ROYAL CANADIAN AIR FORCE
EDMONTON, ALBERTA

The BCATP bases created their own sub-cultures. RCAF trainees, most not long out of high school, produced their "school" yearbooks, complete with cartoons, class photographs, and slightly wry comments on their officer "teachers". This cover was on the Christmas 1942 issue.

**BRITISH COMMONWEALTH
AIR TRAINING PLAN STATIONS**

Through the National Selective Service, the government controlled the workforce. Jobs could only be filled through the NSS and there always seemed to be more forms to fill in.

thought, repeated to them regularly in their newspapers, that their system of price controls, rationing, and allocation of scarce labour was the most effective in the world. Those who could remember the chaos that had resulted from ineffective measures in the First World War may have reflected that even government was capable of learning.

While the war had overwhelming popular support, many people worried about their neighbours. Suspicions about those who didn't appear to conform ran deep, and

wartime patriotism permitted no dissent. There were Communists and Nazis, Italian Fascists, and even some supporters of Japan around the land, or so people feared. There were divisions within ethnic groups, religious sects whose loyalty was suspect, and pacifists and conscientious objectors who wanted others to protect their freedom. Those who were different, those whose lack of Britishness seemed suspect in a country that still thought of itself as very British, roused suspicions, and in wartime the aliens, outsiders, and outspoken were sometimes subject to harsh treatment. Tolerance was in scarce supply.

Even before the outbreak of war, Ottawa bureaucrats had laboured for months over the Defence of Canada Regulations, a set of draconian rules that were to come into force

Vancouver was one of the very few Canadian cities that might have been subject to air attack — if Japan's aircraft carriers had survived the battle of Midway. Citizens carried gas masks, studied bomb types, and prepared for the worst.

under authority of the War Measures Act as soon as the federal Cabinet decided. The DOCR allowed the government to control freedom of expression through censorship, control, and suppression of the press; to arrest anyone, Canadian citizen or not, who might be acting in any manner threatening to the public safety or the safety of the state; and even to punish any criticism of the government likely to prejudice recruiting for the armed forces. The regulations also obliged enemy aliens (German citizens, for example) to register with the police, who had power to intern all for whom firm proof of serious disloyalty or subversive activity existed. Internees were subject to special treatment under the rules of war and were entitled to have their interests watched over by a "Protecting Power", a neutral nation. But the distinction between internees and criminals was ordinarily not clear to average Canadians.

As Germany moved towards war in the last days of August 1939, the first lists were drawn up of organizations to be shut down and of individuals to be arrested as potential dangers to the state. The RCMP, which was in charge of public security, had its mind made up: it proposed to outlaw all Nazi, Fascist, and Communist organizations and newspapers, all foreign-language political organizations of Fascist or Communist affiliation, and the English-language Communist press, and it wanted to arrest key members of such organizations. During the Depression, the Mounties had devoted most of their efforts to penetrating Communist organizations, for the collapse of capitalism had emboldened Marxists across the country and had brought large numbers into the party ranks. The Hitler–Stalin pact of August 1939, clearing the way for the Nazi invasion of Poland, reinforced every concern the government had about Communists. But the Mounties were much less up to date on potential enemy agents in the German and Italian communities, and their suggestions demonstrated a startling lack of sense. For example, there were problems in fast action against Italians, External Affairs officials pointed out. Foreign diplomats in Canada were protected by international law, the activities of consular officials within the Italian community were not illegal, and it would surely be a mistake to seize members of Italian Fascist organizations, at least so long as Italy remained neutral. The Communists posed a different problem. Might it not be better to wait until the attitude of Canadian Communists to the German–U.S.S.R. pact could be determined before arresting party leaders?

Reluctantly the Mounties agreed to wait, but known supporters of Nazi organizations such as the National Socialist German Workers Party or the German Labour Front were quickly rounded up. The Defence of Canada Regulations, put into force on September 1—nine days before Canada went to war—gave the government all the weapons it needed, and 303 Germans

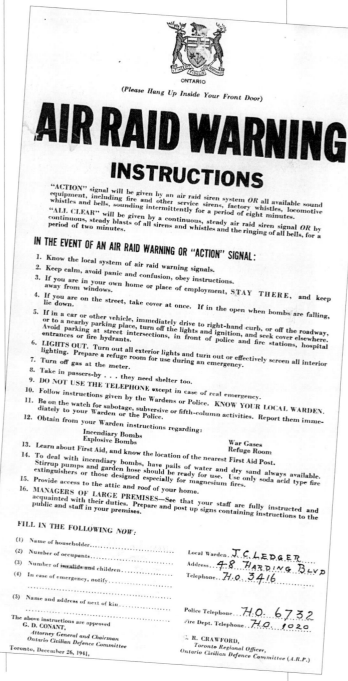

The fear of air raids was real, though it defied logic and the capabilities of wartime aircraft, and the government created elaborate air-raid warning schemes. Blackout curtains were essential, even if (as in point 11) they made it harder to watch out for saboteurs.

and German Canadians were arrested on September 4, again while Canada was still at peace. The public cheered this crushing of the alleged Nazi conspiracy, and the calls for still tougher action were loud. Ontario's attorney-general, Gordon Conant, worried that the "time-honoured principle of British justice, that a man is innocent until proven guilty makes it impossible to curtail the activities of these slimy, subversive elements which are at work not only in this province, but throughout the entire country." In fact, while some of those swept up were convinced Nazis, many were guilty of little more than nostalgia for the old country and were quickly released.

But after Hitler's legions conquered France in May and June 1940 and stood menacingly across the Channel from Britain, there was panic in the land, and the RCMP, fearful of subversive activities like those that reputedly had aided the *Wehrmacht*'s advance, again acted with a heavy hand. Another 350 Germans were arrested and, since Italy had joined the war at Hitler's side in June 1940, more than 500 Italians. Many of the Italian Canadians arrested were simple people who had joined the suppressed organizations for reasons of homesickness; others, however, were spies for the Italian secret police or middle-class individuals who revelled in the power and connections they received through their associations with the Italian consulates and the Fascist Party. No apology was necessary for their internment.

Nor was any needed for the arrest of domestic Fascists in English and French

In North Vancouver's shipyards, Air Raid Precautions (ARP) members formed an auxiliary fire department, much to the satisfaction of officers, executives, and small boys.

The extent of wartime mobilization was impressive, and parades and inspections, designed to encourage Canadians to persist in the struggle, were regular events. Here, CWACs take their turn on parade on Winnipeg's Main St., in 1944.

Canada, those who had worn black or green shirts and offered Nazi or Fascist salutes at their rallies. At the same time the government banned the Communist Party, which had been trying, the RCMP maintained, to "create dissatisfaction and sabotage"; over the next months 133 of its leaders were arrested and placed in preventive detention. Most would not be freed until almost a year after Hitler had invaded the Soviet Union and made Communist Russia an ally of Canada; the ban on the party did not lapse until the end of the war.

So fearful was the mood in the late spring and early summer of 1940 that paramilitary organizations designed to watch over "subversive elements" seemed to be springing up everywhere. In Saskatchewan, a province that had seen a strong Ku Klux Klan movement in the late 1920s, the Liberal provincial government established the Saskatchewan Veterans Civil Security Corps to act "as a deterrent against defeatism" and to check any "subversive talk and action". The

Wartime Boomtime

At the end of 1943, the Canadian Chamber of Commerce commissioned a thorough survey of Kitchener and Waterloo, Ontario, to find out what had happened to this largely urban area during four years of war. In 1939 the area's businesses and factories had employed 9,239 male and 4,288 female workers; by the end of 1943, 3,198 men and 131 women had joined the armed forces, but employment had nonetheless increased to 11,411 men and 6,824 women, a net addition to the work force of more than 8,000. At least 1,200 of those new workers had come from farms in the area, or one from almost every second farm. Despite this loss of labour, farm income had increased from $2,300 a year in 1939 to $3,700 in 1943.

But the real change, amounting to almost an "industrial revolution", the Chamber of Commerce wrote with pardonable hyperbole, took place in the city. Manufacturing sales more than doubled, from $53.7 million to $115.5 million, and the manufacturing payroll increased from $10.9 million to $24.6 million. Wages in manufacturing went from $1,076 a year to $1,708, and middle-income households in Waterloo (those earning between $1,500 and $2,600) increased from 29 to 45 per cent of the population. The Chamber concluded that even after purchasing war bonds and war savings certificates of $17.5 million, "there can be no doubt that in material comforts the population of Kitchener-Waterloo lives, on average, considerably better than it did in 1939—in spite of heavier taxation. . . ." The same survey demonstrated very clearly that Waterloo's people desperately wanted to build onto the gains they had made, and that, while there might be some apprehension about the future, they had every expectation that they would be able to afford consumer purchases—refrigerators, clothing, and vacations—out of their wartime savings. As the survey concluded, if everyone "succeeds in realizing his objectives as stated, the post-war demands of Kitchener-Waterloo can absorb successfully the number of workers then likely to be seeking jobs. . . ."

Wartime employment put money into people's hands and, with little in the way of goods to purchase, Canadians did their duty buying war bonds. Spurred by ads like this, Kitchener-Waterloo's contribution by the end of 1943 was $17.5 million.

Saskatchewan government and many key citizens feared that a heavy ethnic population made the province especially vulnerable, and the 6,500 men of the corps investigated reports of suspected espionage, pro-German speech, and idle talk. More seriously, "foreigners" with good jobs that might have gone to Anglo-Saxons were almost automatically suspect, and Ukrainian organizations and newspapers were watched closely.

The Saskatchewan Corps effectively accomplished nothing, other than to persuade residents that vigilance was being exercised, but its interest in Ukrainian-Canadian organizations was shared by federal agencies. Long before the war, the Ukrainian community's leaders had been sharply divided between pro-Soviet and anti-Soviet factions. Many of the Communist sympathizers had been caught in the round-up of party members in 1940 and their organizations had been closed down, but once Hitler invaded Russia in June 1941, the pro-Communist Ukrainian Canadians quickly became supporters of all-out war. Many anti-Soviet Ukrainians, on the other hand, now looked to the Nazis to liberate Ukraine from Stalin's yoke. The latter attitude could not be readily condoned in wartime Canada, and through the Nationalities Branch of the Department of National War Services the federal government launched a major propaganda campaign at Ukrainian Canadians, engineering a united front of non-Communist Ukrainian organizations under "safe" leadership.

Japanese Canadians were the next ethnic group to fall under suspicion. Since 1931 Japan had been expanding its control over Manchuria and China, and the pace of Japanese intelligence-gathering activities in North America had stepped up. By early 1941 American codebreakers had cracked

Great War vets too old for overseas service were enlisted into the Veterans Guard and used most often to guard POW camps—like this sentry at Wilcox, Sask. Fortunately, most of the POWs were glad to be out of the war.

Tokyo's "Purple" code and discovered efforts to recruit spies among Issei (first-generation) and Nisei (second-generation) Japanese Canadians and Japanese Americans. Such information, largely ignored before Japan's sudden and effective attack on Pearl Harbor on December 7, 1941, now became critically important. Moreover, public opinion in British Columbia, where almost all of Canada's 23,000 people of Japanese origin resided, was desperately

Wartime Movies

With no television to entertain the nation, and with travel limited by gasoline and tire shortages, movie houses filled a huge social need. Every theatre was packed each night (but never on Sunday) and Hollywood films like *Mrs. Miniver* drew tears from those who admired the American interpretation of British pluck. British films like Noel Coward's *In Which We Serve* (a thinly disguised story of the sinking of Lord "Dickie" Mountbatten's HMS *Kelly*) were enormously popular. Canadians especially cheered James Cagney and Dennis Morgan in *Captains of the Clouds*, an American film about the Royal Canadian Air Force and the British Commonwealth Air Training Plan. Cagney played a troublesome Yank who joined the RCAF and rebelled at discipline but eventually sacrificed himself for the greater good—the ultimate wartime message. So important did Ottawa think this film that it put virtually the entire resources of the BCATP at director Michael Curtiz's disposal, and Air Marshal Billy Bishop, the vc-winning fighter ace of the Great War, was happily corralled into appearing in the film, pinning wings on graduating flyers. Other stars of wartime note were Betty Grable, the blonde pinup who decorated Canadian soldiers' barracks every bit as much as American ones, Tyrone Power, Errol Flynn, Paulette Goddard, and Veronica Lake, the sexy actress whose trademark was a tress of hair over one eye.

Of tremendous importance to Canadians is the Warner Brothers production now being filmed in Canada . . . with the co-operation of the Royal Canadian Air Force . . .

CAPTAINS OF THE CLOUDS

Filmed in Technicolor with
JAMES CAGNEY - DENNIS MORGAN
and a cast of thousands
DIRECTED BY MICHAEL CURTIZ

fearful of an invasion. The police arrested a small number of Japanese Canadians immediately after Canada's declaration of war on Japan but this did nothing to calm the public's fears. In January 1942, Ottawa took tougher measures and seized fishing boats, radios, and rifles. And the next month Ottawa caved in to the increasingly hysterical calls for action and ordered the evacuation of all people of Japanese origin from the Pacific coast. Over the next months, the newly established British Columbia Security Commission had the RCMP move the entire Japanese-Canadian community to ramshackle towns in the interior; the evacuees' property was sold for sacrifice prices; and some 700 men, those who had actively proselytized for Japan's victory or had protested too vigorously against the government's repressive policy, found themselves interned at Angler in northern Ontario. The iron heel of ruthlessness had been well and truly applied, and public opinion in British Columbia, left, centre, and

Japanese Canadians were evacuated off the British Columbia coast and moved inland after Japan entered the war. This camp at Hope, B.C., was one of the main relocation sites.

THE PROVINCES

Quebec

When 1945 began, many Quebeckers still seethed at Ottawa's latest broken promise. "Conscription if necessary," Mackenzie King had said in 1942, after the rest of the country had voted to relieve him of his no-conscription promise to Quebec. But who could argue that, with a million men in uniform, it had been necessary to force a few thousand NRMA men to fight in Europe? As usual, French Quebec took it personally. It did not help their traditional faith that Cardinal Villeneuve had sent them a pastoral letter denouncing Hitler and isolationism: "Let us cultivate among ourselves the spirit of heroes, and let our sons, purifying their intentions, learn to die for justice and that faith."

A year before, Quebec voters had shown their opinion of Villeneuve's advice by narrowly restoring the once discredited Maurice Duplessis and his Union Nationale. Cleansed of any reformist illusions, Duplessis promised to battle Ottawa and its huge wartime grab for taxes and social programs. Low taxes and Church-run hospitals and orphanages were what most Quebeckers wanted. Even the Church could take lessons from "Le Chef". Faced by a powerful Catholic delegation demanding stiff enforcement of temperance laws to stop the spread of alcoholism, especially among women and the young, Duplessis pledged to do all that was humanly possible to end such evils—though, he added, he "could not put aside the principles of Christian charity."

Nationalists like René Chaloult insisted that Quebec's social problems were the fault of Ottawa. An excessive war effort had drawn innocent farm girls to the city, destroying the core of French-Canadian culture, the family and the farm. Quebec was experiencing 250 illegitimate births a month, and the debauched women worked in government munitions factories. But that did not stop Quebec City from boosting itself as an ideal headquarters for the new United Nations. A promoter, Armand Viau, promised that $10 million would build three new buildings for the U.N., and a new hotel and more houses would follow. In a more traditional approach to growth, Duplessis promised to resume work on the road to Chibougamau Lake in hope of a mining boom and possibly a tourist influx.

One of the biggest events of the year, in a province passionate about politics, was a by-election in Beauce county, up the Chaudière River. Known for their frugality, Beauceron voters found themselves plied with scotch, paving contracts, and rural electrification, as well as a rich flutter of five- and ten-dollar bills. Visiting reporters were appalled by the corruption, but Duplessis's candidate won easily. Beaucerons kept their reputation for preferring hard cash to speeches—or perhaps, in a county where 3,000 of the 23,000 voters were called Poulin, the victorious Georges-Octave Poulin already had a big edge.

right, was virtually unanimous in hailing the government's actions.

All these steps against enemy aliens and others, however incompetently or unfairly handled, were at least understandable: Germany, Italy, and Japan were at war with Canada. The Communists, in particular, had campaigned against the war until June 1941, and used their influence with trade unions and ethnic groups to try to spread discontent. But how could the banning of the Jehovah's Witnesses be explained? What reason could there be for jailing the mayor of Montreal? And why would the premier of

Ontario try to get a professor at the University of Toronto fired?

The professor in question, Frank Underhill, was a well-known historian and gadfly, a ready man with a well-thought-out speech for any occasion. A socialist, Underhill had spoken at the YMCA's Institute of Politics and Economics at Lake Couchiching, Ontario, in August 1940, and in the course of his remarks he had said that the Canada–U.S. Permanent Joint Board on Defence, created by Mackenzie King and President Roosevelt a few days before, meant the severing of ties between Britain and Canada and the strengthening of Canadian-American links. There would have been nothing startling in such a comment in peacetime, but in the middle of a war, when Britain's survival was in doubt, Underhill's words roused enormous fury in the press. Angry university officials moved to get rid of the troublesome professor, egged on by the Liberal provincial government of Mitchell Hepburn. What saved Underhill, aside from protests by faculty and students, was the intervention of the federal government. One official in the Department of External Affairs wrote the prime minister that a public controversy over Underhill's sacking would "have most serious repercussions" in the United States, "where it would dismay and disappoint our

German POWs brought to Canada spent their war in frustrated safety. Johannes Maron (fourth from right), a member of the Bowmanville, Ont., POW hockey team of 1942–43, emigrated to Canada after the war.

The mayor of Montreal, Camillien Houde, here in a familiar oratorical pose, encouraged his compatriots to resist national registration in August 1940. Ottawa promptly locked him up for the duration.

friends and encourage and strengthen the hands of those who are critical of 'British Imperialism'. . . ." In wartime a few words by a professor could have international ramifications, or so it seemed, and the provincial government and the university quickly backed off. Underhill survived, but the idea of freedom of speech had suffered a blow.

Another such blow, demonstrating that even elected officials were not safe, fell on the mayor of Montreal, Camillien Houde. A large, homely man who resembled a well-known wrestler, "The French Angel", Houde was enormously popular with his working-class constituency. It was this popularity that led the federal government to act when he spoke out in August 1940 against the country's national registration, undertaken under

the National Resources Mobilization Act of June 1940 as a prelude to conscription for home defence. This, he said, was "a measure of conscription" made by a government that in the general election in March had said it was against conscription. "I ask the population not to conform, knowing full well what I am doing presently and to what I expose myself." Little more than forty-eight hours later, Houde was under arrest—"The federal government," Mackenzie King said, "cannot afford to have its laws defied by one of Mayor Houde's prominence"—and confined in preventive detention at Petawawa, Ontario. His "sacrifice" accomplished nothing, for Quebeckers registered in exactly the same proportion as their English-speaking compatriots. Houde was not released until 1944, little chastened by the experience, and he promptly resumed his political career to the cheers of his constituents.

Houde's arrest demonstrated just how concerned Ottawa was that nothing be done to jeopardize Quebec's tepid support for the war. That is the only possible explanation for what was likely the most serious breach of civil liberties during the war, the suppression of an entire religion. On July 4, 1940, the Canadian government passed an order-in-council declaring the Jehovah's Witnesses organization illegal. Membership in the Witnesses, something hitherto enjoyed by 7,000 Canadians, was now a crime. The Witnesses' offices in Toronto, their meeting halls across the country, and the organization's property were seized and handed over to the Custodian of Enemy Property. Over the next three

Big Bands and Boogie-Woogie

The war was the heyday of radio in Canada, and the radio became the greatest disseminator of popular music. New recordings, while occasionally available in music stores, were scarce thanks to wartime shortages, so Canadians danced—or simply listened—to the radio whenever live bands were unavailable. CBC's "Sweet and Low" featured Mart Kenny and His Western Gentlemen, the national network's "Rhythm Time" was the first to showcase "the Brown Bomber of Boogie-Woogie", a very young Oscar Peterson, and "The Victory Parade" brought big bands to radio every week. The music was designed for jitterbugging or for dancing close, and everyone, it seemed, listened on NBC to songs like Bing Crosby's "I'll Be Seeing You" and "Deep in the Heart of Texas", or the Andrews Sisters' "Rum and Coca Cola". The Mills Brothers ("You Always Hurt the One You Love") and the Ink Spots ("Don't Get Around Much Anymore") were probably the most popular black quartets, while Tommy Dorsey, Benny Goodman, Harry James, and Les Brown led American bands of great renown. Glenn Miller and his band had a legendary reputation. Miller's standards, such as "In the Mood" and "Chattanooga Choo-Choo", were incredibly popular and have remained so, although Miller—on active service as an entertainer—died in a wartime airplane crash. Other singers, like Dick Haymes ("You'll Never Know"), Kay Kyser ("Praise the Lord and Pass the Ammunition"), and even the 1920s star Rudy Vallee ("As Time Goes By"), had large followings in Canada.

In the big cities, every high-class hotel, such as the Château Laurier and the Hotel Vancouver, had its own band; in addition, ballrooms like the Roseland in Winnipeg, the Trianon in Regina, the Alexandra in Vancouver, Montreal's Victoria Hall, and Toronto's Palace Pier featured dance bands every Saturday night. At Victoria Hall the staple was the Johnny Holmes Orchestra, while at the Palace Pier the big Dixieland band of Jimmy Davidson was the regular house group.

Overseas in Britain, soldiers, sailors, and airmen flocked to hear the Empire's favourite singer, Vera Lynn, who had a special place in the hearts of Canadian servicemen and servicewomen. Her beautiful voice made tunes like "The White Cliffs of Dover", "We'll Meet Again", "It's a Lovely Day Tomorrow", "I'll Be with You in Apple Blossom Time", "Wish Me Luck as You Wave Me Goodbye", and "When the Lights Go On Again" poignant and powerful enough that, even fifty years later, they bring tears to the eyes of all who served.

years, Witnesses were arrested in large numbers and spied on by the RCMP, and their homes and businesses were raided. Why? The Witnesses, knocking on doors and proselytizing on street corners, had attacked the Roman Catholic Church sharply for its doctrines and policies, and in Quebec especially the church hierarchy was furious at their "damnable heresies". Cardinal Villeneuve appealed for action in the spring of 1940 and the justice minister, Ernest Lapointe, anxious to maintain the hierarchy's lukewarm support for the war effort, promptly had the ban issued and enforced. Not until late 1943 were Jehovah's Witnesses allowed to practise their faith openly, and even then some parents who refused to allow their children to salute the flag continued to be harassed. There was some public and parliamentary outcry at the Witnesses' treatment, but the disheartening fact is that there was so little. A country that was fighting for freedom and liberty abroad sat virtually silent while religious liberty was suppressed at home.

There was one additional area where Quebec concerns predominated. Once the war began, Canada's policy towards European refugees, already harsh and restrictive, became more so. French-Canadian opinion had been unwavering in its opposition to the admission of Jewish refugees from Hitler since 1933, a position that was shared by many in the rest of the country. This did not change with the beginning of the war. Anti-Semitism flourished, with unspoken quotas limiting the numbers of Jews in universities and in certain professions, with some private clubs and resorts flatly closed to Jews, and with prejudice openly expressed. The King government, its majority dependent on Quebec seats and its policy devoted to bringing a united Canada into the war and

Anti-Semitism was as Canadian as maple syrup, or so it seemed. This 1939 sign in Ste. Agathe, Que. was only one overt manifestation of such bigotry.

keeping French-speaking and English-speaking citizens away from each others' throats, had no interest in letting the increasingly desperate Jews of Europe, adults or children, into Canada. The bureaucrat in charge of immigration, Frederick Blair, bluntly described official policy in 1940: "the interest of Canada is to prevent Jewish people from coming to Canada."

After Dunkirk, when Britain asked Canada to accept German and Austrian nationals—many of them anti-Nazi Jewish refugees—rounded up there for internment in Canada, Ottawa reluctantly agreed, but only after deciding that a German was a German, anti-Nazi or not. The Jewish deportees were initially put in camps with German POWs; later, when they were separately housed, it was still behind barbed wire and under armed guard. Not even reports of Nazi extermination camps, widespread by 1943, markedly changed the government policy or public sentiment: in that year the Canadian Institute of Public Opinion reported that 80 per cent of Canadians opposed any attempt to bring large numbers of immigrants, let alone refugees, to Canada. For example, Ottawa's announcement that Canada would admit a few refugees from Spain and Portugal helped fuel Quebec opposition leader Maurice Duplessis's claim that the King government planned to bring 100,000 Jews to Quebec in return for election contributions from Canadian Jews. The actual number was 450. One demobilized soldier, outraged by the attitudes he found still thriving in Canada, told a writer of his "second war" at home: "My best pal in France was a Jewish boy." Rabbi Abraham Feinberg drew the proper conclusion. The soundest hope for Canada, he wrote, lies "with the men who are bleeding side by side for Canada, and know how trivial 'race' and creed really are!"

Part of the Canadian concern about "foreigners" and immigration undoubtedly arose from fears about an uncertain future. In the face of all the evidence to the contrary, most Canadians never doubted that the democracies would win the war. What frightened them was what would follow the return to peace. Would there be jobs for the boys coming home from overseas? Was Canada destined to consolidate the huge economic gains made during the war? Or would the country slide backwards into the morass of the Depression? Public opinion polls repeatedly made it clear that security was the watchword. People wanted jobs, they wanted social benefits, and they wanted returning veterans to get a fair shake. The Depression could not be allowed to return, and if the Liberal government of Mackenzie King could not guarantee Canadians a better future, there were other political parties that claimed to be ready to do so.

THE PROVINCES

Ontario

Ontarians who were around in 1945 would recall VE Day and VJ Day, maybe the June election, and perhaps the Ford strike in Windsor, with its illegal but ingenious car blockade. But they all swore they would remember Ontario's great January blizzard, the worst in a century. Twenty people died, mostly from heart attacks while shovelling. Toronto's Transportation Commission demanded a ban on all private vehicles on city streets. When streets were still clogged four days later, Mayor Fred Conboy and TTC Commissioner Norman Walker resumed the traditional debate about whose gross negligence had let the citizens suffer.

Ontario's 1945 election was less educational than edifying. The CCF began the year by expelling two of its elected members as crypto-Communists. Mitch Hepburn, resurrected as Liberal leader after retiring in 1943, was notorious for his red-baiting during his successful 1937 campaign. Now, to his obvious delight, he became the Communists' hero against both the "social-Fascist" CCF and "the real Fascist," Conservative premier George Drew.

Buoyed by opinion polls and their success in leaping from obscurity to a near-victory in 1943, CCFers had been confident of victory as soon as Drew revealed his true-blue right-wing views. Instead, Drew played his version of Mackenzie King's game—offering Canada's richest province plenty of reforms but also good old conservative values. As well, he made it tough for soldiers overseas to vote—with a federal election in progress, few people even noticed. Why try the inexperienced and turbulent CCFers when Drew sounded conservatively progressive?

Late in the campaign, CCF leader Ted Jolliffe accused Drew of Gestapo-like tactics in allowing a provincial police squad to collect dossiers on 16,000 CCFers. This, said Drew, was "a clear and unadulterated lie". In fact, Jolliffe's "Gestapo" charges were accurate, but he lacked enough hard evidence, and the announcement backfired with voters. Wasn't this the kind of wild statement that a Conservative vote would avoid? Besides, said A.A. MacLeod, a Communist member of the legislature, "You can't fertilize a field with a fart." (MacLeod was later a speechwriter for Ontario Tory premier Leslie Frost.) Both Jolliffe and Hepburn were beaten. The CCF, said *Time*, "took a terrible shellacking", and George Drew laid the foundations for his party to run Ontario for another forty years.

CHAPTER FOUR
PREPARING THE PEACE

The memories of the Great Depression hung over wartime Canada and shaped the politicians' and bureaucrats' planning for peace. Ideas that had seemed unthinkable in the 1930s suddenly became possible during the war.

(Left) The Canadians taken prisoner when Hong Kong fell on Christmas Day, 1941 suffered unspeakable conditions for almost four years. Captain Stanley Banfill (left), an army doctor, saw his son for the first time when he returned home to Montreal in October 1945.

(Above) This Liberal candidate in the 1945 election covered all the bases, but Tory Toronto did him in, sending an RCAF veteran to Ottawa.

MIKE CARSON RETURNED HOME AT THE END of the war bound and determined that a parade down Main Street was not going to be enough for veterans like him. A Cape Bretoner who had joined the navy at sixteen, he remembered that the men who had survived the fighting had gained confidence. They all wanted "something better than what they had left, and no one was going to stop them. They weren't going back on the streets, to be without work and without dignity again." His was a very common attitude. So too was Joe Levitt's. A soldier who had won the Military Medal in Normandy, Levitt had been a young 1930s radical and would become a history professor. "The propaganda of the thirties," he said,

"had always been that the government had no money, couldn't do anything about it, and that's the way things were. But the war taught people a lot. It was a matter of common sense and simple to understand that if the government could find money for war, then they could find it for peace."

It wasn't only veterans who wanted a better life. Alf Ready, a union member at Hamilton, Ontario's Westinghouse plant, was haunted by the memory of the Depression's unemployment. "That made you want to secure the union. You had a fear that you had

Returning soldiers were full of uncertainties, and this artilleryman, surrounded by his family, seems well aware of the difficult transition he faces. So does his mother!

Tommy Douglas led the CCF to victory in Saskatchewan, the first social-democratic government ever in North America. Douglas's homely speaking style and wit greatly helped persuade voters to trust the party.

during the Depression, that you didn't want to face it again. It's a horrible feeling when you and your wife have got nothing. . . . My own people lost their home, my wife's people lost their home. . . . After a while, these were the reasons why political parties like the CCF took off." The general election of 1945, held in June just after VE Day and with the war against Japan still under way, was to decide which party would lead Canada into the brave new world of peace.

Wherever they lived, whatever their occupation, religion, sex, or mother tongue, Canadians wanted the gains they had earned during the war to be preserved into the peace.

This was made clear by some of the first opinion polls taken in Canada. In October 1943, Canadians were asked if they wanted "to see many changes or reforms made in Canada, or would you rather the country remain pretty much as it was before the war?" Almost three in four called for reform, a number much higher than the 52 per cent in the United States and the 32 per cent in Britain who believed their society needed to change. And people were worried. In July 1944, the Canadian Institute of Public Opinion asked people if they expected a postwar job that would pay more, the same, or less than their present job. Only 17 per cent said they expected to earn more, 45 per cent said the same, and 33 per cent said less. What was striking was that the "earn less" category had risen by 14 per cent since a poll in December

The CCF's national leader was M.J. Coldwell (centre), a Saskatchewan schoolteacher. On a visit to Britain in 1944, he is surrounded (left to right) by Clarence Gillis, MP; David Lewis, the CCF national secretary; P.E.Wright, MP; and Frank Scott, the national chairman.

1943, while the "earn more" group had fallen from 30 per cent. And those were the optimists—the pessimists feared that there would be no jobs at all.

The same concern was demonstrated in the rising support for the social democratic Co-operative Commonwealth Federation. The CCF had received only 8.5 per cent of the vote in the 1940 general election, but it made converts as the war went on: in 1943 it formed the opposition in the Ontario legislature with thirty-four seats; in August it won two federal by-elections; and in June 1944 the CCF under Tommy Douglas won power in Saskatchewan, becoming the first socialist government in North America. More striking still, in a Canadian Institute of Public Opinion poll in September 1943 the CCF had narrowly led the Liberals and Conservatives in voter preference. With its emphasis on the little guy, on social welfare measures such as family allowances and medical and hospital insurance, and on tough controls on profiteering, the CCF seemed to reflect the mood of the people. As historian John English noted, Canadians hoped that the war "would bring not Armageddon but the new Jerusalem". David Lewis and Frank Scott, key CCF planners, declared in their 1943 book, *Make This Your Canada*, that "This war is becoming a people's war." Canadians, "roused by the burdens and sacrifice, are finding their own strength, sensing their own potentialities, and seeing their role of leadership in the revolutionary process."

The Conservative Party certainly did not see the change in attitudes during the war as "a revolutionary process", but even the Tories could not ignore what was happening. With their strength in Parliament weak and their relevance somehow ebbing away, the Conservatives tried to make their mark in 1941 by resurrecting former prime minister Arthur Meighen as party leader to head a campaign for Total War, the polite 1940s name for military conscription. But Meighen lost a federal by-election in York South, a supposedly safe Toronto seat, to a CCF high school teacher who had called for conscription of wealth and for social security. The Tories seemed hopelessly adrift until, at an unofficial party meeting at Port Hope, Ontario, in the summer of 1942, younger Conservatives seized the party helm and changed direction. The "Port Hopefuls" called for social welfare, medicare, and collective bargaining rights for workers, stunning many of the party's traditional supporters. "Half a loaf," said party stalwart and president of the National Trust Company J.M. Macdonnell, "is better than no bread at all"; the Conservatives had evidently decided that if social welfare could help them beat the CCF, then they were for it. In December a national leadership convention selected John Bracken, the Liberal-Progressive Premier of Manitoba, as leader and at his request changed the party's name to Progressive Conservative. The "Pro and Con" party, critics jeered, didn't know if it wanted to go forwards or backwards.

The Conservatives' change in direction had left the governing Liberals as the only major national party still wedded to traditional economics. Mackenzie King, the seemingly permanent prime minister, would have objected to that characterization; after all, during the Great War he had written *Industry and Humanity*, a book that laid out his idea of a course towards the reconciliation of workers and bosses. Moreover, his government had brought in old-age pensions in 1927, had produced the first deliberately stimulative deficit budget in 1939, and had secured a constitutional amendment to allow the establishment of unemployment insurance in 1940. But as the war dragged on, no one remembered. "What have you done for us lately?" the public seemed to be saying. In truth, the King government had been so preoccupied with creating Canada's war effort and trying to avoid the imposition of conscription that it had paid scant attention to shifting tides of opinion. Not until 1943, when the Liberals in Ontario were swept from power by George Drew's Tories, not until by-elections were lost wholesale in August, not until the opinion polls in September demonstrated once and for all the CCF's rise, did the government realize that home-front politics required attention. Of course, King and Company had one major advantage— they were in power, and they had a civil service full of ideas at their command.

Ideas were desperately needed if the Depression years were not to be repeated. The "dirty thirties" had seen Canadians thrown out of factories, resource industries, and office work by the hundreds of thousands, and left to sink or swim. One day they had a job; the next day they had nothing—no unemployment insurance, not even a small termination allowance to ease the shock. Farmers suffered just as badly, as export markets dried up and domestic consumption collapsed. On the Prairies, drought and grasshoppers devastated the wheat economy, leaving whole regions with little to wear and nothing but gophers to eat—until old clothes, salt cod, and spoiled apples arrived by the trainload from charities in the east.

In the face of this unparalleled crisis, the country's welfare system was primitive. The federal government pointed to the British North America Act, the country's constitution, which it said made welfare and social policy provincial responsibilities. The provinces, with their tax bases very small and their economies in ruins, could offer only a pittance to the municipalities that had to bear the brunt of swelling welfare case loads. Most towns insisted that those on welfare work for their mite, and so the unemployed dug holes and filled them in again in Calgary or sawed wood by hand while chain saws stood idle in the works department yard in Winnipeg. It was "make-work" with a vengeance. Churches and charities tried to fill the gap with soup kitchens and small cash handouts, but the demand simply outran the supply, and thousands of young men "rode the rods" to the balmier climate of the west coast to sit out the storm. What made the situation all the more painful for those who had always had jobs was that they blamed themselves. "If only I had saved more in the 1920s," people said. "If only I was more enterprising in finding work." If only the capitalist system had not failed.

But the system had failed, and now that Canada was at war, the politicians and officials realized that unless they offered the country a better future they had no hope of extracting a major effort from Canadians.

Aside from efforts in the early months of the war to consider how veterans could best be dealt with, the first planning for the postwar period was undertaken by an advisory committee of notables from academe, business, and labour. The Committee on Reconstruction had been established in March 1941 by British Columbia's Ian Mackenzie, the Minister of Pensions and Health, whose department also had responsibility for

The wartime dream of Canadians was for a comfortable house with overstuffed chairs, a rug, a dining-room set, and three bedrooms upstairs. In the postwar boom, the dream was to become reality.

Marriages, Divorces, Births

	Marriages	Divorces	Births
1939	106,266	2,073	237,991
1940	125,797	2,416	252,577
1941	124,644	2,462	263,993
1942	130,786	3,091	281,569
1943	113,827	3,398	292,943
1944	104,656	3,827	293,967
1945	111,376	5,101	300,587
1946	137,398	7,757	343,504
1947	130,400	8,213	372,589
1948	126,118	6,978	359,860

Source: F.H. Leacy, ed., *Historical Statistics of Canada* (Ottawa 1983).

The striking figure during the war and immediately after is the tiny number of divorces, a product of stiff federal legislation that essentially limited the grounds for divorce to provable adultery. In some provinces, moreover—notably Quebec—Parliament had to approve the ending of a marriage. Even at the end of the war, therefore, the increase in divorces, while highly significant in percentage terms (divorces were 400 per cent higher in 1947 than in 1939), remained very small numerically.

Equally interesting to note is that while marriages and births increased once the war had ended and service-men and servicewomen returned home, in neither case was the increase extraordinary. The 1946–48 marriage figures, for example, are comparable to those from 1940–42; the birth numbers increased all through the war, though the beginning of the "baby boom" is apparent in 1946 and 1947.

The war and postwar years saw a baby boom swell the country's population. One subsidiary reason for the increase was better medical care, such as these baby respirators used at Vancouver General Hospital in 1943.

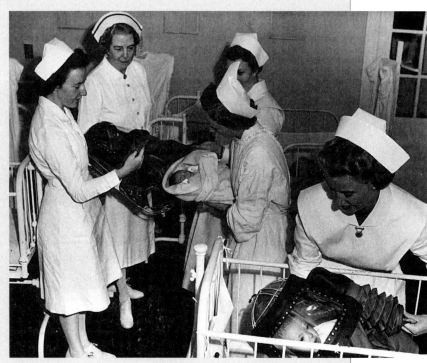

preparing for the re-establishment of veterans. For the civilian side of reconstruction planning, Mackenzie brought together Principal Cyril James of McGill University, J.S. McLean of Canada Packers, and Tom Moore, president of the Trades and Labor Congress. James, a British-born expert on banking who had studied and lived in the United States before coming to McGill, became the chair, and he soon persuaded the government to give him a small budget and the right to hire a staff.

Before long, the James Committee had

In urban areas, countless thousands lived in apartments or flats. This welcome-home party for one returned soldier was in one of the three rooms of a typical apartment.

begun to grow. Its main appointee was Leonard Marsh, a gentle, CCF-supporting English economist who had taught at McGill for a decade and whose studies into Depression social problems had established his academic reputation. Marsh ran the research program, and his task was to find ways in which Canada could create "adequate employment opportunities for the returning soldiers, as well as for the men and women who will no longer be required in the munitions factories." That was the problem; if it was not successfully faced, then "the country would inevitably be confronted by rapidly mounting unemployment and widespread dissatisfaction." The spectre of the 1919 Winnipeg General Strike, the great surge in radical labour unrest that had followed hard on the heels of the Armistice of November 1918, hung over the planners.

The question was, who would determine the postwar direction? By 1942, as the James Committee continued its work and as the House of Commons established a Special Committee on Reconstruction and Re-establishment, the civil servants began to realize that Principal James had stolen centre stage from them. James always had an eye on what could advance his own interests, and knew almost nothing of Canadian politics and the intricacies of the constitution. When he called for a Ministry of Economic Planning to handle all postwar preparations (a move that the key deputy ministers believed would steal power from their own departments), the mandarins struck back. The original James Committee on Reconstruction had its name altered to the Advisory Committee on Reconstruction, a slight change but a clear reduction in status. More important, instead of reporting to Ian Mackenzie, the committee was now responsible to the prime minister, who had no use for James—"an ass of a fellow," he said after one unpleasant meeting with the principal. As a result, the James Committee's effective master became the senior mandarin, the clerk of the Privy Council, Arnold Heeney. And to make the victory all the more apparent, the mandarins set up their own recon-struction committee under Dr. William A. Mackintosh, a powerful Queen's University economist who had moved to Ottawa at the outbreak of war.

But the James Committee, neutered though it had been in the bureaucratic infighting, had one last laugh. At the beginning of December 1942, Sir William Beveridge, the distinguished British social planner, had released a report in England calling for universal cradle-to-grave social security. Surely, James told Ian Mackenzie, Canada should have its own Beveridge Report. The minister agreed, and Leonard Marsh was asked to prepare a report for presentation to the House of Commons' special committee. For a month, Marsh and a few of his experts locked themselves up in a room of the Château Laurier Hotel in Ottawa. Brainstorming night and day, writing feverishly, Marsh had his first draft within a month and had a final version ready in March 1943.

The Marsh Report, as it quickly became known, proposed to change Canada irrevocably. It began by setting out the maxims on which the rest was based: employment was the first and greatest need in a social security program for a modern industrial state; social security had to be underwritten by the whole community; to get economic stability, purchasing power must be kept up when the munitions plants shut down; and social security spending of $100 to $500 million could help keep the economy functioning.

There was more, much more. Marsh wanted to see worker training programs and a huge national program of public employment projects to provide work at the war's end. He called for universal national health insurance, a policy that Ian Mackenzie's department had been studying for some time. He wanted universal contributory old-age pensions and,

demanding that children have "an unequivo-
cal place in social security policy", he proposed family allowances of some $7.50 per
child each month.

The plans advanced by Marsh and his
experts would be expensive, possibly as
much as $900 million a year—or some 60
per cent more than the whole federal budget
in 1939—and the drafters tried to deal with
their critics in advance. Social security payments, the report argued, "are not money
lost. The social insurances . . . are invest-
ments in morale and health, in greater family
stability . . . in human productive efficiency."
It had yet to be proved, Marsh argued, "that
any democracy which underwrites the social
minimum for its citizens is any the weaker or
less wealthy for doing so."

Critics of the report were outraged by
this argument, and businessmen angrily
denounced Marsh for offering the people
"pie in the sky". Who would pay? Where
would the money come from? Why should
anyone believe what a leftist university professor said, anyhow? Charlotte Whitton, the
country's best-known social worker and a
Progressive Conservative supporter, prepared the Tories' official response in a book
called *The Dawn of Ampler Life*. What Marsh
proposed could only be harmful, Whitton
argued, for it would make Canadians dependent on the state and would destroy initiative. Family allowances might well prove so
attractive that the weakest in society would
be encouraged to have more children. Whitton's arguments, tinged with eugenic attitudes not unknown to the Nazis, did not
sound much like the ideas advanced at Port
Hope by Progressive Conservatives. For its
part, the CCF-leaning *Canadian Forum* pronounced the Marsh Report "the price that
Liberalism is willing to pay in order to pre-

vent socialism." Attacked from the right,
tepidly cheered by the left, Marsh had determined the agenda for the public debate.

All this should have meant that Mackenzie King, the great compromiser who had all
but patented middle-of-the-road governing,
could pick up the Marsh Report and run
with it. But his cautious finance minister,
J.L. Ilsley, saw only the terrifying cost of
Marsh's recommendations, and urged the
prime minister to make clear that none of
them were government proposals. Although
King's diary was full of ruminations on the
need for more social security, this most cautious of politicians knew when to rein in the
enthusiasts. The war came first, for one
thing, and King's highly developed sense of
public propriety made him balk at trying to
buy votes while men were dying overseas. "I
said I would never allow an appeal to the
people on social security measures at a time
of war with a view to bringing them to support the government because of what it
would pay out of the public treasury," he told
the Liberal caucus in Parliament shortly after
the Marsh Report became public.

But King was nothing if not pragmatic,
and he was able to forget his principles if the
need was clear. There was the rise of the CCF
in the Ontario elections, the loss of the
string of by-elections, the unfavourable
opinion polls—by August 1943 it was obvious that something had to be done if the Liberal Party was not to lose power. Even
though the war was under way, the party had
to be refurbished and readied for the next
election.

In September 1943, the National Liberal
Federation met for the first time since 1939.
One of King's secretaries was J.W. Pickers-
gill, a Manitoban who had joined the
Department of External Affairs shortly

The Ups and Downs of Public Opinion

Opinion polls came to Canada in 1941 with the Canadian Institute of Public Opinion, an offshoot of the organization created by Dr. George Gallup in the United States. The CIPO polls, which were sold to newspapers, for the first time charted changes in attitudes and political support with some accuracy. Although somewhat less scientific than they claimed to be at the outset, polls demonstrated very clearly the split between French Canada and English Canada over conscription; they also showed, quite predictably, that the strongest support for conscription existed among those over fifty—those certain not to be called up—while the weakest enthusiasm was among males of military age. The polls also tracked the rising support for social welfare measures, and the concern about the postwar period that accompanied the rise in CCF popularity, which peaked in September 1943. The government listened and turned to the left.

The government also undertook its own polling, often using CIPO to undertake secret polls under contract to the Wartime Information Board, the government's propaganda agency. The WIB routinely passed its polls to the Cabinet. Other arms of government also carried out opinion surveys. Even soldiers overseas were quizzed about their attitudes to officers, to the war's course, and to demobilization. Not surprisingly, they largely disliked officers, confidently expected victory, and wanted to return to Canada the day war ended.

Opinion polls graphically demonstrated the rise and fall of the wartime CCF. In September 1943 the social-democratic party led the Grits and Tories, and the next year Tommy Douglas (centre) took power in Saskatchewan. But anti-socialist propaganda cut into the CCF vote, and the party ran a poor third in the 1945 federal election.

before the war and had been assigned to work in the Prime Minister's Office. Although he was a civil servant, Jack Pickersgill had a deep interest in politics and elections, and he soon impressed King with his progressive social views. He had learned the best way to put those views to the prime minister. In one memorandum written shortly before the party meeting, Pickersgill hit the right note:

> Once the war is won, the voters are not going to vote for a political party merely because it did a good job in winning the war. They are going to vote for the party they think is most likely to do what is needed to provide the maximum employment and a measure of social insurance in the future. The record of the government will help only if that record is joined to a program already partly carried out; a program which is a tangible proof of continuing action.

Fired up by Pickersgill's memo, the prime minister denounced the Tories and CCF to the assembled delegates, hailed his own record, and promised a better future for all. And the delegates whipped through a series of resolutions that promised generous benefits for the boys overseas at war's end, and a national scheme of social insurance to include protection against poverty resulting from unemployment, accident, ill health, old age, and blindness. They called for a better old-age pension plan, and urged the government to consider family allowances as a contribution to "a healthy nation with good family life and adequate support for the raising of children." All that remained was to pass the legislation—or so it seemed.

At the end of 1943, King's ministers considered what to do next. There was agreement on the need for three new government departments: Reconstruction, National

Jack Pickersgill was one of Mackenzie King's key assistants, writing speeches, offering policy advice, and helping to create the social welfare program. When in doubt, said official Ottawa, "Clear it with Jack."

Health and Welfare, and Veterans Affairs— key departments in implementing any new policies for the peace. But what would the policies be? Finance minister Ilsley came to the Cabinet with a carefully argued scheme that had been produced by the powerful bureaucrats who worked for him. If the nation's tax system could be revised in conjunction with the provinces to ensure that Ottawa received the funds it needed, then a social security system could be put in place: family allowances, unemployment assistance, better old-age pensions, and possibly health insurance. There had to be government construction projects to create jobs and, in almost the sole departure from the Marsh Report, industry should be given substantial tax credits to ensure that it invested large sums in the immediate postwar period.

Ilsley's prescriptions, soon put into the draft of the Speech from the Throne to open the 1944 session of Parliament, galvanized Mackenzie King, who took credit for them all. The proposals rounded out "what I have worked for through my life, namely . . . it should become the duty of the State to work out some scheme of social justice which will see that opportunities are widened for the many and that at least for all . . . there should be a minimum standard of life. . . ." No fool, King knew that there would be "a great fight over this by wealthy classes. . . ."

To King's surprise, the fight began in his own Cabinet, with Ilsley leading the charge. An upright, honourable lawyer, and likely the only finance minister in history to be popular with his fellow Canadians, Ilsley perhaps had not quite realized how far his officials had pushed him until he saw the draft throne speech. People would say the government was "seeking to outdo the CCF", he complained, and many might simply decide to support the Tories. Other ministers protested too, and King, shaken, agreed to remove any definite promise on health insurance. As a result, it would be a quarter-century before medicare became a national program.

Still, the Speech from the Throne, intoned by the governor general on January 27, was a quantum leap forward towards social welfare: "The post-war object of our domestic policy is social security and human welfare. The establishment of a national minimum of social security and human welfare should be advanced as rapidly as possible." No previous government could have made such a statement; it was testimony to the way the war had changed the country's understanding of its needs. There were to be family allowances, and an effort to seek agreements with the provinces for health insurance, and a national contributory old-age pension plan. Priorities were demobilization, rehabilitation and re-establishment of veterans, reconversion of the economy to peacetime uses, and insurance through pensions and health coverage against the major hazards of life. Only a patchwork of special policies had existed before. For the first time, a Canadian government was accepting responsibility for the social welfare of the people.

———•—•———

The centrepiece of the proposals was family allowances. The idea of helping families with young children was not new. Several European countries had implemented similar schemes decades before, and Canadians had been talking about them since the 1920s. But however important people considered their children, however much they realized that family size and poverty were inextricably linked, there never seemed to be enough money for family allowances. In a society that operated on conservative and traditional views of the state's role, there had been widespread concern about the impact of such state intervention. It took the war to change attitudes.

For one thing, too many young men reporting for army medical examinations were in ill health. Bad teeth, tubercular lungs, rickets—the litany of diseases was endless. Perhaps milk, vitamins, and good food could have improved the health of a generation. Family allowances could help provide those basic necessities.

Also, workers whose pay had been frozen in November 1941, at a time when labour was in short supply, were increasingly restive by 1943. The National War Labour Board, which had been created to keep labour, business, and government pulling together in the interests of the wartime economy, suggested in a confidential report to the Cabinet that a family allowance be paid to each worker with children instead of loosening wage controls. A scheme based on payment for each

child would direct the money where it was needed, while preserving the principles of the wage freeze.

Furthermore, the sacrifices of war and the memories of the Depression had combined to make the pressures for social reform very strong by 1943. The CCF's convention in 1942 had endorsed the idea of family allowances, and at least one member of Parliament had raised it in the House of Commons. The Marsh Report had popularized the idea, and the National Liberal Federation had endorsed it as well.

The Economic Advisory Committee— the key bureaucrats—liked the NWLB idea because it resolved a problem while preserving the anti-inflation policy of government. The Cabinet, however, was divided. Quebec ministers, hailing from a province well known for its large families, were in favour, but their support troubled other ministers who looked instinctively on family allowances as a devious way of giving federal money to French Canadians. That aspect did not bother the prime minister; what did was that "to tell the country that everyone was to get a family allowance was sheer folly; it would occasion resentment everywhere. Great care had to be taken in any monies given out from the Treasury. . . ." The whole idea seemed to be in jeopardy until Jack Pickersgill again stepped in.

Pickersgill's father had served in the Great War, been gassed, and died soon after the war's end. His mother had raised and educated a large family on the pension paid

A London, Ont., family (with only six of its ten children on the doorstep) receives its ration books in 1942. These were the people for whom family allowances meant a chance at a better life, through better food, clothes, and housing.

127

to her as a veteran's widow; what, after all, was the difference between this pension and family allowances? King grasped the point at once—pensions differed only in amount, not in principle, from family allowances. The Pickersgill pension had saved a family in Winnipeg in the 1920s. Family allowances could save countless families across the country, and let other children stay in school to get a good education.

King now began to support the idea vigorously. Officials in the finance department backed him because family allowances— soon earmarked for all families, not just those of war workers—would put money into the hands of parents, who would spend it on milk, baby food, children's shoes, and playpens. That could help the economy in the critical period of reconstruction. As Pickersgill put it in a memo in January 1944, "the economic problem after the war will not be to produce what we need, but to find markets for what we must produce if we are to avoid unemployment. The provision of family allowances would almost certainly result in a considerable net addition to the home market both for food and manufactured goods." The cunning Pickersgill argued that "some of the more reactionary elements in the Conservative party" would be certain to oppose the measure, while CCFers would be unhappy because family allowances weakened the argument for higher wages. Both reactions would help the Liberal Party.

Then there was the "trash" argument against family allowances. The poor would get the money and spend it on drink or sin. Some might, said Clifford Clark, the Deputy Minister of Finance, "but such bad effects should be far more than offset by the opposite kind of effect on those recipients who for the first time are given 'hope' and the ambition to better themselves and improve the lot of their children." At a decisive Cabinet meeting on January 13, 1944, King weighed in: "I thought the Creator intended that all persons born should have equal opportunities. Equal opportunity started in days of infancy and the first thing, at least, was to see that the children got the essentials of life. . . ." Enough of the ministers agreed, and family allowances went into the Speech from the Throne.

The draft bill, not prepared until June 1944, called for a "baby bonus" of $5 a month for children up to five years of age, $6 for those from six to nine, $7 for those from ten to twelve, and $8 for those from thirteen to fifteen. Rates were reduced for families with more than five children, and the cost of the measure was estimated to be some $200 million a year (or almost 40 per cent of the entire pre-war federal budget, for this single program). The payments involved today seem tiny. In 1944, however, the average wage for a factory worker was about $25 a week—a family with four youngsters could expect to receive the equivalent of another week's wages each month. Strikingly, the allowance was to be paid to the mother, giving many women the very first money that came directly to them, rather than from the often grudging hands of their husbands.

The scheme was to come into effect on July 1, 1945. "This would make certain they would not come into force until after the elections," King said. "I did not like the idea of spending public money immediately before an election . . . people were likely to be more grateful for what they were about to receive. . . ." The doubters in the Cabinet tried once more to scuttle the bill, but King prevailed. "Some of his colleagues still think they can go out and shoot a deer or a bison

The Bloc Populaire

When Mackenzie King announced a plebiscite on conscription in early 1942, Quebec was outraged. Promises against compulsory overseas military service, orators cried, had been made repeatedly to Quebec in 1939 and during the 1940 election; now the devious Liberals were asking all of Canada to release them from pledges made to French Canada alone. There was enough truth in that claim to spur the creation of a popular movement to campaign for a "*Non*" vote in the plebiscite. Out of La Ligue pour la Défense du Canada, which captured more than 70 per cent of the Quebec vote for the "*Non*" side, came a new political party, the Bloc Populaire Canadien. Formed in September 1942 and championed federally by the neutralist and nationalist Liberal MP Maxime Raymond, the Bloc spent the next two years organizing and working out a program that was a mixture of progressive social reform and conservative nationalism. Led in the Quebec provincial elections of 1944 by the young journalist firebrand André Laurendeau, the Bloc made little impact as Maurice Duplessis and the Union Nationale swept back into power. It was the same story in the 1945 federal election. Although the sending of home defence conscripts overseas in November 1944 spurred an enormous outpouring of anger in Quebec, it did not last. Voters clearly recognized that Mackenzie King had held conscription off as long as possible, and in the June elections King captured Quebec. The Bloc won only two seats on 180,000 votes as it fell victim to the difficulties new parties always seem to suffer, and had completely disappeared by the next federal election.

Still, the wartime experience was critical for Quebec. Just as the Great War had demonstrated that the Conservatives could not be trusted to protect Quebec interests, so had the Second World War shown that the Liberals—in Quebec nationalist eyes—were no better. That would be remembered when the Quiet Revolution began in 1960 and when the Parti Québécois, combining social reform and conservative nationalism much as the Bloc had done, took the field at the end of the 1960s.

The leader of the provincial wing of the anti-conscriptionist Bloc Populaire was firebrand journalist and intellectual André Laurendeau, here speaking in Montreal during the 1944 Quebec election. His impassioned oratory failed to win his party much support, perhaps because conscription did not seem likely in July 1944.

THE PROVINCES

Manitoba

Manitobans were very conscious that, although few provinces were farther from the war, few had done more. Winnipeg's Grenadiers had been sacrificed at Hong Kong; other city infantry battalions, the Royal Winnipeg Rifles and the Queen's Own Cameron Highlanders, had fought in North-West Europe. The Camerons had landed two years earlier, at Dieppe; the Rifles had been among the first to land on D-Day. Both had fought the brutal battles south of Caen and at the Scheldt, and in 1945 they had taken part in Simonds' drive into Germany. The 12th Manitoba Dragoons had driven armoured cars in Italy; the Fort Garry Horse had landed its amphibious tanks on D-Day and had fought to the very end in Germany.

As Manitoba welcomed its men home, people wondered about their future. Once theirs had been the keystone province, with its major city the third largest in Canada. But was it now the province history had passed by? Or was it simply a prosperous, settled province which had matured beyond providing Confederation with crises—Louis Riel, the general strike in 1919, the French–English conflict over Manitoba schools?

Certainly the agenda for 1945 was sternly practical and impressively positive. Minnesota's experiment with "soil cement" would provide its equally flood-prone neighbour with good, cheap roads. Rural electrification aimed at supplying power to 650 farms that summer, bringing the poles right into the yard at a cost of $150 to $200 to each farmer. In turn, that would be a $630,000 boost to Manitoba's timber industry; since prime red cedar poles could not be found, the Manitoba Power Commission was prepared to creosote the province's own jack pine and give it a chance.

S.J. Farmer's CCF was supposed to have a chance too, when Manitobans went to the polls on October 25. Apart from the Communists, running as the Labour Progressive Party, the CCF was the only alternative to a tired Liberal-Conservative-Farmer coalition that could trace its roots almost back to the previous war. As so often happened, however, Manitoba responded as a replica of Ontario. It listened politely to Premier Stuart Garson being denounced as head of a big-business government, and calmly re-elected him to continue his practices.

for breakfast," he complained to a journalist friend, and then headed to the Liberal caucus to silence the remaining opposition.

In the House of Commons, the family allowance bill drew fire from the Tories, just as Pickersgill had predicted. Herbert Bruce, a Toronto physician who had served as lieutenant-governor of Ontario before winning election to Parliament in the 1940 election, denounced the measure as a "bribe of the most brazen character, made chiefly to one province and paid for by the rest." The bill was aimed at Quebec, he charged, and would be used in "bonussing families who have been unwilling to defend their country." A conscriptionist, Bruce could not understand French Canada's lukewarm attitude to what many in Quebec saw as a British war. Progressive Conservative leader John Bracken himself called the baby bonus "a political bribe", and Ontario Premier George Drew denounced the measure, as did Charlotte Whitton.

"The erratic, irresponsible, bewildered of mind, and socially incapable, feeble-minded and mentally affected parents are definitely the progenitors of many of our largest families," the great social worker said. Payment of cash grants would only "perpetuate this menace" and, even worse, extend "the uneven rate of natural increase" of new racial stocks. This appalling rhetoric embarrassed many, not least Conservative MPs like John Diefenbaker and Howard Green, who broke party discipline to support the measure. Yet when the family allowance bill went to second reading not a single member, Liberal, Conservative, CCF, or Social Credit, opposed it.

Why? The reason was obvious: the voters wanted it. Even though opinion polls in 1944 showed a general retreat from the reformist zeal of 1943, family allowances remained very popular. A Gallup poll found that 57 per cent of Canadians approved the baby bonus, including 81 per cent in Quebec. Predictably, opposition was highest among older people; of those in their twenties, almost 75 per cent thought family allowances a good idea. Critics were disarmed as well by the government's data, which demonstrated that the Maritimes and the Prairies, not Quebec, would be the main beneficiaries. Quebec paid 34 per cent of federal taxes but would receive only 33 per cent of family allowances; the Prairies, by contrast, paid 7 per cent of taxes but would get 21 per cent of the baby bonus. Ontario, regularly painted as the "milch cow of Confederation" by its politicians, would get only 29 per cent of the family allowance money in return for its 47 per cent of taxes paid. In Quebec the Dup-

The end of the war left many Europeans shivering in the ruins. The Salvation Army was one of the organizations collecting clothes and blankets for shipment.

lessis government, returned to power in 1944, insisted that men, the heads of the family, get the family allowance cheques, and Ottawa had to agree. The government decided that in the north the RCMP would hand out the equivalent value of the baby bonus in food, clothing, and ammunition for the 30,000 Indian and 5,000 Inuit youngsters.

So the family allowances became law, and preparing for their implementation in mid-1945 came to occupy most of the time of the newly created Department of National Health and Welfare. Birth certificates or their equivalents had to be found and submitted with an application, and parents scrambled to find the necessary records. Wisely, the department decided to test the system in Prince Edward Island, running the registration there early to get the kinks out of the system. One Charlottetown mother, Mrs. Frank Doyle, had in all eleven children, seven of them under fifteen years of age and therefore eligible. "I use forty-three quarts of milk a week," she said, "and still my children don't get enough milk."

In the first year of peace, as Canadian industry beat its swords into ploughshares, the monthly production of children's shoes rose from 762,000 to 1,180,000 pairs, and there were

similar increases in every other measurable index of production for family needs. Along with unemployment insurance, the baby bonus laid the groundwork for the welfare

In 1945, the King government ran for re-election on its wartime record and its promises of a "New Social Order" for the future. The campaign was helped by social legislation put on the books during the war.

state and, with the better wages that more and more unionized workers brought home, helped spur economic growth.

Not until the 1950s and 1960s, however, with the adoption of universal old-age pensions, hospital insurance, the Canada Pension Plan, the Canada Assistance Plan, and medicare, would the rest of the edifice of cradle-to-grave security be complete.

———•—•———

Expensive as they were, family allowances were only one of the major spending measures the Liberals pushed through Parliament in 1944 and 1945. The National Housing Act aimed to generate $1 billion in new construction, and Ottawa had appropriated $275 million to get building under way. The Industrial Development Bank had $75 million to help business retool for peace, while the Export Credit Corporation had authority to issue insurance on up to $100 million in exports. There was $225 million to maintain the wartime floor prices on agricultural products and fish. Including the Veterans Charter, which provided a host of benefits to the men and women who had won the war, the Liberal government appropriated $3.12 billion to cushion the shock of returning to peace.

There was one additional measure, though it had no legislative effect. In April 1945, the government issued a White Paper on Employment and Income. Prepared by Dr. Mackintosh, by 1945, a senior official in the new reconstruction ministry, the White Paper declared that "the maintenance of a high and stable level of employment and income" was "a major aim of government policy." To achieve this goal, the government "will be prepared, in periods when unemployment threatens, to incur deficits and increases in the national debt. . . . In periods of buoyant employment and income, budget plans will call for surpluses." The theories of John Maynard Keynes, the great Cambridge economist, had been accepted in Ottawa, and budget deficits— before the war the equivalent of mortal sin— now were just another economic tool.

———•—•———

Despite the huge sums allocated for the postwar period, despite the country's superb war effort and the generally skilful management of it by the Mackenzie King government, few expected the Liberals to return to power in the election that had to be held in 1945. No wartime government had much credibility for peace—there had been too many hard decisions, too many dead overseas, too much resentment of controls and privation at home, too much bitterness between French and English Canadians.

In Ontario, the Maritimes, and the west, that bitterness had been inflamed by sharp divisions over the role played in the war by French Canadians. Servicemen and their families were furious at the government, and at Mackenzie King in particular. Despite the substantial contribution to the three services made by French Canadians, much larger than in the Great War, many in English Canada lumped all French Canadians together as slackers. For their part, Quebeckers who had believed King's pledges against conscription felt betrayed by the prime minister's plebiscite of 1942 and the conscription crisis in November 1944. How could any politician, any Liberal, ever be believed again? Nationalist politicians moved into the vacuum, and the Bloc Populaire Canadien—even though it was led by the wooden Maxime Raymond, a former Liberal MP—made enough gains to give it as much as 9 per cent of the total Canadian vote. Or so opinion polls said.

If the Liberals were in trouble, no other party stood high. The Progressive Conservatives were saddled with a weak leader, John Bracken, whose speeches were even more boring than those of Mackenzie King. Stiff and stilted, he seemed very much a lone westerner in a party directed by Ontarians. His views on conscription were those of his party, but his supposedly progressive beliefs had become suspect thanks to the family allowances débâcle.

The 1944 Saskatchewan election took place while the First Canadian Army was fighting in North-West Europe. Arrangements, here caricatured by The Maple Leaf's *Les Callan, were made for soldiers to vote.*

The Co-operative Commonwealth Federation, led by M.J. Coldwell, a Saskatchewan schoolteacher, was better directed, and its policies were more forthright and coherent. Perhaps it was their clarity that began to frighten so many Canadians. Business groups had mounted an expensive and sustained attack against the CCF, decrying it as a "National and Socialist" party that aimed at the nationalization of all industry, banks, and land. "Our Next Big Threat? . . . Having Defeated the Dictators Abroad Are We to Forfeit Our Freedoms at Home?" asked ads published by the Public Information Association. "Social Suicide", a pamphlet paid for by a coalition of large business groups and delivered to every door in the country, contained racist slurs directed at CCF party strategist David Lewis, a Russian Jewish immigrant. The attacks worked; the CCF lead in the opinion polls in September 1943 dwindled in the face of the onslaught to 29 per cent in September 1943, 24 per cent in January 1944, 22 per cent in January 1945, and 19 per cent in May 1945. Even though Tommy Douglas led the new party to power in Saskatchewan in June 1944, the CCF had begun to lose support on the Prairies and among farmers nationally by the beginning of 1944. The Progressive Conservatives peaked at 30 per cent in June 1944 and held steady near there, while

THE ONLY SASKATCHEWAN VOTER IN THE COMPANY — HAS TO BE RIGHT UP UNDER JERRY'S NOSE!

SASK. ELECTION BALLOT BOX

YOU'RE LATE

NO 1 POLL

LES. CALLAN
BELGIUM

WHO SAID **DEMOCRACY** WAS "DECADENT"?

King and the Liberals hit 36 per cent in September and, surprisingly, remained at that level until April 1945, the conscription crisis notwithstanding. By May—with VE Day heralding the end of the war in Europe, with the election campaign in full flight, and with the general election scheduled for June 11—the Liberals were on the rise.

Mackenzie King's campaign featured the slogan "Build a New Social Order", an explicit reminder that the Liberals were the party that had given Canadians unemployment insurance, family allowances, a pledge of full employment, and the Veterans Charter. As the prime minister, now seventy years old and very tired after six years of war, put it, the main task of a re-elected government would be to maintain full employment and

In the 1945 federal election, the ballot box was taken to soldiers in hospitals, as at Deer Lodge in Winnipeg. Surprisingly, given the supposed conscriptionist sentiment in the forces, more servicemen voted for the Liberals than for the Progressive Conservatives and the Co-operative Commonwealth Federation.

social security. His government "did not leave these problems to be solved after the end of the war. . . . The necessary laws," he said to the voters, "are on the statute book; the necessary departments of government have been established; and our policies are in actual operation." That was powerful advocacy, and the Liberals hammered it home by ostentatiously advertising the family allowance scheme and urging all to fill in the forms so money could be sent out. Liberal candidates in Ontario received notification of the amount the baby bonus would pour into their constituencies each month: $153,000 for Welland, $132,000 for Cochrane, to a total of $6 million in all. Skeptical of political promises, many citizens refused to believe that the cheques actually would come.

The Conservative campaign sadly miscalculated the public mood. Convinced that the Anglo-Canadian bitterness towards Quebec could be exploited, Bracken campaigned on a pledge to send home defence conscripts—the much-despised Zombies—to fight the war in the Pacific, to give "practical application to our policy of equality of service and sacrifice." The difficulty was that the war against Japan was not seen as a priority by most Canadians. People wanted to get on with their lives, they wanted their men home from Europe as soon as possible, and they wanted a better life. Even the Conservatives' claim to "stand four square for private enterprise and individual freedom" jarred ordinary Canadians who wanted the social welfare benefits the Liberals had implemented. The CCF may have expected to capitalize on those sentiments, but it could not. Overconfident, its members had little idea of how badly the party had been hurt by the campaign against it.

The Progressive Conservatives received a boost on June 4 when George Drew won a smashing re-election victory in the Ontario provincial election. The handsome Tory leader took 66 seats while the Liberals, led once more by the mercurial Mitch Hepburn, fell to 14. The startling feature, however, was that the CCF, the opposition in the last provincial Parliament, dropped to a mere 8 seats. The Tories went into the last week of the federal election convinced that they were on a roll.

The result of the election on June 11 disappointed them. The Conservatives captured only 27 per cent of the vote and 67 seats, winning just one new rural seat, Bracken's own riding of Neepawa, Manitoba; the CCF had 15.6 per cent of the popular vote and 28 seats; Social Credit won 13 seats, and the Bloc just 2. The Liberals, however, captured 125 seats on 41 per cent of the vote—enough for a small majority—including 53 seats in Quebec. Francophones had presumably decided that King was the best of a bad lot—or enough of them had to give historian Gordon Rothney the perfect title for an article in *The Canadian Forum*, "Quebec Saves Our King".

Despite the lingering fury over conscription, the armed forces realized that the war was over and gave King's party 35 per cent of the service vote, 3 points more than they gave the CCF and 9 more than they gave the conscriptionist Tories. But one Liberal suffered their vengeance. Later, soldiers boasted that they had switched their official residences to the Saskatchewan city of Prince Albert: when their votes came in, Mackenzie King's narrow majority dissolved and the CCF took his seat. Unctuous as ever, King lamented, "cruel it should be my fate, at the end of the war, in which I have never failed the men overseas once, that I should be beaten by their vote."

The overall result may not have seemed a resounding endorsement of King's policies, to be sure. But Winston Churchill, the great war leader who had been Britain's saviour, would have been delighted to do so well—Churchill's government was smashed by Labour in July 1945.

The Mackenzie King government had

Federal Election Results

	Liberal	PC	CCF	Social Credit	Other
March 26, 1940					
Seats	181	40	8	10	6
% popular vote	51.5	30.7	8.5	2.7	6.6
June 11, 1945					
Seats	125	67	28	13	12
% popular vote*	40.9	27.4	15.6	4.1	12.1

*Percentages do not total 100% due to rounding.

The Mackenzie King Liberals managed to keep power in both war elections. The first was a huge landslide, one of the largest majorities to that time. The second was closer but the Liberals still maintained a small majority, a remarkable feat after the strains of six years of war. Especially noticeable was the Conservative drop in popular support between the two elections, although John Bracken's Tories increased their seat total. Equally important, the CCF almost doubled its popular support (although the election result was far below the 29 per cent it drew in a September 1943 opinion poll) while more than tripling its seats. The key to the 1945 election was Quebec, which, despite its unhappiness with the imposition of conscription in November 1944, gave its votes to Mackenzie King.

Indeed, King's war record firmly established him as one of Canada's great prime ministers. Never a powerful orator, a wily politician who was always too tricky by half, he nonetheless was a strong leader. He picked powerful Cabinet ministers and gave them their head. He created a strong bureaucracy and took its advice. And above all, he understood that a country as divided as Canada had to be steered very gently. Conscription appealed to many in English-speaking Canada, but if it stirred riots in Quebec, how could that possibly benefit the war effort? By moving cautiously, by coaxing, by using the carrot instead of the stick, the prime minister pushed and prodded Canada towards a magnificent war effort. In the 1945 election, the Canadian people grudgingly recognized his accomplishment.

run an effective war effort. It had begun the process of creating the welfare state. And once they cooled down, Canadians began to realize that King had held the nation together despite the strains of war. The Liberals had won power again, and they had done so because they recognized that the Canadian people, conditioned by war, wanted a more interventionist government. As King wrote privately to one of his party's senators, "When account is taken of the inevitable misunderstandings and grievances which develop in the course of a long war, it is, I believe, little short of miraculous for a wartime government to survive an appeal to the people at the close of the struggle."

CHAPTER FIVE

OUT OF UNIFORM

The greatest single challenge of 1945 was to wind up the war and absorb a million men and women in uniform. How would a country that had known mass unemployment absorb all those demobilized defenders? Plans had been made almost before the war effort began. But would they work?

(Left) Canada was no land of plenty in 1946, but for these war brides and their regiment of children at a Christmas party in Calgary it was starting to feel like home.

(Above) Dormitories for veteran students recalled wartime barracks life. Universities quickly came to realize that they had never had students as highly motivated as the vets.

Wars NEVER END NEATLY, AND VERY seldom end as people expect. For most Canadians, the real war stopped on VE Day, 1945. Hitler and Germany were the enemies they understood, and both were now defeated. Those in Europe wanted to come home; those at home wanted a more normal life, free of rationing, shortages, and the increasingly intrusive directives from the Wartime Prices and Trade Board. It had been six years; enough was enough.

But of course the war wasn't over. The Canadians who had survived beatings and starvation in Japanese prison camps, or who were flying Dakotas over Burma or stoking boilers in HMCS *Uganda* as she headed for the Pacific, knew Japan was still fighting. So did people in British Columbia. Eighty of the thousands of Japanese incendiary balloons launched in 1944–45 had landed on Canadian soil, most of them in B.C., though one got as far as Nelson House, Manitoba. Three were shot down by the RCAF. None did noticeable damage, but defence experts worried secretly that they might have been used to spread typhoid or anthrax. Since Pearl Harbor three and a half years earlier, Americans knew all too well that there was a war in the Pacific; with the actual invasion of the Japanese homeland, Canadians would learn first-hand what it had been like to fight on Iwo Jima or Okinawa.

Even in Europe, the peace was less than certain. Would the Germans really accept unconditional surrender? Or would the Allies have to battle the same kind of underground resistance the Germans themselves had faced in France, Poland, and other countries? Would the Allies have to remain in Germany as an occupying army? What if they had really defeated and occupied Germany in 1919, instead of sending their armies home? Would there have been a Second World War? Canadians might not want to be part of an occupying army, but neither could they go home with the job unfinished.

———+·+———

While he was representing Canada in San Francisco at the founding conference of the United Nations, Mackenzie King kept a careful eye on voters back home. On April 4, 1945, he announced two predictable and pre-planned decisions about the rest of the war. Canada would do a lot less to defeat Japan than it had done against Germany, and certainly less than the service chiefs wanted; and those who fought Japan would be volunteers. The response was predictable. Toronto's *Globe and Mail* called the decision not to conscript "despicable"; the Conservative opposition denounced it as appeasement of Quebec. *Time* magazine was shrewder; King, it suggested, "had cut himself a bumper harvest of political hay"—Quebeckers were not the only ones who refused to get excited about a Pacific War in its final stages.

Another King decision was even more significant for the future. So far, Canadians had done almost all their fighting alongside the British, although a small joint unit of Canadians and Americans had fought for a while in Italy. In the Pacific, Canadians would serve alongside the Americans. Canadians must not be seen to be helping Britain regain her Far Eastern colonies. A new 6th Division, under the popular Major-General Bert Hoffmeister, would train in the U.S. with American arms and equipment. The RCAF's "Tiger Force" would fly Canadian-made Lancasters to bomb Japanese targets, but a lack of airfields in the North Pacific

Mackenzie King, here addressing the San Francisco conference that created the United Nations in the spring of 1945, represented a more powerful Canada than had ever before existed.

meant that only two squadrons would serve in 1945; the other six would stand by. The navy had the most ambitious plans. Though its heavily gunned but short-range Tribal-class destroyers would have served better off the coast of South-east Asia than in the broad expanses of the Pacific, fighting Japan was the admirals' chance to try out the cruisers, escort carriers, and big destroyers they wanted for a peacetime fleet.

As it turned out, the government's volunteer principle led the navy into a memorable humiliation. After months of refits and weeks of tropical heat, the crew of HMCS *Uganda* were fed up. When Ottawa insisted that they be given the choice of serving or returning to Canada, it was no contest: two-thirds of the sailors voted to go home. On August 10, as the rest of the Allied fleet watched, an embarrassed Captain Rollo Mainguay gave orders for the cruiser to weigh anchor for Esquimalt. Seldom had a warship crew voted itself out of action. The move was in poignant contrast to the day before, when British Columbia–born Lieutenant Robert Hampton Gray had taken off from a British carrier and, minutes later, crashed his damaged fighter into a Japanese destroyer and sunk it. Gray's posthumous Victoria Cross was Canada's thirteenth of the war, and the last. No one had asked the former medical student whether he wanted to serve. Nor did the sailors of HMCS *Prince Robert* insist on their rights. Ordered to Hong Kong as the war ended, 85 per cent of the crew agreed with their captain that rescuing Canadian prisoners of war from Japanese hands was more important than thirty days of shore leave.

Getting 30,000 soldiers and 15,000 airmen to volunteer for the Canadian Army Pacific Force and the RCAF's Tiger Force proved easier than expected. Veterans of the war in Europe who volunteered for the Pacific would be first in line to come home to Canada. In addition, Ottawa promised thirty days of uninterrupted leave, and extra pay for Pacific service—30 cents more than a private's $2.00—though only 25 cents more for women, whom the army paid at 80 per cent of the male rate.

In fact, by the time the first Canadian soldiers were getting used to training in the heat of Fort Benning, Georgia, the war was over. On August 6, an American bomber dropped a twenty-kiloton atomic bomb on Hiroshima, and another was dropped on Nagasaki on August 9. On August 8, as agreed with their Western allies, Russian forces began sweeping across Manchuria. On August 10, at considerable personal risk from fanatics and his own generals, Emperor Hirohito decided to save his people and surrender. On August 14, all hostilities ceased. Just after 7:00 P.M. that day, Mackenzie King met reporters in his East Block office. "This is the greatest day in our history," he announced. In Washington, President Truman announced that August 15 would be VJ Day. Canada, of course, conformed.

"IT'S ALL OVER!" exulted The Maple Leaf, in a headline that covered its entire front page. Canadian newspapers echoed the news, enthusiasm growing as the word spread westward. Across Canada, civic authorities remembered the shambles of Halifax in May and took careful precautions, while in Halifax itself police and service authorities took prompt action against revellers. The navy provided its members with a dance band and an ample supply of beer and hamburgers. In a few places, warm weather and a lack of police led to trouble. In Windsor, Ontario, a mob of 2,000 rampaged through the lobby of the Prince Edward Hotel. Crowds in Saint John demolished a bandstand. At Sudbury, where miners resented their wartime alternative of working underground or being conscripted, there was steam to release. A

142

boisterous crowd started a fire on the post-office steps, drove off firemen, shattered liquor store windows to get at the contents, and had done $40,000 damage by dawn. "Everybody was downtown and drinking right in the streets, right out of the neck," a witness recalled. "You never saw so many drunks in your life . . . and guys walking around in duds they'd taken out of clothing stores, and carrying on like crazy." But on the whole, Sudbury was the exception.

On September 2, Japan's formal surrender took place aboard the U.S. battleship *Missouri*. Canada's representative, Colonel Moore Cosgrove, enlivened the proceedings by signing on the wrong line.

VJ Day found Canadians still scattered around the globe, from RCAF flyers with British squadrons in the Burmese jungle to soldiers manning remote stations of the Northwest Territories and Yukon Signal System close to the Arctic Circle. As Mackenzie King had complained during the 1944 conscription

The celebrations marking the end of the war with Japan were quieter than those for VE Day. Perhaps that war had seemed less of a threat—or perhaps the atomic blasts that ended it seemed too terrible to be celebrated. In tiny Smoky Lake, Alta., however, flags waved.

crisis, tens of thousands of uniformed personnel were scattered across Canada, in depots, bases, and camps, and even standing guard against an enemy that now would certainly never come. Regional politics had helped spread wartime spending and the military establishments that went with it. By August repatriation from Europe was in full progress but thousands remained in postwar chores, from graves registration to dismantling equipment for disposal and, occasionally, for shipment home.

Canada had begun planning for demobilization almost before it mobilized. Brigadier H.F. McDonald, a one-armed Great War veteran and chairman of the

Canadian sailors from HMCS *Prince Robert come ashore at Hong Kong as part of the liberating forces at the end of August.*

Canadian Pension Commission, wrote the first memorandum in October 1939, and his minister, Ian Mackenzie, needed little coaxing. A First World War captain, Mackenzie had built his political career as a friend of the veterans. In 1939 Mackenzie King had demoted him from National Defence to Pensions and National Health because of departmental scandal, frequent binges, and seeming incompetence. A proud man, Mackenzie was determined to rise again. Planning after the First World War, he insisted, had been "slipshod and inappropriate". In his view, he could surely do better,

and Parliament agreed. Through the Canadian Legion and other organizations, veterans were already a powerful lobby. The war would make them stronger and would make MPs even more responsive.

Like Ian Mackenzie, most of those involved in shaping Canada's demobilization policies between 1939 and 1945 were Great War veterans. Some had been active in veterans' organizations like the Legion and the Army and Navy Veterans. They remembered how they and other returned men had felt short-changed in 1919. Sir Robert Borden's Union government had worried more about the national debt than about rewarding former soldiers. Mackenzie also remembered how veterans had squandered their discharge gratuities on having a good time, ending up

The Cabinet minister who directed Canada's planning for veterans was B.C.'s Ian Mackenzie, shown here with a Chinese-Canadian worker.

had got nothing beyond a modest gratuity, a clothing allowance, and a year's free medical care. Even if the country could afford it, argued Robert Borden—and it couldn't—handing out more would simply prolong some of the worst features of army life: dependency and loss of initiative. Though the Borden government had made land and low-cost loans available to veterans willing to become farmers, through the Soldier Settlement Act, the program had been run on strict business principles. Thanks to high costs, low farm prices, marginal land, bad luck, and their own mismanagement, half the soldier settlers had quit the land by 1930.

Demobilization planners struggled, like

dependent on soup kitchens and charity.

While Canadian pension rates for widows, orphans, and the disabled had been the highest in the world, few of the veterans had been so disabled that they collected the full amount. As for able-bodied veterans, they

Wearing U.S. uniforms issued by the GIs who liberated them, some of the first Canadians to return from the POW camp in Niigata, Japan, wait for transportation home. A few weeks of good food and medical care had begun to fatten them up.

other wartime policy-makers, to learn from previous experience. Some lessons were positive. The First World War had left Canada with a network of veterans' hospitals and more experience in rehabilitating disabled soldiers than the U.S. In 1933, R.B. Bennett had ended a decade of grumbling by creating the Canadian Pension Commission out of three warring agencies. Thus there were good precedents for meeting the needs of widows, orphans, and disabled veterans.

The real problem would be getting close to a million men and women out of uniform and into civilian jobs. What if, as many feared, the war was simply an interlude in a continuing depression? Legislation was quickly passed decreeing that veterans could claim their pre-enlistment jobs. That had been done in 1919 too, though many soldiers who returned to their old jobs soon quit; it would have helped if they had been guaranteed the higher pay and added seniority they would have gained by

Kriegies and Hong Kong Vets

By the time the war ended, 8,995 Canadians had become prisoners of war, three times as many as in the 1914–19 conflict. The majority—6,433—were soldiers, including 1,685 who had survived the Japanese capture of Hong Kong on Christmas Day 1941, and 1,946 left behind at Dieppe on August 19, 1942. Another 2,475 were in the RCAF, most of them bomber crew members shot down over Europe. The RCN contributed 87 sailors, many of them survivors of the *Athabaskan*, lost in a battle in the English Channel on April 28, 1944.

Until the Nazi regime disintegrated in 1945, the great majority of Canadian prisoners experienced only boredom, overcrowding, and the depression some christened "barbed-wire disease". Canadian Red Cross food parcels, faithfully delivered, kept most of them healthier than other prisoners, though none claimed to be well fed. By 1945 many prisoners had enrolled in education courses sponsored by the Canadian Legion, and a few had even worked on university credits. A tiny handful beat impossible odds and escaped.

Another handful, often captured agents or unlucky escapers, fell into the loathsome horror of German concentration camps. Some of them, including Frank Pickersgill, younger brother of Jack Pickersgill, were killed after horrible ordeals. Then, in 1945, as Germany collapsed, thousands of Canadians joined forced marches as their captors drove them ahead of the advancing Russians. Short of food, at times strafed by Allied aircraft, some exhausted men were kept moving only by the knowledge that their side was winning.

Canada's Hong Kong prisoners faced an infinitely worse ordeal. *Bushido*, the Japanese soldier's code, taught that a soldier who surrendered was a worthless wretch. Even if they had been treated like Japanese soldiers, as the Geneva Convention required, they would have been hungry and beaten. Instead the Japanese army ignored the convention, punished and starved its prisoners, denied them food parcels, mail, and basic medical care, and turned all who could move into slave labour, first in Hong Kong and then in the coal mines, docks, and shipyards of Japan itself. Malnutrition, disease, savage punishment, and despair killed 174 of them. Gaunt, exhausted, tortured by hunger, beriberi, pellagra, and savage guards, most survivors believed they would have perished if the two atomic bombs had not ended the war in August 1945.

Repatriation planners expected released prisoners to be changed by their experience. Several staying home. But what about veterans who had never had a civilian job? Hundreds of thousands had quit school to join up; others had been part of the great ragged army of unemployed. Would men who had been sent to fight for freedom and a better world settle for a return to bread lines or soup kitchens, and riding the rods? Mackenzie King and his colleagues were just as worried about government borrowing as the Borden government had been. In the earlier world war, the national debt had quadrupled to $2,978 million in 1919; between 1939 and 1945, it had almost quadrupled from $5,113 million to $18,443 million. But they had an even bigger worry: what would happen if a million veterans didn't like postwar Canada?

Much of the planning for veterans fell to an ad hoc body of bureaucrats known as GACDAR— the General Advisory Committee on competing committees planning for the worst, soon reported that Germany's prisoners were in better shape than expected. Content to be pushed to the head of the repatriation queue, "ex-Kriegies" (from the German term *Kriegsgefangener,* or "war prisoner") insisted they wanted no fuss. Many cut short the medical exams that might have supported later disability claims. Years of confinement left them irritable with their families, and often preoccupied with food, but usually the symptoms faded.

After their far worse ordeal, Hong Kong prisoners had all these problems in aggravated form, plus symptoms of deep malnutrition and tropical diseases few Canadian doctors could recognize, much less treat. They too found the pressures of family and friends hard to take. "My only desire was to crawl into a hole like a groundhog and close out the human race," recalled William Allister, a Winnipegger. Some used alcohol as an escape, though most put their lives together again—only to find their ordeal had left them prey to high blood pressure and early heart attacks. Years of struggle for pensions and benefits lay ahead. In 1945, though, it was enough to have outlived horrors that few Canadians have experienced.

The Canadian soldiers captured at Hong Kong at Christmas 1941 spent almost four years in brutal captivity. Starved, beaten, overworked, these survivors— shown at the moment of their release—had lost weight, teeth, and years of freedom. Most would suffer from debilitating disease the rest of their lives.

In Hong Kong's POW cages, British and Canadian captives cheer the arrival of their liberators. A few days before, Japanese guards patrolled along the wire.

Demobilization and Re-establishment—formed in January 1940 with Brigadier McDonald in the chair and an adult educator and veteran, Robert England, as secretary. Like most planning groups, GACDAR spent too much time on ideas that never materialized, including elaborate schemes to extract skilled men from the services as key players in restoring a civilian economy, and a hopeless proposal to delay demobilization of the unskilled and least employable. The influence of the veterans' lobby paid off most in their determination to meet as many of a veteran's social and economic needs as anyone in the 1940s could foresee. Whether or not all Canadians deserved a new era of social security, the veterans certainly wanted it for themselves.

In 1944, advice from GACDAR and its successors led to a new Department of Veterans Affairs, with Ian Mackenzie as minister and another veterans' activist, Walter S. Woods,

as his deputy. The Veterans Charter, pushed through Parliament in the 1944 session, offered Canada's servicemen and servicewomen more than American veterans gained from the GI Bill of Rights. Some benefits were more generous versions of those offered in 1919: the clothing allowance was $100, not $35, and the war-service gratuity was a tax-free $7.50 for each thirty days served in the western hemisphere plus 25 cents for each day served outside the hemisphere. To make up for the lack of home leave, soldiers with overseas service got an extra seven days' pay for each six months spent abroad. A private soldier who served for three years, two of them overseas, could count on a lump sum of about $512, a healthier sum then than now. Veterans got a year's free medical treatment and lifetime care for any service-related condition. They could also buy up to $10,000 in life insurance, usually without a medical examination. For disabled veterans, of course, there would be pensions, free hospital and medical care for their disability, and an even better effort than in 1919 to find them jobs and

The "Guinea Pigs" of East Grinstead

If soldiers ever talked of their fears, it was their dread of never being a "real man" again that topped the list. That horror might result from the wicked anti-personnel mines the Germans strewed wherever their enemy might walk; it could also come from the dreadful disfigurement suffered by survivors of burning bombers and "brewed up" tanks. For such men, the burn hospital in East Grinstead, in Surrey, England, became a beacon of hope. It was there that Sir Archibald McIndoe brought his skills as a plastic surgeon and his brilliance as a healer. Human wreckage was sent there for years of reconstructive surgery.

McIndoe and his Canadian assistant, Wing Commander Ross Tilley, earned fame for their work, but the real heroes of East Grinstead were the 630 patients, 170 of them Canadian. It was the patients who insisted that no one feel sorry for them: there was always someone worse off. Officially McIndoe insisted on calling them the Maxillonians; they preferred to be known as the "Guinea Pigs". The president of their association boasted that his mouth was so ruined he could hardly talk; the secretary's hands were so burned he couldn't write; and the treasurer's feet were so badly burned he couldn't run away with the money.

McIndoe had the wits to see that a hospital was the worst place for his patients. He made the Guinea Pigs visit local pubs until people there got used to them. He sent them to London theatres in groups of ten, then in ones and twos. A workshop paid them union rates to make precision parts for aircraft. Canadian officials at first assumed that the men would want to go home to Canada as soon as possible, but only two volunteered. Others wanted everything East Grinstead could do for them before they faced their family, their friends, and their deepest fear: that no woman would ever look at them again.

Journalist Nancy Figueroa described a typical case: an airman, age nineteen, who had crashed in Italy: "The right eye is gone. The left hangs from its socket. There are no eyebrows, eyelids or ears. The nose and mouth are obscure." Four years later, "He isn't the dashing young man he once was, but my stomach doesn't roll when I look at him. There are eyelids, eyebrows, a nose and lips that smile." Later, the young man married and had two children and, though blind, became a business success. There were failures, too—but some of the bravest victories of the war began at East Grinstead.

The pioneering reconstructive surgery at East Grinstead soon found practitioners in Canada. At the Department of Veterans Affairs' Sunnybrook Hospital in Toronto, as at other DVA hospitals across the land, plaster casts showed what could be done to repair the horrific damage of battle.

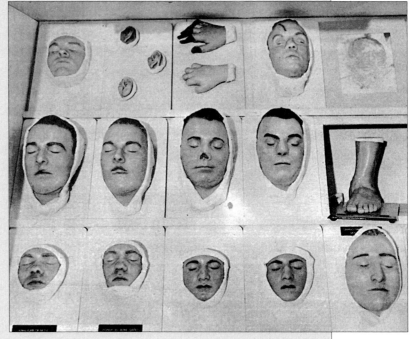

economic self-sufficiency. In all, the Veterans Charter would cost taxpayers $1.2 billion, $752.3 million for the war-service gratuity alone.

Farming was still a major way of life in 1945. Thousands of veterans had left farms and thousands more dreamed of a farming future. They needed capital, but not the crushing debts the Soldier Settlement Act had loaded on veterans of the earlier war. The Veterans' Land Act offered low-interest loans (up to $4,500 for land and $1,500 for stock and equipment, at 3 1/2 per cent) to veterans who wanted to farm or even to run a market garden. An even bigger innovation offered education or vocational training programs to any ex-serviceman or ex-service-woman who wanted them. In the earlier war, vocational training had been restricted to disabled veterans and only a tiny handful of them got help to go to university. This time a veteran who wanted to finish school or get a university degree or learn a trade would be supported for as long as he or she had served in uniform. Veterans who didn't take advantage of the Land Act or free education could claim a re-establishment credit, or "rehab grant", equal to the value of their basic gratuity, to be used to buy, maintain, or furnish a home, or purchase and equip a business. Only NRMA men who had neither volunteered nor been forced overseas would be refused. With that popular proviso, Parliament approved both the war-service gratuities and the rehabilitation grants in a single day.

With Canada's new unemployment insurance scheme in effect since 1941, returning veterans would qualify after only fifteen weeks of work, as though they had been contributors from its inception. If they could not find work, they could claim an out-of-work benefit for up to twelve months, depending on their length of service. A similar benefit provided limited income to veterans who had started farms or businesses, while they waited for a financial payoff. Another innovation was the 1942 Reinstatement in Civil Employment Act, guaranteeing veterans their former jobs under conditions "not less favourable" than if they had never joined up; returned soldiers would not be reinstated as office boys or elevator operators after six years in the army. Almost 200,000 veterans reported reinstatement in their old civilian jobs. Writing in 1948, Walter Woods could report only four charges brought against uncooperative employers under the Reinstatement Act, and only two convictions. And after a few months of wavering, the government did the decent thing: though their pay in the services had been lower than men's, women veterans would have exactly the same benefits.

The government's 1943 polling had told it to be still more generous in benefits to veterans and to make sure people knew what those benefits were. It succeeded. By April 30, 1945, polls showed that 55 per cent of respondents thought veterans' benefits were "about right"; another 31 per cent thought they were "not enough". Perhaps not, but no belligerent did better. A quarter-century of brutal experience had taught the King government some lessons that Robert Borden hadn't figured out. Not only must veterans feel they got a fair shake, so must the country. Besides, funnelling thousands of veterans into trade schools and universities would ease the huge pressure on the job market and give the country a fresh stock of educated professionals and skilled workers. The rehab grants would give the economy a burst of consumer spending when otherwise it might easily sag back into a depression. As they lost their war contracts, factories would have a powerful incentive to switch to making anything from stoves and refrigerators to chesterfields and bedroom suites. Renewed production meant new jobs. Not everyone would find the work he or she wanted, but there would be work for all.

Some demobilization begins the moment armed forces are organized. Within days of enlistment, even fresh recruits start trickling home with undiscovered ailments, disabling injuries, or merely misconduct discharges. About a third of the armed forces had been discharged before the fighting stopped. In Canada demobilization got into high gear months before the Nazi collapse, after a heated Cabinet debate led the government to order the release of thousands of men and women to ease a desperate civilian labour shortage. In turn, that renewed the long debate about which service members should be released first. Groups and individuals pestered politicians for priority. Carl Eayrs was typical. Writing to the prime minister, he asked that his nineteen-year-old son come home to finish high school. Every interest group had a claim. The Canadian Lumberman's Association predicted that the crippling lack of timber for new homes would continue until the Canadian Forestry Corps came home. The coal-mining industry insisted that miners should have accelerated discharges to relieve labour shortages in the pits. From a business viewpoint, the first out of uniform would ideally have been skilled workers and those with the most recent labour-market experience. In practice, that would have favoured those with the least service, while any surviving "breadliners" who had joined in 1939 would have been the last out of uniform. But men and women in uniform, and their veteran allies, urged a fairer principle: first in, first out. Pre-war mass unemployment had convinced the veterans that only the early birds would get jobs. Zombies and latecomers should wait their turn.

By late fall of 1945, the overseas forces were starting to return home in a flood, their trophies prominently on display.

(Left) Everywhere the crowds gathered to welcome their men, pressing close, as here in Winnipeg.

Fairness generally won out. Priority for demobilization would be based on two points a month for service in Canada and three points a month for service overseas. Married men and any women in uniform got special priority. (None of the services wanted women in peacetime.) Volunteers for the Pacific campaign would come home first, with ex-prisoners and the wounded. Compassionate cases and "the satisfaction of critical manpower requirements in industry and the professions" would have some priority, but on the whole the point system prevailed. An Industrial Selection and Release Board had the right to order priority release of service personnel. The RCAF, the service most affected, reported 7,638 applications for early release: 1,892 had already been released, 3,849 recom-mendations were approved, 1,709 cases were rejected, and 188 airmen refused to go back to their old jobs.

Repatriation was complicated, of course, by an acute worldwide shortage of shipping, partly because of the Pacific War, but chiefly because of the success of the u-boats. While Canada had hurriedly constructed a wartime fleet of merchant ships, none of them was designed to carry passengers. Nor were the navy's corvettes, frigates, and destroyers. Canadians would have to await their share of berths on the battered passenger ships that had survived the war.

Like Sir Arthur Currie in 1919, General Harry Crerar insisted that as many as possible of his regiments return intact. It would make

POWs from the Far East were frequently in fragile physical and mental states. These repatriates at Calgary, including men of all services, were given hot drinks and cigarettes by Red Cross workers.

War Brides

In 1940, their first year in England, Canadian soldiers and airmen had entered 1,221 marriages. While the RCAF and RCN imposed no restrictions on their members' marriages, the army insisted that men in the ranks and even young officers needed permission to marry, and generally discouraged it. After several cases of bigamy, soldiers were asked to declare their current marital status. Their fiancées needed certificates of good character, and the pair had to wait two months. Overseeing of marriage regulations was dumped on the unit chaplain. One recalled the pain of telling a pregnant fiancée that her lover already had a wife and three children; another soldier, with a dependent mother and plans to marry an English woman, was pursued for paternity payments by the wife of a British soldier. Financially, observed the chaplain, "He is getting himself into deep water." Roman Catholic chaplains did their best to discourage mixed marriages, and French-Canadian padres engaged in a keen unofficial competition to keep their units free of war brides.

By the end of 1946, there had been 44,886 Canadian service marriages in Britain. The vast majority of "war brides" (though there were war husbands too) were British, though Canadian airmen, sailors, and soldiers also married 1,886 Dutch women, 649 Belgians, 100 French, 26 Italians, 7 Danes, and, despite the prohibition on fraternization, 6 Germans. Between August 1944 and the end of 1946, 61,088 members of service families came to Canada, far more than the 48,000 GI brides and children who went to the United States. Canadians, of course, had been overseas far longer than the Americans. And some of them left more than a memory; by August 1945, British courts had notified Canadian authorities of 414 child maintenance orders. The Toronto *Telegram* transferred the balance of its British War Victims Fund—more than $50,000—"for the immediate relief . . . of the children, legitimate or otherwise" of Canadians who had served in Britain during the war.

Despite the best efforts of Alice Massey, the wife of the Canadian high commissioner, and a Canadian Wives Bureau established in 1944 at Canadian Military Headquarters in London, the adjustment problems were enormous.

Far from home, sometimes for five or six years, Canadian servicemen naturally formed relationships overseas. More than 47,000 married, the great majority in Britain. These war brides and children, en route to meet their husbands and fathers, may have been misled by the Canadian National Railways' meal service—most Canadians made do with fewer than six pieces of cutlery at dinner.

demobilization an "administrative dream" and "a tidy show from start to finish". Moreover, he argued, "there can be no more stabilizing influence in any community than the presence of 'all ranks' of a unit that represented that locality overseas". Generals were not immune to notions of social engineering. As in 1919, the unit-cohesion policy encouraged rumours that even conscripts in fighting units got home early. In fact, NRMA men were replaced by soldiers with over fifty demobilization points.

In June, units started handing in their tanks, artillery, and other equipment at depots established outside Arnhem and Nijmegen. Officials from the War Assets Corporation sold what equipment they could, some disappeared into the black market, and most ended up as scrap metal. In July, when the last ex-prisoners of war and Pacific Force volunteers had left for home, the rest of the army and RCAF began moving from Holland to Britain. Reinforcement units, hurriedly converted into repatriation depots, were responsible for providing medical and dental examinations and documentation. Whether in their units or at the depots, officers did their best to keep restless soldiers and airmen busy with sports, education, entertainment, and unwelcome doses of drill. Canadian Press reporter Ross Munro reported on a "khaki university", modelled on the earlier war's "University of Vimy Ridge", that offered vocational and university courses. Welfare officers claimed that each soldier could see two live shows and two movies per week. Staff officers insisted that units provide two to three hours a morning of physical training and drill. Soldiers and airmen sat through lectures on citizenship, public affairs, and the generous re-establishment benefits their country had prepared for them.

In England, Canadian authorities worried that bored, frustrated soldiers would repeat the round of bloody demobilization riots that had marred Canada's reputation in 1919. There was only one major episode. At Aldershot, billed in peacetime as "the Home of the British Army", 30,000 Canadian soldiers grumbled about poor food, pay office snafus, and especially the garrison town's downtown merchants. On July 4 a small mob of Canadians looted shops and marched on the local jail. Despite a sharp warning from the local commander, the next night they went back. This time, army provosts got tough. Censors reported that most soldiers approved. "It's given us a damned bad name," wrote a private, ". . . it would have been allright if they'd burned the Barracks down but instead they took their spite out on honest Shopkeepers. Everyone of these guys should get at least five years don't you think?" Courts martial convicted six soldiers and handed out sentences ranging from seven years to sixteen months. (Three of the offenders had been Pacific Force volunteers, already scheduled for quick return to Canada.) By the end of March 1946, Canada had paid $41,541 to compensate riot victims. Bearing no grudge, Aldershot gave Canadians the freedom of the city.

July also brought Veterans Affairs minister Ian Mackenzie to Europe, accompanied by DVA officials who would interview applicants for senior positions in his department and check into the points system and repatriation problem. "Canada is determined to get every man home as quickly as humanly possible" was his message, but not everyone agreed it was happening. Every soldier had heard a rumour of a freshly arrived Zombie sent home while a five-year man was stuck working as a clerk or cook. Unfortunately *The Maple Leaf* fed the rumour mill by publishing complaints that Crerar's "home by units" policy got Zombies home before volunteers. Lieutenant-General Simonds fired the editor, Major Doug MacFarlane, when he refused to retract the claim. The editor, complained Simonds, "refused to adhere to the principle that a balanced expression of opinion as opposed to his own personal opinion, should govern the editorial policy of The Maple Leaf." Within the points system, insisted Simonds, conscripts and volunteers would be treated the same—and he ordered the paper to report that. While a free press has a sacred right to tell lies, Simonds seems to have written the truth.

That was small comfort to bored, homesick soldiers. There was trouble at Utrecht in September when a squabble between a

THE PROVINCES

Saskatchewan

A year after its electoral triumph on June 15, 1944, Saskatchewan's brand new CCF government was in a real fight with Ottawa and with those traditional farm villains, the banks.

A combination of great growing years and wartime prices had quintupled farm incomes from their starvation base in the Dirty Thirties, and persuaded creditors that a debt-ridden Saskatchewan farm might finally be worth owning. Tommy Douglas and his novice ministers took power amid a blizzard of foreclosure notices. Anyone else might have pointed to Ottawa's constitutional power over banking and credit, issued some plaintive protests, and sat back. Douglas, a former bantamweight boxer as well as a Baptist minister, brought in a Farm Security Act under the provincial power over property and civil rights. Creditors would have to leave farmers their home quarter-section (160 acres) and forget about collecting interest payments whenever (as would happen in 1945) nature wiped out the harvest. Horrified at this socialist assault on "the sacredness of contract", the CPR, Hudson's Bay Company, and Dominion Loan and Mortgage Association demanded that Ottawa use its power of disallowance to overturn the act.

Given three weeks to prepare a legal defence, the diminutive Douglas went on the radio to appeal for public support against "this invasion of our democratic rights by the financial barons". The resulting flood of letters persuaded the federal Cabinet to back off and leave the Supreme Court and the Judicial Committee of the Privy Council to strike down the act. By the time that happened, the worst of the crisis was past.

But Ottawa had other ways of punishing the CCF. A $17 million loan for seed grain that had been conveniently overlooked since 1937—as long as Saskatchewan was run by fellow Liberals—was now "overdue". Regina must pay $6.3 million at once, said federal finance minister J.L. Ilsley, and the balance in five equal instalments. Meanwhile, federally collected taxes would not be forwarded. Furious letters between Regina and Ottawa made no difference.

What made life possible for the CCF was prosperity. Suddenly, times were good. Provincial treasurer Clarence Fines promised a $33,000 budget surplus for 1945, and found he had $2.2 million left over after retiring $3 million in debt, and spending $700,000 to acquire new businesses, $785,000 to help co-ops, and $155,000 to provide health and hospital care for the blind, old-age pensioners, orphaned children, and women on mothers' allowance. One of the CCF's new acquisitions—Saskatchewan's biggest power company, Dominion Electric—cost $693,000 (about double its annual earnings).

Canadian soldier and a Dutch civilian turned into a full-scale brawl. Canadian provosts arrested soldiers and civilians alike, and disarmed Dutch police. Both sides blamed themselves. Major-General Holly Keefler condemned "certain misguided soldiers"; Burgomaster C.A.W. Ter Pelkey responded apologetically, "It was a matter of girls. [T]hey are always the beginning of trouble."

The only good solution was to bring the Canadians home. Though the British and Americans controlled shipping, Mackenzie King thought he had won President Roosevelt's agreement to a "strict chronological priority"—Canadians who had been in England since 1939 would come home before Americans who had arrived only in 1942. Ottawa was horrified to learn that it could count on bringing home only 132,000 in the first six months, including prisoners of war. But as it worked out, concern about morale and discipline—and the early end of the Pacific war—helped achieve a year-end average of 30,000 repatriations a month. Whitehall wanted the Canadians out of England almost as much as Ottawa did.

Canada brought home a total of 346,080 servicemen and servicewomen from Europe and 40,217 from the Far East and the Pacific, and most of them were back before the end of 1945. Among them were 10,254 sick and wounded and 6,332 ex-prisoners of war, 1,504 of them from Japan and Hong Kong. Along with returning Canadians came most of the 44,886 women and men they had married overseas during the war, and the 21,358 children of these unions.

Some soldiers and airmen with lots of points had to stay behind. Officers, cooks, clerks, and mechanics often had long overseas service, but without them the army and air force could not function. Some few

remained to answer for wartime conduct. A Canadian court martial at Farnborough convicted three Dieppe prisoners, members of the Essex Scottish, of betraying their comrades. Lance-Corporal Adrien Demers from South Granby, who had absented himself for three years in wartime England, got two years' hard labour. Having promoted himself to sergeant-major, the man had persuaded his English wife that he had a soft office job.

Canadians were not the only people to face retribution. In Germany, a Canadian court martial convicted Kurt Meyer, an ss major-general, of inciting his men to kill eighteen Canadian prisoners of war, and sentenced him to hang. Conscious that not all their own men had clean hands, senior officers commuted Meyer's sentence to life in prison. After nine years in Dorchester

Overseas, vengeance was exacted against those who had collaborated or cohabited with the Nazis. Women who had been too friendly with the occupiers often had their heads shaved, as at Almelo in The Netherlands.

Penitentiary, including a brief interlude advising the Canadian army on how to fight the Soviet army, Meyer was released in 1954.

There remained the unpopular business of occupying Germany. At the end of 1944, Ottawa had reluctantly agreed to provide eleven squadrons of the RCAF and 25,000 soldiers for the initial phase of adjustment and disarmament. The army reconstituted its 3rd Division as its Canadian Army Occupation Force (CAOF), found 10,000 volunteers, and added another 8,000 soldiers with fewer than fifty repatriation points. While many excellent soldiers and airmen volunteered for occupation duties, a few just wanted to continue their wartime rackets, and others doubted whether they would ever find as much rank, pay, or power on "civvy street", and looked forward to lording it over the enemy. As for the "low points" men, they only wanted to go home.

After weeks of reorganization in Holland, the CAOF moved into Germany in June and July, relieving the 2nd Canadian Division. Major-General Vokes, a plump, outspoken extrovert from the Permanent Force, commanded Canada's occupation troops. He loved his job but few others shared his joy. Postwar Germany was a ruined, starving country. Even volunteers for occupation duty complained about short rations, bad cooking, limited leave, and plenty of nothing to do. Strict Allied rules against fraternization with the conquered Germans, the perpetrators of the horrors of Belsen and Auschwitz, had seemed reasonable at first, but homesick, lonely soldiers wanted company. Ottawa

Towns big and small staged massive welcome-home parades for their regiments. Oshawa, Ont., welcomed back the Ontario Regiment, its armoured unit, on November 29, 1945.

ignored Crerar's suggestion that a battalion of CWACs do clerical duties and provide "girl-power for unit parties". By the end of 1945, Canada had brought home most RCAF units. Despite bitter British protests and General Vokes's regrets, the army's occupation force began heading for Canada in February 1946. Sit-down strikes in army and air force units helped speed the process.

Almost everyone arriving from Europe landed at Halifax, though the *Queen Mary*, *Mauretania*, and other huge ocean liners that had survived the war dropped Canadians at New York, and smaller passenger ships carried troops upriver to Quebec and Montreal. The CNR and CPR insisted on drafts of 225 people, the passenger capacity of one of their troop trains. A hundred old passenger cars were refitted and leased to the Armed Forces Sleeper Company. When huge ships docked, like the *Ile de France* in June, the railways mobilized 148 sleepers and 23 diners, leaving civilian travellers to sit up all night in a day coach or beg for a vacant hotel room.

Local officials and volunteer agencies took on the task of organizing a civic welcome. Haligonians, who would have had to spend a year at the docks to welcome every ship, were condemned, as in 1919, for their shabby welcome. Other communities tried harder. At stations along the main line, people met troop trains with slices of apple pie and tubs of ice cream. Of course, the biggest crowds gathered to greet a hometown unit. At Windsor, crowds were so thick that the Essex Scottish could not march up Ouellette Street. The 1st Canadian Parachute Battalion found the throngs so dense at London's station that some troops had trouble struggling out of the cars. In Toronto, mothers, wives, and other relatives jammed into the ranks until there were more civilians than troops. Mayor Saunders looked down at lipsticked veterans carrying children, pocketed his speech, and simply shouted, "It's nice to see you fellas."

As in 1919, Toronto boasted the country's largest and most efficient discharge depot. Troop trains pulled into the Exhibition grounds. Relatives waited in the grandstand in alphabetical blocks while a band played to ease the wait. Troops marched in, broke off to find their families, and re-formed to collect pay, ration cards, travel documents, and passes for thirty days' leave. Civilian volunteers with cars offered to drive families, or to provide a bed for the night. The Legion was on hand with coffee, cigarettes, and sandwiches. The telephone company provided a bank of phones and the Ontario government picked up the tab for long-distance calls.

Whether they were met by crowds or by a little knot of people at a prairie whistle stop, returning veterans had eyes only for their families and the sweethearts they had left behind as long as six years before. Perhaps everyone expected too much. No matter how they yearned for each other, husbands and wives had grown apart. Despite four or five years away, some parents assumed that a son or daughter was still a child. Children left as infants were troubled by the uniformed stranger who would invade the kitchen and their mother's bedroom. Older children expected a war hero and discovered an ordinary man who could not talk about killing Germans even if he had done so. Like earlier veterans, returning men and women found that home news mattered more than anything they could bear to say about the war. They were coming back from places only veterans could know. At home, there was no

Fast and steady speeds my lathe
So Hitler gets a closer shave!

BRAVE MEN SHALL NOT DIE BECAUSE *I* FALTERED

This message is issued by the Department of Munitions and Supply for Canada

FOR YOUR *Christmas* AND OUR *Victory*

Season's Greetings

With a Gift of War Saving Stamps to help make a Happy New Year ~

Spirit of Total War, F.B. Taylor

s/L Hal Gooding, D.F.C., A.A.M., Paul Goranson

Potato Peelers, Leonard Brooks

Sergeant P.J. Ford, Charles Comfort

sharing the memories of paralysing cold in a bomber over Germany, or the smell of the foc's'le messdeck in a corvette, or the sound of friends cooking in a burning Sherman tank. Only other veterans understood and, for some, their company was soon all that made homecoming tolerable. Some never adjusted to the ordinariness of home and peace. Nova Scotia author Donald Ripley recalled a local war hero who became "a sort of twilight zone social guerilla, wrestling with peace and drinking with old buddies at the Legion, while hating day-in-day-out ordinariness." Still, most returnees realized that that was a trap. When a veteran cared more about the future than the past, his demobilization was complete. The second battle, a veteran of the earlier war had said, was winning a new life.

"The Lord Helps Those Who Help Themselves", the sign says. Still, veterans needed government help to reintegrate into Civvy Street, and demobilization centres tried to provide it.

In planning his department, Mackenzie had talked of a vast information network to brief veterans on their future. Demobilization centres would bring together experts on every aspect of government policy, from university education to life insurance, with a special emphasis on job-finding by the Department of Labour. As usual, it was easier for officials to teach than for their clients to learn. "The average fighting man of the Second World War . . . often expected more than the country could give him," wrote the navy's official historian, Gilbert Tucker. "Cases were known where officers, in good faith, had led their crews to suppose that the moment they landed back in Canada the best of everything was to be handed to them— farms, automobiles, continued exemption from income taxes, almost anything they wanted."

Mackenzie's dream of friendly, efficient rehabilitation centres could not entirely escape bureaucratic tradition. Montreal's centre, reported Blair Fraser in the September 1945 issue of *Maclean's*, resembled a soup kitchen. Veterans waited on benches in a basement for up to an hour for a chance to register, and for another hour while their service files were located. War-service gratuity payments depended on record-keeping; the air force was the best, Fraser was told, and the navy was the worst. Despite a promised thirty-day turnaround for pension decisions, Fraser found that the Pension Commission took more like three months— though any eventual payment was retroactive, and taxpayers, he admitted, deserved some protection from fraud and extravagance. And he had praise for DVA officials who kept a restraining hand on how veterans

SENIOR ARMY OFFICER
Who satisfactorily filled command and staff appointments, including one of the most difficult in Canada, is seeking employment. Can prove organizing and administering ability in both civilian and army life. Very successful in personnel management. Pre-war employment has ceased to exist. Position is sought where real ability can earn a real salary.—Box 65, Saturday Night.

Every vet worried about finding a job; some who had proved themselves in major wartime positions made an asset out of their experience.

spent their rehab grants. "Racketeers have been waiting with their tongues hanging out for the thousands of youngsters who . . . will be coming back to get these Government credits."

Some groups who thought they had done much to win the war would be disappointed. Civilian pilots who had trained aircrew or flown aircraft to Britain as members of Ferry Command found that service medals and veterans' benefits were reserved for those in uniform. Fifteen thousand Canadians had joined the Merchant Marine and 1,200 had died or been injured when their ships were sunk, but they were not in the Royal Canadian Navy. They could qualify for medals but their generous wage scales and special war-risk bonuses for serving in dangerous waters were deemed sufficient compensation, without benefit of the Veterans Charter. A little grudgingly, the DVA allowed merchant seamen most of the benefits, from pensions to the Veterans' Land Act loans, available to veterans. Naval returnees, jealous of merchant navy pay, made no common cause with those they had tried and frequently failed to protect.

The 25,000 seriously disabled survivors found a chain of veterans' hospitals, job placement programs, and even free legal representation in preparing their pension appeals. But nothing made disability easy. No device could stop the phantom pain of a lost leg, or the frustration of a missing arm. Morale-building lectures were too trite to ease the lonely life that faced some of war's sadder victims. Still, the DVA offered vastly more patience and flexibility than its predecessor in 1919, and its care would continue for a lifetime.

There were hundreds of thousands who lined up for Veterans' Land Act loans, signed up for university courses, or used their rehab grants to start businesses. Some learned the hard way why their land had never been farmed before, or that calling a business "Vet's Drycleaning" or "Veterans' Taxi" was no guarantee of customers. A Winnipeg policeman who had commanded a company in action found himself once again pounding a beat and writing parking tickets. A private who remembered his service career as an uninterrupted battle with authority returned to take over his father's company and prospered.

Some veterans had no family reunion. Parents, even wives and children, had died during their long absence. Wartime romances had ended in "Dear John" letters. Marriages consummated during a week's furlough and remembered by a few dog-eared snapshots had withered in the years of separation; others collapsed when the partners finally saw each other again, and saw what the war had done. Between 1939 and 1945, divorces in Canada rose by 150 per cent, and the rate soared even higher in the first two postwar years. Half a century later, the divorce problem seems invisible; to contemporaries it was a scandal. The *Toronto*

The war had left thousands disabled by wounds, and the Canadian people promised—and genuinely tried to provide—continuing care. On the hospital ship Lady Nelson, *this nursing sister was attending to a relatively happy patient.*

Daily Star called its hometown the "Reno" of Canada and claimed that a special court would have to dispose of a case per hour to clear the backlog. In British Columbia, one marriage in ten ended in divorce. In Quebec, where Roman Catholic principles prevented the legislature from legalizing divorce, unhappy couples had to petition the Canadian Senate for a private bill. Despite the enormous cost and difficulty, petitions increased fivefold. Even for veterans, no one dared change the law.

The war had been hard on fidelity. Most men who had left with the 1st Canadian Division in December 1939 did not return until late 1945. Others were away for two, three, or four years. Many, possibly most, were utterly faithful to their wives in Canada, as their wives were faithful to them. But others formed lasting relationships overseas. One of them, an army brigadier who had fought through Normandy to The Netherlands, left a frank account of why he divorced his Canadian wife in favour of a Dutch woman. A marriage breakup made a further military career almost impossible in

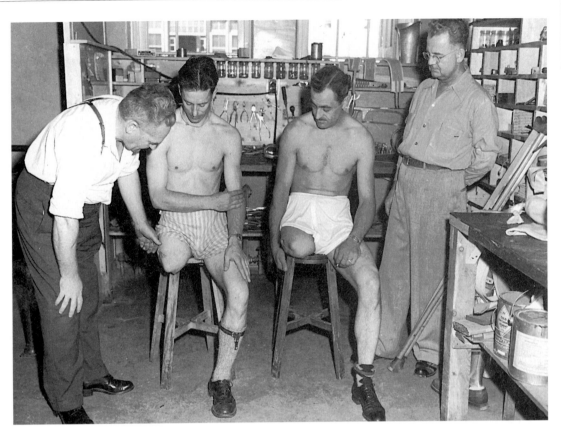

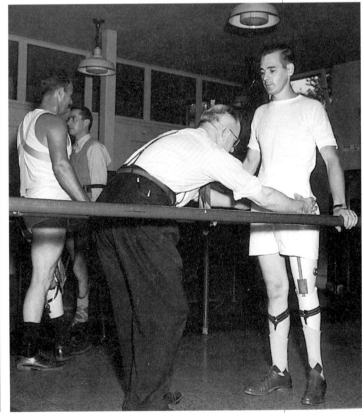

(Above) Those who had lost limbs were fitted with the latest in suction-socket prostheses by the Department of Veterans Affairs, and underwent months or years of physical therapy.

(Right) Learning to use a false limb was only the first step. Many vets turned to the War Amps—a support group founded after the Great War—for help in the hard days ahead.

1945. "That some Canadian senior officers in England consoled themselves with English women was well known and sniggered at," wrote C.P. Stacey and Barbara Wilson in *The Half Million*. So did their juniors.

Wives in Canada worried and waited, and sometimes gave up on waiting. The myth that women must preserve their chastity while men could do as they pleased survived in the media but not in practice. "[F]rom what I see in the courts," a Supreme Court justice complained to *Maclean's*, "I am forced to the conclusion that women's morals are slipping badly. There is no such thing as the 'double standard'. Many women seem to have adopted the man's standard. Fear of consequences is no longer the strong deterrent it used to be; knowledge of birth control is widespread. I can't estimate its effect on our country, but I do know it won't be good."

Then there were the war brides who had married Canadian servicemen overseas. Once in Canada, war brides faced especially tough adjustments. Arriving at Halifax, often with a child or two and almost always without their husbands, the women confronted an unknown country and long journeys before they reached their homes. Most would remember the big trains, the heaping servings of food, the vast distances, and the efficiency of the Red Cross, which took charge of their cross-country travel. One woman recalled being awakened for her first glimpse of Lake Superior—and it was still in sight eight hours later. Perhaps nothing could have prepared city-bred brides for the loneliness and hardships of prairie homesteading, or even of living in a remote Manitoba or British Columbia town. Imagine the transition from an English city or even a farming village to a prairie homestead in midwinter, with an unheated biffy near the barn and the nearest neighbour a mile away. In smaller communities, war brides were often met with deep suspicion and ill-concealed resentment for capturing the hearts of hometown heroes. And the heroes themselves often had a different status out of uniform than they seemed to have as RCAF fighter pilots or army corporals. Mavis Gallant, then a young reporter with the *Montreal Star*, reported that the most difficult adjustment of all was for English women who had married French Canadians. The barriers of language, culture, and religion between them and their adopted

Far from home and in a very unfamiliar society, war brides had to make major adjustments. These arriving mothers and children in Toronto look suitably apprehensive.

families would never come down. The chaplains of French-Canadian regiments who competed for the lowest rate of "mixed" marriages may have been kinder than they seemed.

Indeed, anyone would have found the transition from Britain to Canada in the mid-1940s a challenge. The sight of grown men reading comic books typified for one woman a country where even major cities lacked a genuine bookstore, where the single audible radio station played little but cowboy music and the tiny public library was managed by a prudish spinster. Wartime rationing and even pre-war custom persuaded many war brides that Canadians ate monstrous quantities of food. Binge drinking and dreary taverns with their "Ladies and Escorts" entrances were a rude surprise to women accustomed to the cosy saloon bar at the "local". The wise ones learned to keep their

Medals and Decorations

To an outsider, a service medal looks like an oversized bronze or silver coin, cross, or star hung from a multicoloured ribbon, a sort of two-dimensional Christmas tree ornament. To a veteran, each medal tells a story of service and some tell of special courage. The first medal was struck by the British to recognize veterans of the battle of Waterloo; soon there was a medal (and a ribbon) for each campaign, with a clasp or bar for each battle. British sailors and soldiers got few other rewards for fighting and dying for the Empire.

During the Second World War, the British issued the 1939–45 Star, a six-pointed bronze medal normally earned for six months' active service overseas. For service in specific theatres around the world they issued similar stars, each with a distinctive ribbon. Like other Commonwealth troops, Canadians qualified. Many Canadian sailors and merchant seamen on convoy duty qualified for the Atlantic Star. Soldiers earned the Italy Star, the France and Germany stars, and sometimes both. Soldiers at Hong Kong earned the Pacific Star. A few Canadians came home with the Africa Star. Airmen who flew over France and Germany in the bomber offensive earned the Aircrew Europe Star. If they flew in support of the campaigns in Italy or North-West Europe, they also qualified for those stars.

The British awarded the Defence Medal, on a flame-coloured ribbon with green edges, for those who stood guard at home and in its threatened colonial outposts. That included many Canadian soldiers and airmen, and a contingent of Canadian firefighters who served during the Blitz of 1940–41 and the v-1 and v-2 bombings of 1944–45. Almost everyone who served in uniform for at least twenty-eight days earned the British War Medal. Canada struck its own, in .800 fine silver, and issued over 700,000, including 4,450 to the Merchant Marine.

As part of its campaign to get more volunteers, in 1943 Canada issued the Canadian Voluntary Service Medal, with a small silver bar (or a maple leaf on the ribbon) for those who served overseas. A drab-looking ribbon and an unpopular political purpose led many service personnel to call it the "Spam", a reminder of something else that came up with the rations.

Medals were issued to all participants. Decorations were awards to individuals for valour, service, or leadership. Supreme was the Victoria Cross (vc), whose dark crimson ribbon indicates service of exceptional valour in the face of the enemy. The George Cross (gc), with its blue ribbon, recognized great courage but not in the face of the enemy. Each service also had its own decorations. The Distinguished Service Cross (dsc) recognized successful naval officers; the Distinguished Flying Cross (dfc) was the reward for a successful fighter ace or a bomber pilot who had brought his crew through a dangerous tour of operations. The army's Distinguished Service Order (dso) might be routine for a successful battalion commander; for a junior officer it meant a near miss for the vc. Other ranks earned other medals. A Distinguished Conduct Medal (dcm) recognized almost enough valour for a vc; a Military Medal (mm) was a little easier to earn. The King government legislated its own family of decorations during the war, but somehow lacked the courage to manufacture and award them.

These medals were earned by an RCAF pilot.

criticisms to themselves, or to save them for their letters home; Old World airs of superiority had never been welcome in Canada. Most of the war brides eventually overcame the transition and enriched the country. Few did so more than Betty Oliphant, the founding head of the National Ballet School; her marriage failed but "Miss O" became the inspiration for generations of talented young people. But the failures, of course, were the audible minority. Happy people have no history.

Any marriage endures stress during wartime. Husbands, warned the Canadian Youth Commission, would find wives who had been acting as heads of the family and might not accept their old subservience. Alternatively, men who were used to taking orders might not welcome renewed responsibility. Single veterans would certainly have a hard time in the old family home, and so would their parents. "Some young veterans acquired habits and points of view that are distressing to their parents," warned the commission. "They have developed a taste for unconventional language, drinking or carefree spending. Their changed social and sexual codes may cause parents great concern." Several veterans recalled for Barry Broadfoot the family embarrassment when years of mess hall habit led them to call, "Pass the f—ing butter."

It was not hard, in 1945, to find issues for returning veterans to tackle. For many civilians, who had accumulated comfortable nest eggs in the years of high wartime wages and limited spending temptations, Canada had never been a better place to live. A veteran with a wife and child and no place to live had a different view. For sixteen years almost nothing had been done to build or renew housing, and, as latecomers, veterans and their families were the victims. Apart from emergency housing, wartime construction had lavished materials and skills on training camps, airfields, and munitions factories. A whole family might now be crammed into a boarding-house bedroom or two, cooking on a hotplate and sharing the bathroom with the rest of the boarders. Landladies, in veterans' memories, schemed to make extra money and trouble. The alternative, doubling up with parents—as many soldiers' families had done during the war—struck most veterans as even worse. The war had also dried up production of cars, furniture, and domestic appliances. With his family sleeping on the floor and his rehab grant ready to spend, a veteran found nothing but high-priced second-hand relics for sale. Car lots looked like junkyards, with old models sitting on bald tires.

Still, housing was the problem that ranked highest in veterans' minds. It spawned speeches, committees, and, in Vancouver, the temporary occupation of the biggest downtown hotel. The housing problem had seethed through the latter years of the war. In every city or town with war factories or military bases, housing had been so scarce that rent rackets were rampant. Some landlords charged "commissions" before tenants could move in; others filled out a lease but charged $500 for a key or forced luckless tenants to buy worthless furniture. Yorkton, a prairie town with a nearby British Commonwealth Air Training Plan school, housed families in garages, basements, and sheds. For two rooms, a landlord could demand $20 a month from an airman earning $40. Early in 1945, the federal government declared Toronto an "emergency shelter" area. Unless non-residents were coming to

work in a war industry or an essential job, they could stay away. No one, declared the emergency shelter co-ordinator, would be allowed to come "merely because they think Toronto is a nice place to live." For haters of Hogtown, it was a thought to remember.

The end of the war solved nothing. Though the administrators of the Land Act claimed that its loans helped build 6,000 new homes and the National Housing Act would eventually transform hundreds of thousands of tenants into homeowners, demobilization planning had not addressed the short-term shelter problem. The hunt

Housing continued to be scarce well into the post-war years. Crowded conditions like this squalid Kingston, Ont., scene were all too common.

for shelter created an ugly tension between veterans and civilians. People who had done well in the war did even better in peacetime by renting a garage or a basement to a veteran. Experts blamed overcrowding for a wide range of social ills, from drinking to children running wild. "The lack of privacy resulting in too close association of the sexes," warned the Ontario Children's Aid Society, ". . . is the cause of childhood delinquency in numerous instances."

Veterans' organizations could do little about a national housing shortage, but they had a long history of working for disabled and dependent pensioners. As in the earlier war, the saddest cases were often those whose medical and psychological problems were ignored, most often by themselves. A wife recalled a husband eventually crippled by an old wartime back injury who had left the army in 1945 with the cheerful comment "No complaints." He felt fit, he was in a hurry, and disability meant comrades who had lost an arm or a leg or part of a stomach. "And those two words," she remembered, "have caused him more trouble than any two words should ever cause anyone trouble." They robbed him of an obvious disability claim. There were thousands more whose cases, undocumented and unprovable, would become the grievances of a lifetime.

In 1945 there could be no measurement of the long-term consequences of the mental and physical strain of wartime service, even for the starved and beaten survivors of the Japanese prison camps. In Britain, where most of the population had shared the risks and terrors of war, the National Health Service was a logical response to a national trauma. In Canada the Liberals had promised a national health insurance plan in their 1945 election platform; not until 1958 would all Canadians have hospital insurance, and full medicare would wait until 1967.

So would the equal status at least some women had enjoyed in wartime. Despite appearances, that equality had never

Government and private contractors tried to build homes for veterans and their families. By December 1946, for example, the POW camp at Bowmanville, Ont., had been transformed into a housing development.

extended to the 50,000 women in uniform. "They serve that men may fight" was the motto of the RCAF's Women's Division, and it applied equally to the navy's Wrens and the army's CWACs. Servicewomen had been separate and different, lower-paid than men and more limited in the trades open to them. Crerar's idea of how CWACs might help the occupation force as "girl power" for parties was an inadvertent reminder of the wartime whispering campaign that the army had recruited women of easy virtue. In fact, like all the women's services, the CWACs worked overtime to preserve morality. The corps' biggest controversy in 1945 had been whether the new CWAC pipe band would have to wear its kilts well below the knee to preserve regulation modesty. Demobilization solved the problem; there would be no band, for all three of the women's services were abolished. "Communal uniformed life does not appeal to most women," explained the director of the WRCNS, Commander Adelaide Sinclair. Civilian employment, she added, would be far more attractive. She would find hers with the United Nations;

Veterans flooded the universities, so wise presidents scouted around for housing. At the University of British Columbia, prefabricated huts from abandoned army and air force camps were pressed into service for the married.

most of her members would become wives and mothers.

Though servicewomen ultimately shared equally in veterans' benefits, they used them mostly to return to the traditional women's world. The Youth Commission warned that women had joined up to escape dependence and monotony, but readers of the *Canadian Home Journal* were reassured by Rica McLean Farquharson that, because they remained "women, in the full sense, the majority of Canada's women who have been in the services admit a dream of civilian living made up of 'a man of my own, a home of our own, a baby—or more—of our own'." The DVA proudly reported that women veterans had not been a problem. Only 3 per cent of women needed an out-of-work allowance, compared to 15 per cent of the men. A higher proportion of women than men took training, but 85 per cent chose traditional occupations—nursing, hairdressing, dress-making, and "commercial". By 1946, 16,000 were married and 20,000 had jobs.

The most notable postwar success was probably free university education. For men and women who hadn't opened a serious book in years, going back to school was no picnic. "I had a wife, children, four years as a bomber pilot, and a nagging sense that listening to a professor who had never been closer to war than a newspaper was kid's stuff," one veteran remembered. Others dropped out; he stuck to it. With fees and books paid for, $65 a month for a single student and $85 for a married man, and a chance to earn more in the summer, thousands of Canadians got an opportunity they would otherwise never have had. Universities gained too. Professors who taught the veteran classes of 1945–50 remembered them as the best students they had ever had.

Having served a national purpose well, Canada's universities would not return to the impoverished obscurity they had known. A generation that appreciated its opportunity for a better education would make sure that its children and grandchildren also had a chance to attend at minimal cost.

Veterans who didn't go to university succeeded too, if they grew from their experience instead of living in it. DVA officials boasted that they took one ex-colonel back to the firm where he had been little more than an office boy in 1939, in hopes that his old employers would see why the army had valued him so highly; they did. More than in the earlier war, military service had often involved training relevant to civilian experience. As a contribution to re-establishing its members, the navy published a booklet listing its trades and their civilian equivalents. There were other accomplishments, from managing the mess accounts to motivating a few wet, shivering men to risk their lives, that could find relevance in postwar Canada.

For all its failings and frustrations, demobilization succeeded in 1945 because Canada itself had changed. Somehow, the government had transcended the nervous anxiety of 1919 that generous treatment would bankrupt the country and transform returned soldiers into greedy dependents. There were other fears in 1945—of riots and disorder, of a vast crime wave perpetuated by gun-toting veterans or by their children, run to seed for lack of a father's stern discipline. None of it really happened, though the fear was more durable than the reality.

CHAPTER SIX
ORDERLY DECONTROL

The controls that had carried Canada's economy so successfully through the war were not needed once victory had been won. But how could they be eliminated? How could the economy be liberated without plunging the nation into chaos? The task fell to the "Minister of Everything", C.D. Howe.

(Above) Having directed Canada's industrial mobilization, C.D. Howe was put in charge of winding down the war effort and organizing the transition to peace.

(Right) Even in 1948, strikers at Vancouver's American Can Co. characterized their struggle in wartime terms.

VETERANS!
IS THIS the DEMOCRACY YOU FOUGHT FOR ?

THE WAR YEARS HAD SPURRED AN INCREDIBLE development in aviation. Aircraft routinely flew across the Atlantic Ocean, tens of thousands of men and women had learned to fly, and giant planes rolled off the production lines. No nation was better placed to take advantage of this new frontier than Canada, or so Canadians believed. The British Commonwealth Air Training Plan had been a success, the big factories at Winnipeg, Vancouver, Montreal, and Toronto had proved they could build aircraft and components from small pilot trainers to giant four-engine Lancaster bombers, and Trans-Canada Airlines, created in the 1930s to serve the Canadian market, was poised to begin civilian flights overseas. Why not make Canada the centre for the new age of aviation?

The government leased Victory Aircraft, the Crown corporation that had built Lancasters at Malton, Ontario, to the A.V. Roe Company, a British firm, which quickly began work on jet passenger aircraft. Another huge factory, at Cartierville, Quebec, was bought by its executives and named Canadair; their intention was to build four-engine passenger aircraft called North Stars. The government placed orders for the products of these plants, thousands of highly skilled men and women found jobs in advanced industries, and the world, or so it seemed, was Canada's oyster. The dream

The war had spurred the industrialization of Canada, and put women onto the shop floors alongside men. This welding shop at Macdonald Bros. Aircraft in 1941 Winnipeg was not atypical of smaller enterprises.

THE PROVINCES

Alberta

In 1945, most of Alberta's oil wealth was still a dream, though gas from the Turner Valley had already added to provincial coffers. Agriculture had helped make Alberta one of Canada's "have" provinces, and the war had been a good time for farmers. The province was Canada's leading hog producer, and Alberta pigs not only invaded traditional Danish markets but increasingly matched Danish quality. Dairy farmers took pride in Alcarta Gerben, a sleek Holstein that delivered 1,410 pounds of butterfat and 27,800 pounds of milk in a year.

In 1945, the Prairie Farm Rehabilitation Administration announced a $2,470,000 plan to reclaim land, most of it in Alberta. A federal-provincial agency little known outside its region, the PFRA was dedicated to battling soil erosion, desertification, and other environmental consequences of a generation of "grain mining" in western Canada. The PFRA would create thousands of jobs and save, it hoped, a million acres, from Medicine Hat to the St. Mary–Milk River water development scheme.

What most Canadians knew about Alberta was that it had a "funny money" Social Credit government that had promised a $25 monthly "dividend" to each adult Albertan. In 1942 Ernest Manning had succeeded his mentor, Bill Aberhart, as both premier and chief preacher for the Prophetic Bible Institute. While banking and credit were under federal jurisdiction, debtor-protection laws designed by Social Credit had made Alberta a wasteland for lenders. Conscious of pent-up demand for borrowing, Manning prudently exempted National Housing Act loans from the provincial debt legislation. About 800,000 Albertans cautiously prepared to join the postwar spending boom.

Within the party, the Social Credit faith burned bright. In December, delegates met in Calgary for the annual convention, reminded their leaders of their pledge of $25 a month, and told them to get going. "You are asking for a declaration of war," declared attorney-general Lucien Mayrand; "Do you want us to go beyond the law and the constitution?" Delegates roared their answer. "Are you prepared to go to jail?" shouted Mayrand; "I am." Louder roars. "The young people in our district will shoulder guns," claimed a young delegate, "... just give us the ammunition." "God willing, we will follow our Moses through the desert and into the promised land," an elderly woman promised. The motion passed unanimously, and delegates gave three cheers and joined in singing "Onward Christian Soldiers." Nothing happened.

proved to be only that, but no one could argue that big thinking and grandiose planning had been lacking in Canada at the dawn of the air age.

The planner, the chief executive officer designated to manage the transition from war to peace, was Clarence Decatur Howe, the Minister of Reconstruction. Soon after the outbreak of war, he took over the newly created Department of Munitions and Supply, and built Canada's industrial war effort into a giant. His department spawned Crown corporations by the dozen to run critical segments of the war effort: to buy scarce silk, to dig uranium, to import and allocate machine tools, to operate merchant ships and build bombers. The department dispensed billions in contracts, with quite astonishing effectiveness. Now Howe, the man who had built the war machine, was the

The end of gasoline rationing meant liberation from irksome controls for drivers—and for gas station operators.

man charged with taking it apart.

When C.D. took over the new reconstruction department in late 1944, he had fully formed views on what was needed. Popular opinion was that, once the war had ended and the armies had returned to Canada, chaos would result, exactly as had happened after the First World War. There would be labour strife, employment would plummet, and, worst of all, the Great Depression would return. Howe believed this was simply wrong. The war had put the Canadian economy through its period of reconstruction, and all that was needed now was a period of "reconversion" to make proper use of what already was in place. As early as 1943 he had told Mackenzie King that "if the present rate of production can be maintained after the war, the absorption into civilian life of the men and women of the Armed Services and in war industry presents no serious problem." He said the same thing in 1945, telling a visiting labour delegation that "there is plenty of employment in this country" and writing to a friend that "1946 will be a good year and 1947 a boom year." There was, in Howe's view, not a surplus of labour but a shortage, and the problem would be shortages of goods, labour, and capital. Government would not have to resort to creating public works projects to put people to work. But was he correct?

In the view of Howe and his staff in the reconstruction department, industry had to be pushed and prodded to convert from wartime to peacetime production. It is hard, he said privately, "for our privileged class in the war plants"—he meant the bosses, not the workers—"to realize the atomic bomb killed Santa Claus as far as they are concerned, and that they must now go to work." The postwar government was not going to purchase everything industry produced, in other words. Still, companies would need help through the transition. This meant an array of incentives—grants, tax concessions, and the carefully timed sale of wartime surpluses, equipment, and buildings—to ensure that business was ready to serve the domestic market, with its pent-up demand, and markets overseas, where countries in Europe and Asia were in ruins.

Critics on both the left and the right shouted their abuse of Howe. CCF leader M. J. Coldwell believed that wartime controls and regulations had worked to limit inflation, prices, and profits; he wanted much of this to remain, though not, of course, controls on wages. John Bracken, the Progressive Conservative leader, believed that Howe was moving too slowly in dismantling the wartime economy, crippling business with high taxation and too much regulation. The businessmen also grumbled about Howe and his heavy hand.

Gradually, however, the structure of regulation began to disappear, and industries were freed. "Lid Is Off on Gold Mining", the *Toronto Daily Star* reported on June 7, 1945, "Sink Shafts Where Ye May." The Wartime Prices and Trade Board began to deregulate goods just as quickly as supplies reached levels where the removal of controls would not drive prices up. Hitherto unavailable commodities came back on the market. The first "wonder drug", penicillin, had been used to treat soldiers with venereal diseases and to control infection in wounds; it would reach the public in August, and the newspapers would soon be full of miracle cures as the near-dead were returned to health. Fuel rationing ended in May, and the 40 m.p.h. speed limit followed soon after. The ration of anthracite coal increased by 50 per cent in September, a vital necessity at a time when most Canadians heated their houses with coal. Restrictions on the use of paper products were lifted on December 31, and newspapers swelled in

War had swelled the federal bureaucracy, and the return of peace did little to chop it back to size. These civil servants from the Department of National Revenue in 1947 knew that continuing government intervention and regulation guaranteed their jobs.

Government-subsidized public housing began to replace big city slums by the end of the 1940s. Toronto's Regent Park development was a vast improvement over Cabbagetown's squalor.

size almost at once. On New Year's Day, 1946, tire rationing lapsed. By February some 300 products had been liberated from controls, including jewellery and taxi rides. Not until 1947, however, were a host of expensive items such as refrigerators and automobiles readily available.

Some controls remained popular. Though it had been evaded by thousands in countless ways, rent control had helped the nation get through the wartime shortage of housing. Now, with the soldiers returning to Canada, housing seemed ever harder to find. Landlords resorted to evicting tenants to free up their properties for reletting at higher rents, and the government had to provide emergency shelters, converted from now empty military barracks in Vancouver, Winnipeg, and Toronto, for thousands of homeless vets and their families. Still, the government's work was successful overall. In the United

States, where controls on almost everything were stripped away in a rush, prices increased by 18 per cent in the twelve months after VJ Day; in Canada they went up only 5 per cent. The critics' complaints, of course, did not end.

Howe persisted on his course. As early as late 1943, he had directed that some wartime industries switch production runs to civilian goods; explosives plants turned to making fertilizers, for instance, on the assumption that increased crops to feed the liberated countries were by then a greater necessity than more bombs. In June 1944, the government made it clear that the accelerated tax write-offs for businesses that built new plants, a device that had helped speed up wartime production, would continue into the peace. The intent was to relieve new investors in private projects from the burden of taxation to assist the conversion and expansion of industry. There would also be low-interest loans to buy new machinery.

In 1945, the Crown corporations began to close down, to sell off their assets, or to merge. Howe shut those that dealt with oil, metals, shipping, shipbuilding, aircraft, timber, and other commodities, twenty-two in all by the end of 1946. He undertook the combination of the Wartime Housing Corporation and the National Housing Administration into the Central Mortgage and Housing Corporation, and sold off all the assets of Park Steamship Company, at war's end the third-largest shipping company in the world. Why dispose of much of the country's merchant navy? To Howe it was simply good sense. The end of the war was certain to produce a worldwide surplus of shipping, and Canadian operating and construction costs were sure to be higher than those of other countries; sell. On the other hand, when it made good

"The Minister of Everything"

Clarence Decatur Howe built Canada's massive war machine from scratch. American-born, an engineer who had become rich by constructing grain elevators, C.D. Howe came to Parliament from Fort William, Ontario, in 1935. Mackenzie King put him in the Cabinet as Minister of Transport at once and, soon after war broke out, created him production czar as Minister of Munitions and Supply. The act that established his department gave Howe unprecedented power to do almost anything to get the war effort going, and he turned to the upper ranks of business for the managerial experts he needed. Most of "C.D.'s boys" worked for $1 a year of federal money, their salaries paid as a patriotic duty by their companies, and all threw themselves into the task. But none worked as hard as Howe, who negotiated with his Cabinet colleagues for the share he needed of the country's human resources, and with Canada's allies for scarce raw materials. On one trip to Britain in December 1940, Howe's ship was torpedoed; he was finally rescued after hours in a lifeboat.

Under Howe's direction, Canada's war factories produced so much that in 1942 the country began giving their products away. A billion-dollar gift of war matériel to Britain was followed by billions more in contributions called Mutual Aid. With the coming of peace, Howe managed the transition to a peacetime economy, as Minister of Reconstruction, with the same skill.

The state became the driving force of wartime Canada, and there was irony in the fact that C.D. Howe—capitalist entrepreneur extraordinaire—was the man who made the engine run.

Clarence Decatur Howe galvanized Canada's war production. The tough Minister of Munitions and Supply, here meeting the workers who produced the goods, knew how to organize and direct the country's business leaders.

sense, he was willing to create new organizations. The war had left the government with huge surpluses of every kind of war equipment, from tanks to trucks, while government offices had regiments of typewriters, filing cabinets, and waste baskets. The disposition of government surplus was handed over to the new War Assets Corporation, a Crown corporation that by 1947 had generated $450 million in sales. Thousands of businesses and farmers purchased army trucks, and some of the enterprising even acquired tracked Bren-gun carriers to haul lumber off their woodlots.

Although the government sold off as many war assets as possible, much expensive wartime equipment had to be sold for scrap.

One of the first tasks facing the government was to get Canadian exports back into markets overseas. The devastated countries of Europe, their cities destroyed by bombing, their fields torn up by tank tracks and shellfire, needed everything North America could provide: food, raw materials, manufactured goods. There was only one difficulty: none had any money to pay for the goods.

The answer was soon found. British negotiators appeared in Washington and Ottawa to seek huge loans on favourable terms. As always, the bargaining was tough, but in the United States a package worth $3.75 billion at 2 per cent interest was the result. The American economy was fifteen times the size of Canada's, but Canada was much more dependent on exports to keep its economy going. The result was that Ottawa offered $1.25 billion—or more than one-tenth of the Gross National Product in 1945—on the same terms as the Americans, and forgave all of Britain's wartime debts to boot. That was a testimony to the government's serious intention to keep Canadians working and exporting—Britain, after all, took almost the entire Canadian production of bacon, eggs, and canned salmon, and high proportions of the exports of wheat, newsprint, and timber. An additional $750 million in credits soon were offered to European customers, for the same reasons. There were a few blinkered denunciations of the government from Quebec, cries that Canada had bankrupted itself for England during the war and now was doing so in the peace. But the *nationalistes* completely missed the point. The choice was simple: either Canada gave its customers the money to buy its goods and kept its people working, or it suffered terrible dislocations. The farmer in Quebec producing butter that was sold to Britain would benefit from the British loan every bit as much as the Saskatchewan wheat farmer. Ottawa had made the right choice.

Canadian exports still dropped substantially from 1945 to 1946, falling by almost a billion dollars to $2.3 billion as the military equipment that had swelled the totals

Crown Corporations

How was Canada to create a wartime industrial complex that could produce the goods the Allies needed? Under the direction of C.D. Howe, the Minister of Munitions and Supply, a vast array of Crown corporations came into existence. The government, through the Wartime Prices and Trade Board, controlled the pricing and supply of commodities and labour, and now, through the Crown corporations, it took control of entire sectors of the economy. Take rubber, for example, a vital wartime need. Once war erupted in the Pacific in December 1941, and the Japanese swept all before them, the Canadian supply of rubber from Malaya ceased. While there was stock on hand, it could not meet the need. Howe's answer was Polymer Corporation, which he located at Sarnia, Ontario, to produce synthetic rubber. It took eighteen months for the plant to hit its stride, but Polymer soon produced 5,000 tons a month. Or take uranium, a metal that until the war was thought to have little value. Howe knew about the work on the atomic bomb from the very outset, and he understood how critical uranium, controlled by Eldorado Mining and Refining at Great Slave Lake in the Northwest Territories, was to its development. He quietly took over Eldorado and made it a Crown corporation, and Canadian uranium fed the Manhattan Project in the United States, which produced the A-bombs that brought Japan to its knees in August 1945. Or take the need to purchase goods for the American troops who were building the Alaska Highway and operating other installations in the north. To supply them, and to prevent American-directed purchases from interfering with Canada's price and wage control system, Howe created North West Purchasing Limited, with its headquarters in Edmonton, Alberta. The purchases it controlled through 1943 averaged $1.25 million a month.

The Crown corporations were everywhere, sailing merchant ships and building Lancaster bombers, controlling supplies of silk and constructing radar sets. A uniquely Canadian device, they proved themselves in the crucible of war. Many survived into the peace, and still more would be created to serve Canadian needs into the 1950s.

disappeared off the market. But without the loans and credits, exports might well have dropped to Depression levels (exports in 1933 had been only $532 million). By 1947 the numbers showed considerable improvement, and the next year, after the negotiation of the General Agreement on Tariffs and Trade created an international regime to govern world trade, exports again were close to wartime peaks.

Unfortunately, imports rose even more dramatically, doubling between 1945 and 1950. The money Canadians had socked away between 1939 and 1945 was burning holes in their pockets. All the luxuries they had been obliged to give up were now available, and they spent as if there were no tomorrow. Fresh fruit, automobiles, refrigerators, jukeboxes and radios—everything imaginable poured in from the United States, in such volumes that by late 1947 the country faced a crippling trade deficit with the U.S., along with a U.S. dollar shortage and a foreign exchange crisis. The economy itself was in good shape, but the balance between exports and imports was out of kilter. It took heroic measures to halt the drain: the imposition of quotas on imports such as household appliances, and the negotiation of a large U.S. dollar loan from an American government bank.

At the same time, diplomats persuaded

the United States government to allow Canada to be a source of "off-shore purchases" under the Marshall Plan—the great plan to supply the Continent and, simultaneously, sell American goods and check Communism. Slow to recover, the European economies had been crippled by a shortage of hard currencies like the American and Canadian dollars. The loans and credits at the end of the war had been used up very quickly, and the only way to continue rebuilding Europe was for the United States to give its goods away. But if, for example, the Americans offered wheat free of charge, the Canadian export market would collapse and prairie farmers would suffer. The answer, worked out in the finance department and sold to the American administration, was to allow Europeans to use their Marshall Plan dollars to purchase Canadian products. Inflationary pressures and increasing shortages in the U.S. helped the American officials to agree. By 1950, as a result, the United States had paid for a billion dollars' worth of Canadian exports, a measure that went a huge distance towards righting the country's trade deficit and dollar shortage.

The combination of measures worked, and the Canadian economy's reconversion to peace proceeded apace. The Gross National Product, $11.8 billion in 1945, was up to $13.4 billion in 1947 and $18.4 billon in 1950. The doomsayers had been confounded, and C.D. Howe, one of the very few who had predicted a great postwar expansion, had been proved right.

—— •+• ——

Not that everything went smoothly at home. The strains of war on the Canadian economy had been pronounced, and unrest was inevitable. Once wage controls came off, once postwar inflation began to pick up steam, once the soldiers, sailors, and airmen returned home, the strikes began in earnest.

There had been major labour disruptions during the war, of course. From a low of 122 labour disputes involving 41,000 workers in 1939, a peak of 402 disputes involving 218,000 workers had been reached in 1943, the year when war-weariness and resentment over controls and rationing peaked. There were steel strikes in Sydney, Nova Scotia, and Sault Ste. Marie, Ontario, for example—disputes that threatened one of the country's most critical wartime materials. In all, almost one union member in three went on strike in 1943. In the last year of the war and in 1946, the number and duration of bitter strikes increased. In part, they were attempts to secure wage gains or to win union security; however, they were also undoubtedly a reflection of organized labour's new strength.

The war had been good for the trade unions. After a decade of depression that had seen union memberships drop or, at best, remain static, the war had produced a boom. A total 1939 membership of 359,000, just 7.7 per cent of the civilian labour force, had doubled by 1945 to 711,000, or 15.7 per cent. As important, Ottawa had sped the centralization of labour by putting workers in all war-related industries under federal jurisdiction, and by 1945 this covered fully 85 per cent of the non-farm workforce. Labour's new strength helped press the federal government into seeking accommodation—in the interests of maintaining industrial peace to keep war production going. When the prime minister met the leadership of the Canadian Congress of Labour in February 1944, the union leaders stressed their desire for harmony, if only they could get legislation in place to assure

Companies large and small faced strikes for higher wages and union recognition. In December 1945, a trio of Santas demanded that Toronto's Brown's Bread put more in the family stocking.

workers the right to collective bargaining. Within a week the government had passed Order in Council PC1003, the so-called Magna Carta of Canadian labour law. PC1003 guaranteed the right of workers to form and join unions, and it promised any union automatic recognition once it had won majority support in a government-sponsored vote. It forbade unfair labour practices, required compulsory collective bargaining and conciliation, imposed a grievance procedure, and affirmed the right to strike. The order was a major advance, but it was not law; it could be revoked at any time. More tellingly, King insisted that PC1003 say nothing about union security: the right of a union shop to employ only union members and to deduct union dues automatically from workers' paycheques. These were issues that meant life or death to union locals and their national organizations. Even so, PC1003 helped the Liberal government mightily in its dealings with organized labour, and it paid off in the election of 1945, when substantial elements of labour supported Mackenzie King's bid for re-election.

The postwar period was not destined to be so peaceful, as issues of union security reached the boiling point—most notably in

the great strike against the Ford Motor Company at Windsor, Ontario, in the summer and fall of 1945. The United Auto Workers Local 200, representing workers at Ford since 1942, demanded a union shop and the automatic check-off of dues to guarantee stability for the union's membership and finances. Although Ford's management in the United States had conceded these points in August 1941, the Canadian company stood on its autonomy and refused, and the strike began on September 12. Strike benefits were a minimal $15 a week for a striker with a family, but the workers' enthusiasm and anger were high. The strikers sealed off the plant, denied entrance to administration and production workers, and shut down the powerhouse. When government officials threatened to use police to break the picketers' lines, strikers and their families and friends—and hordes of frustrated motorists caught in the middle—wedged hundreds of automobiles and trucks into the plant's entrance. Not since the Oshawa strike of 1937 against General Motors had a labour dispute so captured the public's interest.

Neither side seemed willing to budge, and union locals and labour councils across Canada began passing resolutions in favour of a general strike to support the workers in Windsor. The last general strike in Canada had occurred in 1919, when the city of Winnipeg had been paralysed by a total withdrawal of services. Mindful of the Russian Revolution just two years before, and fearing that Canadian Bolsheviks would launch a similar workers' revolution, the government had called up the militia and ordered a squadron of the Royal North-West Mounted Police to intervene. That general strike was crushed with armed force, special legislation, and speedy deportations. No one, least of all the union leaders, wanted to see 1919 repeated in 1945; moreover, even Canadian Congress of Labour leaders believed that Communist militants were exploiting the Ford workers in the party's own interests. To organized labour, a general strike meant certain repression. Although it took two membership votes to do it, in mid-December the Local 200 strikers accepted their leaders' advice to return to work and wait for the results of arbitration.

Mr. Justice Ivan Rand of the Supreme Court of Canada—a man, said Windsor Member of Parliament Paul Martin, "who I believed reflected progressive ideas"—was named as arbitrator. Rand toured the plant and held hearings before issuing his report at the end of January 1946. The judge made it clear that he saw both labour and capital as necessary partners in economic development, and that he understood that his decision would determine whether Canada's postwar labour relations would be determined by "war or reason". He was for reason, and his report proposed a substantial compromise.

There was to be no union shop at Ford. A union shop, Rand stated, "would deny the individual Canadian the right to seek work and to work independently of persons associated with any organized group." That was a blow to labour, but it was assuaged by the granting of the dues check-off: dues would take their place alongside other payroll deductions. "I consider it entirely equitable," Rand wrote, "that all employees should be required to shoulder their protion of the burden of expense for administering the law of their employment, the union contract; they must take the burden along with the benefit." If the union's finances were secure, then the union would mature and become responsible. If the union did not mature, and if it allowed wildcat strikes, then the check-off could be rescinded.

The Rand Formula, as it became known, seemed to satisfy almost everyone. Management expressed pleasure that the union shop had been denied. Labour declared the "modified

Everywhere, union recognition was a key demand, along with paid vacations.

union shop", with all workers paying dues, a victory. David Croll, a prominent Liberal MP who had quit the Ontario Cabinet in 1937 to walk with the Oshawa strikers was well pleased: Rand "has taken management-labour disputes out of the brick-and-tear-gas stage. His decision has delivered potential members to the union and given it union security. And to the company he has given a measure of security as well, protection from wildcat strikes."

The Ford settlement did not stop all strikes—indeed 1945 saw proportionately more time lost than any year since 1919, and 1946 was worse yet. Some unions, especially Communist-dominated ones, remained militant; some managements, notably in the steel industry, continued to profess their devotion to the old dog-eat-dog principles of capitalism. A national steel strike in 1946 demonstrated that the struggle continued. In Sault Ste. Marie and Sydney, the workers shut down the plant. In Hamilton, Stelco tried to continue in operation as the workers put the plant under siege; when the company tried to send workers and supplies in by boat, a strikers' navy headed them off; and former RCAF pilots among the union membership took to the air in light planes to drop leaflets urging Hamiltonians to support the strikers. In fact, the local community did support the strikers, merchants contributing food, restaurants catering meals, and the union's women's auxiliary keeping the picketers supplied with coffee and sandwiches. The result, predictably, was the Rand Formula and a small wage increase.

By 1950, 90 per cent of Canadian unions

As late as 1947, strikers (here at the St. Lawrence Starch Co.) wore their battledress to garner public sympathy. Sometimes it worked.

The national steel strike of 1946 was another major war between capital and labour. Hamilton's Stelco plant was besieged by workers who tried to shut down management's continued operations.

operated under the Rand Formula, and shop stewards no longer had to chase after their members to extract their dues. Union membership all across the country continued to grow. In 1954, it hit its peak—33.8 per cent of the non-agricultural workforce belonged to trade unions. The war had sparked a revolution in labour relations, and a booming economy was soon reflected in the paycheques workers brought home each week.

Some politicians and bureaucrats in Ottawa believed that the war had also revolutionized relations between the federal government and the provinces. Through the 1930s, the antiquated provisions of the British North America Act had all but eliminated the possibility of strong federal action to deal with the Depression's ravages from province to province. Neither R.B. Bennett nor Mackenzie King was especially ready or able to tackle mass unemployment, but for both the constitution's division of powers provided a ready excuse. Ottawa had most of the taxation resources, even though laissez-faire and free-enterprise governments had never chosen to use them for fear of frightening off foreign investment and creating problems with business. The provinces had the power to levy income taxes and deal with social welfare questions, but most had done little or nothing, thanks in part to conservative ideology and the same fears that forestalled federal attempts at raising taxes.

In 1937, as the Great Depression continued to choke the nation's economic recovery, King had established the Royal Commission on Dominion-Provincial Relations to examine the state of the federation. The Rowell–Sirois Commission's report arrived in Ottawa in February 1940. The commissioners proposed a radical restructuring of Confederation; fiscal power would be centralized in the federal government and, in return, Ottawa would take full responsibility for unemployment and much of the cost of welfare, while providing grants to enable the provinces to offer services from roads to public health at a national average. In essence, the Royal Commission proposed taking power from the provinces in return for subsidies that would help the various provinces enjoy equal levels of services. The difficulty was that Ontario, Alberta, and British Columbia all believed that they would be cheated of their rightful share of the pie. When a dominion-provincial conference took place in 1941, at a time when the war demanded that Ottawa have full fiscal control in order to mobilize the national economy, the Royal Commission proposals failed to secure agreement. The "three saboteurs", premiers Mitchell Hepburn of Ontario, William Aberhart of Alberta, and Duff Pattullo of British Columbia, had derailed the war effort, or so newspapers charged.

Ottawa still needed more money to fight the war, and Walter Gordon, a young accountant from the family firm of Clarkson, Gordon who was working in the finance department, hit on the idea that gave the federal government the solution. Ottawa would impose the income and corporation taxes it needed to pay for the war, even if this impinged on provincial areas of jurisdiction. In return, it would agree to give every province that surrendered its taxation rights for the duration of the war an annual payment equal to the revenue raised from those sources. Given the public's support for the war, and its scant patience with provincial politicking in a time of crisis, this was nothing less than blackmail. But it worked, and Ottawa got the money it needed to win the war.

What about after the victory? Planners in Ottawa believed they had run a superb war effort, and they convinced themselves that wartime unity and patriotism had put paid to provincial posturings. They had imposed federal standards on labour, they had controlled wages and prices fairly across the land, and they had the plans for reconstruction and peace all ready to roll. All they needed was full control over the fiscal levers, to match the grip they had on the levers of power. As the Minister of Finance said in 1944, it would be "quite impossible for the Dominion Government to manage . . . if we had to go back to our pre-war taxing system." Ottawa had to concentrate taxation and spending authority in its hands to give the nation's economy the firm direction it required. Centralization was the answer. The Dominion-Provincial Conference on Reconstruction that began in August 1945 would show whether the provinces agreed.

Mackenzie King came to the meeting on August 6 carrying a small "Green Book" that laid out the government's plan. Federalism was to be restructured to give Ottawa the power it had exercised during the war, power that now would be used to safeguard Canadians, not from Hitler and Tojo, but from the evils of privation. What he wanted, King said, was an agreement. There was to be no coercion, no attempt to ram the Green Book proposals down the throats of the provincial leaders.

The premiers looked on calmly, some of them inwardly infuriated by the prime minister's presumption. Lieutenant-Colonel George Drew, the Ontario Progressive Conservative premier, was a man with very fixed views. Like C.D. Howe, he believed that Canada was on the threshold of a great boom; unlike the Liberal government in Ottawa, he emphatically did not believe that only Ottawa knew how to manage this coming growth. Nor, under Canadian federalism, did it have the right to do so.

Drew found his ideological soulmate in

Having taken charge of so much during the war, the federal government found it hard to let go. Ontario's George Drew, shown with his wife, Fiorenza, fought bitterly against Ottawa's plans to control the economy and social services.

Quebec's Union Nationale premier, Maurice Duplessis. Centralization was evil, believed Duplessis, and a threat to *la survivance* of French Canadians. Other premiers—Liberal A.S. MacMillan of Nova Scotia, Social Crediter Ernest Manning from Alberta—were cool to Ottawa's scheme. Only Tommy Douglas, the CCF premier of Saskatchewan, and Liberal Stuart Garson of Manitoba were genuinely enthusiastic; their provinces had suffered so much during the Depression that, to them, this plan seemed like manna from heaven. As for the rest of the premiers, they watched and waited and wondered what their electorates wanted.

The conference went badly right from the beginning. Drew demanded time to study the proposals, which at first blush seemed, he said, to be directly counter to the basis on which Canada had been founded. Duplessis offered a heartfelt "me too", and the Green Book proposals, which included a national health care scheme, were sidetracked to a co-ordinating committee for study.

When the conference reconvened in April 1946, it was only to bury the Green Book. Drew denounced Ottawa's proposals as contrary to Ontario's interests, while Duplessis compared them unfavourably to the works of Mussolini and Hitler. Others among the premiers chimed in, and instead of building a unified economic scheme, Ottawa had to scramble over the next months to find viable stopgap measures as its wartime emergency powers gradually disappeared. It offered a scheme of "tax rentals" to the provinces—a complicated plan that gave Ottawa the sole right to levy income, corporation, and succession taxes, and in return handed a lump sum to the provincial governments. Ontario and Quebec predictably refused to go along, insisting on their right to levy their own taxes. The attempt to give the Canadian people effective, rationalized, centralized government dissolved in bitterness and acrimony, scuppered by the "Drew–Duplessis Axis".

In the flush of enthusiasm and confidence in their economic strength, buoyed by the success of the war effort and by C.D. Howe's brilliant management of the transition from war to peace, few Canadians worried very much about the demise of the Green Book proposals. There were jobs, there was money in the bank, there were goods in the stores. The greatest Canadian economic boom in history had begun, and federal-provincial squabbling seemed to amount to nothing more than a very small cloud in the blue skies of prosperity.

The Drew—Duplessis Axis

George Drew was elected premier of Ontario in 1943. A veteran officer of the Great War, he was tall, straight, good-looking, and the embodiment of all that was British. Maurice Duplessis was his antithesis. Short, swarthy, and dumpy, Duplessis had governed Quebec through the last years of the Depression until the Liberals drove him from office in the fall of 1939. Returned to office in 1944, he continued his career of preaching Quebec autonomy and attacking the centralization of government that Canada's war effort required. This unlikely duo ought to have been at each other's throats, yet as Canada began to prepare for the conversion to peace they found themselves increasingly in alliance.

The issue was the government's desire to alter the federal-provincial relationship to ensure that Ottawa had the money and powers to control the economy. Duplessis hated any such centralizing effort—he had opposed the introduction of family allowances in 1944 as an intrusion into the provincial sphere—but so too did Drew. Ever since the 1870s, Ontario had always resisted the federal government's attempts to seize power for itself. George Drew was ready to continue the tradition. He openly despised King, who, in his view, had been appallingly weak during the war, and had catered to Quebec at every turn. He loathed French Canadians as wartime slackers, and feared that Quebec's higher birthrate might submerge British Canadians in a French-speaking sea. He also had only contempt for the "brains trust" of civil service mandarins with whom King surrounded himself. His provincial treasurer told him that the federal plans would "kill the goose that lays the golden eggs"—Ontario, in other words—and Drew agreed. Over the objections of the poorer provinces, over the protests of those who wanted the health-care scheme Ottawa had included in its plans, the two powerful premiers combined to thwart King's proposals at dominion-provincial meetings in 1945 and 1946. The Drew–Duplessis "Axis", a deliberately unflattering phrase coined by the Liberal press to suggest the alliance between Hitler and Mussolini, had prevailed.

Quebec's Union Nationale premier, Maurice Duplessis, shown nose-to-nose in 1948 with rotund Montreal mayor Camillien Houde, was always a vigorous opponent of Ottawa's wartime intrusions into provincial jurisdiction.

CHAPTER SEVEN

NEW CANADA, NEW CANADIANS

It was a new Canada in 1945, but did anyone know it? What was life like for Canadians in the year the war ended? Did people grasp their changed possibilities, or did they cling to familiar institutions and values?

(Above) By 1947, cars like this Studebaker were rolling off the assembly lines in bedazzling streamlined designs. "Which end is the front?" asked children.

(Right) Jews had been unwelcome in Canada during the 1930s, and reports of wartime death camps did little to improve attitudes. But some escapees made it from neutral Portugal, including these refugees, who landed in Montreal in April 1944.

IN A HUNDRED YEARS, PROFESSOR GRIFFITH Taylor of the University of Toronto's geography department told readers of *Chatelaine* in January 1945, Canada would have forty million people, with the densest population around Calgary, largely because it had the best reserves of coal for heavy industry. The political centre of the British Empire perhaps might move from Europe to "the better protected Canadian section". There might, of course, be a "world state" in which all nations and diverse racial groups would live harmoniously, though there was always the possibility of a "prolonged cultural and economic struggle in which Occidental will be ranged against Oriental." *Chatelaine* promised its readers (mainly women) that frozen fruits and vegetables were here to stay and that "when material becomes available, a household freezer may be as much a necessity as a refrigerator or washing machine." *Maclean's* claimed that Canadians would soon be sitting at home watching their first television sets. "You'll see a bright, clear picture on the screen . . . a *moving* picture, with sound. Maybe it will show you a hockey game. Maybe a musical show. Maybe a drama, or a fashion parade, or an event that is taking place on the other side of the world!"

In 1945, that future started to take shape. In Burnaby, outside Vancouver, moviegoers could visit Canada's first "auto theatre", a thirteen-acre lot with spaces for 6,090 cars. With gas rationing still in effect, they might prefer radio, with the Happy Gang, Andrew Allan's Stage series, the barn-dance music of Don Messer and the Islanders, and "Hockey Night in Canada" with Foster Hewitt, to say nothing of Saturday-night dance shows from local hotels and Sunday-morning sermons from local churches. Fresh from the Army Show, Johnny Wayne and Frank Shuster began writing and producing "The Johnny Home Show", mixing wit and official propaganda

Ten years of depression and six years of war had left people hungry for appliances and home furnishings. Even the most practical items were part of the long-awaited "better times".

on repatriation. In October 1945, A. Davidson Dunton was named chairman of the Canadian Broadcasting Corporation, with a salary of $15,000. He promised to put zip into programming, keep peace with the ninety-two private but CBC-regulated stations, and get politics out of the corporation. Dunton also hoped to draw expatriate Canadian stars back from the United States.

While Dunton's ten CBC radio stations depended on commercials for a quarter of their revenue, the ninety-two private stations had little other income. Advertisers had waited impatiently for peace so that they could turn the miracles of technology into a consumer's cornucopia. Dow's Styron would be the "Nation's No. 1 Plastic". Koroseal, used for wrapping food parcels and rifles, would be available for shower curtains and fold-up raincoats. With new synthetic materials, shoe soles would last four times as long as leather. *Chatelaine* promised women that nylons, long silk dresses, rubberized girdles, and wonderful new windproof and waterproof fabrics would soon be available. So would the fine oils essential for perfumes and cosmetics.

Hollywood still monopolized most people's entertainment dollars; radio absorbed their time. Apart from the six-team National Hockey League and the Canadian Football League, even professional sports had faded from the national passion they had been in the 1920s. Professional theatre had died in the 1930s, and only a few stalwarts joined Dora Mavor Moore in 1946 in trying to revive it with the New Play Society. Local stages were occupied by enthusiastic amateurs vying for the ultimate accolade at the annual Dominion Drama Festival. A few professional actors made a meagre living performing radio plays on the CBC and

The CBC began planning for the introduction of television soon after the war. "Space Command", with actor Austin Willis, drew on the fifties' wide-eyed optimism about scientific technology.

its French-language arm, Radio-Canada. French Canadian playwrights and performers had to reckon as well with the hostility and occasional censorship of the Church.

Still, there had been some wartime milestones. If English-speaking Canada had diverted much of its musical talent to the simple rhythms of military brass bands, Quebec had chosen 1942 to launch its original Conservatoire de Musique

Canadian culture was no hardy plant in early postwar Canada, but Dora Mavor Moore, founder of Toronto's New Play Society, fought to keep it alive.

The New
PLAY SOCIETY

DORA MAVOR MOORE,
founder and director
presents its Third Series of Six Plays

"WHAT EVERY WOMAN KNOWS"
by Sir J. M Barrie

Thurs - Fri - Sat . . . Sept. 25 - 26 - 27
ROYAL ONTARIO MUSEUM THEATRE

•

followed by these outstanding plays
MACBETH (Shakespeare)
CHARLEY'S AUNT (Thomas) — Oct 9-10-11
JUNO and THE PAYCOCK (O'Casey) — Oct. 23-24-25
AMPHITRYON 38 (Giradoux) — Nov. 13-14-15
— Nov. 27-28-29
(Presented by the MONTREAL REPERTORY THEATRE)
COVENTRY CHRISTMAS PLAY — Dec. 11-12-13

•

TICKETS — MOODEY'S   90 King St W — El 1098

in Montreal. Schools and universities responded to growing wartime prosperity by offering more courses in music, theatre, and art, subjects hitherto dismissed as "frills". More than anything, the emergence of trained, self-confident performers would transform the arts in Canada. Meanwhile, if symphony orchestras in Toronto, Montreal, and Vancouver were conservative in their tastes, an increasing share of their audiences had never heard of Debussy or Scriabin, to say nothing of Canada's Claude Champagne or Healey Willan, and Ernest MacMillan of the Toronto Symphony Orchestra might have escaped national fame if he hadn't had the distinction of a knighthood.

In the 1930s, the Canadian Radio League had become Canada's first cultural lobby, pressuring Ottawa to create what became the CBC. Performers might denounce the

The Canadian Broadcasting Corporation

The war helped launch the golden years of Canadian radio. After the dress rehearsal in special-events coverage of the Royal Visit in 1939, Canadian Broadcasting Corporation staff followed the armed services to war. A Canadian, Ernest Bushnell, organized British shortwave broadcasting to North America. A six-ton van, "Mobile Unit No. 3", sent three programs a week back to Canada. Other crews visited Canadian camps and bases. On D-Day, Matthew Halton and Marcel Ouimet were only a wave behind the first assault landing on the beaches. Their voices and others—those of Bob Bowman, Peter Stursberg, Benoît Lafleur—brought the war home. By 1941, daily news coverage had doubled to 20 per cent of the broadcast day.

In return for a tax on each radio set (collected door to door), the CBC provided programs, operated stations, and made and enforced the rules for Canada's private broadcasters. By 1945, the CBC owned and operated ten of its own stations, most of them members of its twenty-four-station Trans-Canada Network. Twenty-nine stations, all but one of them private, were linked for two and a half hours of programming in the evenings-only Dominion Network. Of course, in the pre-television era, evenings were radio's peak listening times. The ten-station French network had yet to reach beyond Quebec and the immediate border regions. A tenth of its programming was taken directly from the Trans-Canada and Dominion networks.

Inaugurated in February 1945, the International Service symbolized Canada's new global commitment. With headquarters in Montreal and two 50,000-watt transmitters at Sackville, New Brunswick, the CBC spoke to the world in English, French, Czech, Dutch, German, Spanish, and Portuguese, and planned to reach around the world and to speak in even more European languages.

The war encouraged the CBC to expand and experiment in every area, from farm broadcasts to children's programs like "Just Mary", by Fredericton's Mary Grannan. It gave work to Canadian musicians, authors, and actors when no one else would. In 1944, 80 per cent of the plays produced by the CBC were by Canadians—by 1947, the proportion was 97 per cent. CBC's Stage series began in 1944, bringing listeners radio versions of Shakespearean classics and new plays. The CBC's symphony orchestra, under Geoffrey Waddington, was probably the best in the country. In 1945 about a quarter of CBC programming was commercial (financed by corporation, but they lived on its cheques. The captivating notion of government patronage of the arts had been born; war, with its in-built temptation for the government to take charge, had nourished the infant. Wartime had also brought the fame of the Group of Seven to a broader audience. Their style of painting lent itself to silkscreen reproduction, and soon hundreds of copies of the works of A.Y. Jackson, J.E.H. MacDonald, and Lawren Harris decorated officers' messes and other ranks' canteens. In the previous war, the private wealth of Lord Beaverbrook had financed the Canadian War Memorial, a project that sent outstanding British and Canadian artists and photographers to record the country's wartime achievements. This time it was the federal government that paid talented artists to produce the nation's war art.

advertising). Radio soap operas were the biggest draw for advertisers, with variety programs, usually American-made like "Charlie McCarthy" or "The Fred Allen Show", coming second. Despite

The war and postwar years were radio's high-water mark, and the CBC reached every home in the nation. One politician who knew how to use the medium was Newfoundland's Joey Smallwood, whose campaign for Confederation achieved success over the airwaves. His signing of the documents that would bring Newfoundland into Canada was just one of the great events covered by the CBC.

pressure, the CBC kept its news broadcasts commercial-free. The French network produced proportionately more drama for its audiences, and more classical music; avoiding conflict with a powerful and censorious Catholic Church was a preoccupation for its managers. The rest of the CBC was very cautious too—or perhaps high-minded.

The war taught a generation of Canadians to trust the CBC, and exposed them to ideas and a world of high cultural expectations as no other medium would. Programs like "Citizens' Forum" and "Farm Forum" explored issues with a balance and maturity few contemporary newspapers would have contemplated. Critics complained that the wartime CBC was too loyal an arm of government—to the extent of refusing time to opponents in the 1942 conscription plebiscite. But on a host of other issues, from anti-Semitism to free collective bargaining, the CBC was more liberal than Liberal.

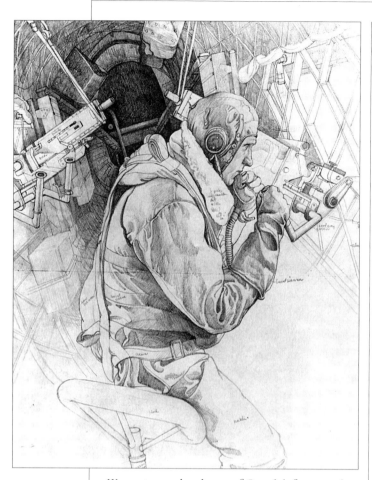

War artists produced some of Canada's finest art, but most of it remains little known to the public. Paul Goranson's pencil sketch Dorsal Gunner *is one splendid example.*

Veteran masters like Harris and Charles Comfort and newcomers such as Alex Colville, Paul Goranson, and Bruno and Molly Lamb Bobak brought a vigorous range of styles to their task. In turn, their work helped fuel the fire of their abstract and modernist rivals, and gave Canada a far livelier postwar art scene than anyone could have expected in 1939.

In 1944, the Federation of Canadian Artists had sought government support for the arts. Also in 1944, the Turgeon Committee on Reconstruction and Re-establishment in Parliament had listened to pleas from art groups to set up a board to promote culture. Nothing happened—Mackenzie King was too old-fashioned to believe that there were votes in symphonies and abstract art—but the idea continued to grow and would eventually yield the Massey Royal Commission on National Development in the Arts, Letters and Sciences, and the Canada Council.

In the 1920s, Canada had briefly been the world's second-largest automotive manufacturer. In wartime, auto plants in Oshawa and Windsor had helped put the British army on wheels. With the war over, claimed *Maclean's* reporter Royd Beamish, Canadians could count on 15,000 civilian cars by November, compared to the normal prewar production of 200,000 a year. The Wartime Prices and Trade Board decreed that the price of a new car would be $1,200, up from $1,000 in 1939, but that it could go higher if the United Auto Workers got their 30 per cent wage increase. The first postwar cars would basically be made from the dies that manufacturers had put away in 1942. Buyers would have to wait until 1947–48 for dramatic changes—wraparound windows, sunroofs, rear-window wipers, seats that could be adjusted up and down. Released from wartime restraints, the big three manufacturers, General Motors, Ford, and Chrysler, could produce a million cars in a couple of years, but thought it would be wiser to go slow. Or maybe it wouldn't; Henry J. Kaiser, an industrialist fresh from wartime experience mass-producing merchant ships, promised that he would produce a small new car for as little as $400.

Cars suddenly mattered more than they had, because part of the postwar world would be the "garden suburbs" that city planners had been promising for decades. Ordinary people, as well as the wealthy, would escape crowded, airless, dirty downtown streets for the fresh air and open space of the country. Families would have their own homes, firmly planted on their own lawns, with schools and shopping only minutes away by car. Canadians would no longer have to leave the land to find the rewards of urban life; they could now take a little of it with them—but only if they had their own cars. It was a dream worth waiting, saving, struggling, even fighting a war for. And it would take shape in Toronto's Scarborough and Etobicoke, Vancouver's Burnaby and Richmond, Winnipeg's River Heights and St. Vital. Montrealers would slip away from the slums of Pointe St. Charles and St. Henri to the South Shore, or westward to Lachine. A steady job, a monthly family allowance cheque, and the family's first car would make it possible.

In its July 1945 issue, *Time* explained the impact of baby bonuses on the Moskaluk family. Metro Moskaluk worked as a cook at an Ottawa hotel and played the bull fiddle in a Hull nightclub to support his wife and eleven children, aged fourteen years to fifteen months. With $5 to $8 per child, Mrs. Lea Moskaluk could count on at least an added $55 a month, and the Moskaluks reported plans to buy a bigger, better home. This one large Ottawa family represented many others; by helping people out of high-cost, low-quality slum housing, the family allowance did more than any single public policy to transform Canada's poor from a majority to a minority.

Women talked of careers but agreed that marriage and family took priority, and students in "home ec" classes at Toronto's Oakwood Collegiate still beamed for the camera as they practised "wifely" skills.

In 1945, there were 5.96 million females in the Canadian population and 6.108 million males. But the power and status gap was very

Some women who had held positions of responsibility in the armed forces or the wartime public service were not content to return to domesticity. One woman vet makes her point to the Canadian Legion's conference at Saskatoon in June 1948.

much greater than the population gap. Few women had achieved status and influence: Byrne Hope Sanders ran the WPTB's consumer branch and would manage the Gallup poll in Canada; Elsie MacGill had designed training aircraft during the war; the crusty Charlotte Whitton had tried to re-shape Canada's tiny social-work profession. For women, paid work routinely ended with marriage, and certainly with child-rearing. Women who wanted a professional career looked almost invariably to such nurturing professions as teaching, nursing, and social service. They faced a future of spinsterhood and half-scornful dismissal as "old maids". Widows could expect poverty if they did

not take refuge in hurried remarriage.

In 1945, the Canadian Youth Commission asked its director, Mrs. R.E.G. Davis of Toronto's Protestant Children's Homes, a consultant with the Catholic Family and Children Services, to study the prospects for youth, marriage, and the family. The war, she reported, had left many women with "the dismal loneliness which followed the departure of a loved one", and the heavy responsibilities of home-making and family life. Any misery seemed to be the woman's fault. As a result, "[t]he dependent, less mature woman" had fallen into extramarital entanglements or, responding to rumours about her husband's infidelity, had retaliated. Alternatively, a wife's increased maturity and self-reliance could be a threat to the husband "when he first return[s] to his role as head of the family." When the housing shortage or a lack of means forced a family to move in with relatives, a wife "found her autonomy, care of her children, even her own conduct scrutinised."

During the Depression, employers had added 200,000 women to the workforce, often because they were cheaper. Between 1939 and 1944, women's share of the workforce had risen from 21 to 27 per cent. Women operated machinery, serviced cars, drove streetcars, delivered bread, and parachuted into occupied France. Their wages, while usually lower than men's, rose well above traditional levels. Domestic workers fled to factories, leaving their middle-class

Canadian Summers

Most Canadians now take annual vacations and paid holidays for granted. Many own a cottage or camp and assume that the summer will include regular weekend treks to a lake, river, or coast, and at least a few weeks away in the summer. More and more even assume that a week or so in a warm climate is a vital interlude in an overlong winter.

These were not common assumptions in 1945. A wealthy minority owned cottages in Muskoka, the Laurentians, downriver at Rivière du Loup, or in some kindred resort region; others planned a few weeks at one of the big, rambling resort hotels that catered to the middle class. However, most Canadians could only dream of spending a vacation in the leisure of swimming and boating.

For most city-dwellers, the summer was a time of recurrent suffocating heat waves and accompanying outbreaks of polio, or infantile paralysis, a horrifying disease that could leave survivors unable to walk or, in some cases, to breathe without the aid of a huge, expensive "iron lung". Mothers were told that it was their fault; the disease was carried, doctors insisted, on unwashed fruit. By the end of the war, air-conditioning had begun to add to the attraction of going to summertime movies. In most communities, sports, movies, and theatre were banned on Sunday, and any other form of public amusement was frowned on during the "Lord's Day". People yearned for the occasional statutory holidays, when they could throng nearby beaches and amusement parks. Most cities and towns had favourite spots, like Winnipeg Beach, Jericho for Vancouverites, or Sunnyside for west-end Torontonians.

One of the early goals of collective bargaining had been "paid holidays"—an annual week or two weeks with pay, and wages for statutory holidays like Christmas and Labour Day, when employers were compelled by law to close down.

Postwar affluence transformed Canadian summers. Car ownership—registrations doubled between 1945 and 1952—gave people the means to get away. Roads were extended farther and farther into "cottage country". More and more people found they could manage a second home—though it might be a primitive cabin—and helped pay off the mortgages by renting their own properties, for part of the summer, to families not quite so fortunate. Two weeks' holiday with pay became a standard benefit for most workers with a union contract and, by example, for many more who had never signed a union card. Instead of heading for local parks and beaches, more and more Canadians jammed the highways, with the children bickering in the back seat and the beer stewing in the trunk. Summers would never be quite the same.

As paid vacations became a standard of postwar employment, more and more urban families discovered the joys and perils of cottage country. Lakes and forests (and mosquitoes) took their place in the Canadian psyche.

employers to bemoan "the servant problem". Educated women took on influential
policy-making jobs where their presence
would have been unthinkable in 1939.
Thirty-four small but well-publicized day-
nurseries gave official sanction to an even
more eccentric idea—that mothers could
hold paid jobs.

What would happen when the war was
over? In January 1943, Cyril James's Advisory Committee on Reconstruction had
asked a subcommittee headed by Margaret
Stovel McWilliams, a prominent author and
wife of Manitoba's lieutenant-governor, for
advice. In her reply, McWilliams insisted
that women must have the right to choose
their work, and claim equal pay and opportunity for advancement. Married women
should be economic partners with their husbands, with access to social security and
morning daycare. At the same time, domestic service should be considered a legitimate
job, with unemployment insurance and
workers' compensation. Women needed
access to vocational training, McWilliams
insisted, though chiefly in their traditional
occupations as nurses, teachers, and domes-
tics. Other postwar projections insisted that
women were mobilizing to be a force for
peace, often behind their heroine, Mrs.
Eleanor Roosevelt, widow of the late American president.

It was clear by 1945 that few women
were going to keep their wartime status, and
that not all of them even wanted to. A 1944
Gallup poll found that 75 per cent of Canadian men and 68 per cent of women believed
that men should have preference in postwar
employment. And that is what happened:
less forcefully than in 1919, but just as insis-
tently, opportunities for women evaporated.
Women in the navy, army, and air force had

no peacetime prospects. As early as 1944,
munition factories began closing down or
got ready to convert to peacetime demand.
Everyone got layoff notices, but the new
postwar jobs would be mostly for men. Journalist Katharine Kent insisted that women
had as much right to jobs as men. But, she
added, "there should be no need for women
to band together as women. They should be
able to act on an equal basis as workers." A
million women who had handled their own
paycheques were not going to go back to the
hand-out system—and thanks to war brides,
thousands of them had been robbed of the
chance of a Canadian husband. Naomi Hastings, a Winnipegger fresh out of uniform,
confessed dismay at the thought of being
treated as a mere stopgap. "Are we, who have
worked with men on equal terms, to be
again surmounted (*sic*) by those invisible
walls and stupid taboos?"

For most Canadian women, the answer
was yes. *Careers for Women in Canada*, a government guide for job-seekers, had cheerful
chapters on "Dressing People", "Feeding
Folk", nursing, teaching, and even drama and
radio work, but its descriptions of professions like dentistry, optometry, and law were
brief and discouraging. When *Chatelaine*
asked its teenage forum about going to university, its members were unanimous about
wanting enough training to earn a living, but
a strong minority thought too much education would deter would-be husbands. The
university-bound majority thought education would put them in touch with more
interesting men and make them better
wives. *Chatelaine*'s Lotta Dempsey acknowledged that young women were finding it
hard to plan careers because they didn't
know which jobs men would have. She
summed up what teenagers told her:

That's okay by us too, because we all hope to marry in our early twenties, and have from two to four children each (no Only Child for us). And only a few girls will want to go on with their work afterward—like those in music, painting, and writing. So most of the vocations we plan will be very useful in our own homes. But we want our men to have good jobs.

Governments and the market dutifully prepared women for their postwar domestic role. *Chatelaine* advised its readers on "What's Ahead in Home Furnishing" in its January 1945 issue, "New Uses for Glass Blocks" in March, "Baby's First Bed" in April. As for what men wanted, Margaret Bishop, wife of the First World War air ace, described it as "the certainty of a compatible job, and the dignity which can only go with economic security." Women, she insisted, should "make sure that the 'Land Fit for Heroes to Live in' is, in fact, eagerly and anxiously awaiting the return of the hero."

What image did Canadians in 1945 have of the ideal woman? The *Canadian Home Journal* asked some male high-school students to pick out Miss Canada from photos of 175 teenage women. The winner was Lenore Johannesen of Winnipeg, 5'8" tall, 127 pounds, with honey-coloured hair and green-grey eyes, reported *Time*. With a little pardonable vanity, Lenore had not worn her glasses for her picture. She would begin Home Economics at the University of Manitoba in the fall. Presumably she fitted the image of the heroine in magazine fiction: more pretty than glamorous; unswervingly faithful, caring, and nice— and invariably successful in snaring the right sort of man.

Male dominance was apparent even in

Some people had no houses at all. In 1947, bailiffs evicted sixteen families from army barracks on Montreal's St. Helen's Island.

Waiting in Canada, women worried about the future when their men returned from the war. John Labatt Ltd.'s advertisement was a useful caution.

the traditionally female domain of child-rearing. Susan Bland's study of wartime advertising found that male doctors, dentists, and scientists, not mothers, were portrayed as "knowing best" about modern child-raising. In *Chatelaine*, psychologist William Blatz of the University of Toronto's Institute for Child Study declaimed on childhood health problems. "Rock-a-bye" mothers threatened a child's character, claimed Blatz; babies must be fed on schedule, not because they cried. Blatz's rigorous prescriptions were already being challenged in 1945 by a popular Boston doctor, Benjamin Spock. "Bringing up your child won't be a complicated job," he assured parents, "if you take it easy, trust your own instincts and follow the directions that your doctor gives you."

One such male expert became a lightning rod of controversy in 1945. A psychiatrist and First World War infantry officer, Brock Chisholm had begun the war as a brigadier and had risen rapidly to be the army's chief doctor. He had insisted on psychological testing for recruits and sympathetic treatment for victims of battle exhaustion. Although he was already a controversial figure in 1945, the government appointed Chisholm to be deputy minister of its new Department of National Health and Welfare. Washington's William Alanson White Foundation chose him as the distinguished scientist to give its 1945 lecture. Chisholm rose to the occasion. His target, well and truly blasted, was anyone who tried to impose dogma on children. By the age of six, he claimed, this kind of teaching "permanently impairs the human's ability to think for himself." A civil servant with an opinion got attention. Billed in English Canada as an attack on Santa Claus, Chisholm's speech provoked fury, especially in

As the baby boom began, and modern child-rearing became a popular subject, women were constantly reminded that the real experts were men.

Quebec. No man of such anti-religious views, declared the Societé St-Jean Baptiste, should be allowed to hold public office. Liberal ministers and MPs from Quebec announced that they would campaign against him. An unrepentant Chisholm repeated his message to journalists: "Unless we mend our ways of thinking we shan't avert the Atomic War which will wipe out two thirds of humanity," he told *Maclean's*. "And if human survival doesn't come under National Health, . . . what does?" Fortunately the U.N. solved the problem: Brock Chisholm went off to head the new World Health Organization. Ottawa could relax.

The war had focused attention on the young. Conventional views that children required two parents had to be reconciled with the need to send men overseas to fight. Little girls, said Mrs. Davis of the Youth Commission, needed a father's love and guidance to adjust to men and marriage, and boys needed to pattern themselves after a father. "The boys who are raised during the war years," she warned, must be safe-guarded against becoming men who were "tied to their mother's apron strings." The Youth Commission's French-Canadian committee worried that children were neglected when mothers worked. There were signs of lessened interest in home-making, "which strikes at the very heart of French Canadian culture". Everywhere, experts complained that the war left children emotionally and physically deprived, whether through overcrowding or because working mothers were too weary and impatient at the end of a long day. While children might seem resilient, Mrs. Davis warned, "after a few years, evidence of considerable disturbance may appear, sometimes in the form of shyness or

The "teenager" was a recent invention, and "hanging out" was a popular pastime. This Toronto diner was typical of postwar Canada, though the big-city prices would have shocked small-town residents.

withdrawal from people, at other times in aggressive outbursts."

Some of the generation too young to enlist had expended their energy, like adolescents before and since, in offending their seniors. Their zoot suits and other extravagant clothes were a deliberate defiance of the cloth-saving regulations of the WPTB. "Old folks" who thought a dance meant waltzes and foxtrots found jive, jitterbugging, and bebop noisy and alarming. Young people who quit school easily found work and high wages in the wartime economy, but by 1945 a few already wondered whether they had prejudiced their future. A twenty-year-old man told the Canadian Youth Commission, "I've a swell job, earning good money. . . . Maybe I was wrong to give up school. I'm not fit for any skilled work. I want to marry but who knows whether I shall be able to afford a home." Some youngsters had to grow up too fast. Social workers told of soldiers' wives burdening their sons with too much emotional responsibility, or pulling their daughters out of school to take over home-making roles.

Still, convention dictated that youth be hopeful. Boys, reported Rica McLean Farquharson, preferred girls who were feminine, while 95 per cent of girls wanted to marry, though most also wanted to carry on their careers after marriage. Both sexes believed in the importance of religion and wanted to know more about Canada. Judging from Youth Commission findings, Canadians could rejoice that the young were tolerant, ready to listen to others, and, in dating situations, quite traditional. Boys preferred girls who did not smoke and who had strong moral principles, while "the modern girl still wants the boy to pay, help her on with her wrap, help her off the streetcar and offer old-fashioned compliments." The young of both sexes believed in racial and religious tolerance, even if their elders had different views.

Wartime rumours of wild promiscuity among women in uniform, reports of VD among men in training camps, and fears that Canadians had experienced moral pollution overseas inspired cries of alarm from pulpits and press. In retrospect, most Canadian behaviour was quiet, orderly, and remarkably conservative. An attendant at Toronto's Union Station caught a serviceman kissing his wife and ordered the couple from the rotunda. After a solemn debate, the city council cautiously decided that it now approved of kissing in public "in general", especially when the principals had not seen each other for a long time. It also censured anyone trying to interfere. But not everyone agreed with such laxity. In Montreal, a new Citizens' Vigilance League claimed over 200,000 members, and a like-minded alderman sent police to warn three women sunbathing on their apartment roof "in garb which left insufficient to the imagination". Landlords, warned the city council, were responsible for their tenants' deportment. Aldermen wanted policewomen to patrol Mount Royal Park after dark, to stop couples from "spooning".

Montreal's morality crusade even extended to the city's $5 million illegal gambling industry, although some supporters protested that it was no worse than Toronto's brisk trade in mining stocks. Ontario's Tory attorney-general, Leslie Blackwell, disagreed; he saw no harm in stock markets but he was ruthless about curbing the growing taste for gambling. Ottawa's Lions Club had collected 8,000 people a night in the civic auditorium, raising $40,000 for a health

A Postwar Crime Wave?

In the rural Ontario community of Ayr, two well-dressed young men mingled unnoticed on the fringe of a conference of ministers until it was closing time at the Bank of Commerce. Then they pulled scarves over their faces, drew guns, and shoved six people into the vault before leaving with $19,000 in cash and Victory Bonds. One of the six, a young farmer, helped the manager light a candle and unscrew a plate on the back of the vault door to get at the lock. "The four women thought we would never get the door open," he reported, a little ungallantly. "They were crying and the air was getting worse every minute."

Canadians in 1945 read a lot about crime in their midst. Did it add up to a postwar crime wave? Do statistics tell the truth?

In 1945, there were 41,965 indictable offences by adults in Canada; in 1946, there were 46,935 and, in 1947, there were 41,600. The sharpest rise was in Ontario, from 17,287 in 1945 to 21,379 in 1946. Other provinces also experienced more crime in 1946, with the conspicuous exception of Quebec, where reported crime fell by over 10 per cent. Juvenile delinquency fell from 5,758 convictions in 1945 to 4,949 in 1946, ammunition for supporters of the popular theory that the firm hand of a man was needed to keep teenagers in line—though convictions had fallen from a peak of 6,920 in 1942, while the number of absent fathers had grown.

Crime statistics largely depend on what police choose to prosecute, but murders are hard to ignore. Did demobilization unleash masses of homicidal veterans? The war years had seen an average of 129 criminal homicides a year, fewer than the average for the previous five peacetime years. In 1945 there were 152 homicides, and 146 in 1946 and the same number in 1947—hardly a terrifying trend for the most serious of crimes.

Certainly the fear of crime (and the rising wealth to pay for civic services) led to dramatic growth in police strength. During the war years, as in the 1930s, fewer than 6,000 police officers guarded Canadians, between 1.2 and 1.4 officers per thousand adults. In 1947, the total zoomed to 11,714, about 2.4 per thousand. Harsh sentences reflected public and judicial fears. In 1939, just 497 criminals had been sentenced to more than 5 years in the penitentiary; in 1945, however, 559 received long sentences, and 708 in 1946—but only 417 in 1947. Total admissions to penitentiary fell from 1,896 men in 1939 to 1,335 in 1945 and 1,635 in 1946. Death sentences rose from 14 in pre-war 1939 to 17 in 1945, though only 14 were actually carried out. Never again would so many die in a year, and after 1958 no more Canadian criminals would be executed by the state.

centre, $12,000 for children's camps, and $27,000 for bombed-out British children, but, said Blackwell, no longer. Instead of winners being offered a 1946 Lincoln Zephyr or a $15,000 fruit farm in "sunny British Columbia", prizes at future charity bingos would be limited to $50. Alberta, Manitoba, and British Columbia echoed Blackwell's views.

In September 1945, federal liquor rationing ended, but provincial controls remained. Quebec allowed drinkers eighty ounces of spirits a month; most provinces raised the limit to fifty-two ounces, while P.E.I. remained officially dry. As a measure against drunk driving, Saskatchewan's new CCF government allowed Reginans to order their liquor ration by telephone. To restrain tavernkeepers from their traditional tricks, beer would henceforth be sold in an eight-ounce glass with a moulded tide line. In P.E.I. doctors undermined the ban (as they had wherever prohibition prevailed) by issuing prescriptions for up to twenty-six ounces of liquor a week, and all the beer a patient could drink. The price of such "scrips" kept impecunious doctors in practice. When Premier Walter Jones tried to liberalize the rules, three ministers defected and the lieutenant-governor refused his assent.

In 1945, drunkenness, vagrancy, and extra-marital sex were all crimes. So were homosexual relations, almost any form of gambling, and "offering liquor to an Indian". Going over Niagara Falls in a barrel was a crime too, though William "Red" Hill followed his family's tradition and bobbed seven miles through the Niagara Gorge on a July night.

Warnings about loose morals and the return of Canada's defenders persuaded many people to brace for a postwar crime wave. After all, most criminals were men of military age, and over half a million such men were coming home. They would join a rising generation that had made "juvenile delinquency" one of the watch phrases of the war years. On the last weekend of August 1945, Ontario thought the crime crisis had arrived. Two gunmen took $11,000 from a Toronto trucking company messenger. Four bandits shot it out with police at a Toronto auto dealership and got away. At Amherstburg, crooks stole $10,000 from the Bob-Lo Amusement Park. Both Bath and Blenheim reported bank stickups. In the following week, Windsor police found a car mechanic and an army sergeant, both stabbed to death, and a tipsy reveller with a serious stab wound. At a Windsor garage, robbers used a hammer to batter a night watchman to death.

At Hallowe'en, juvenile crime reached its annual climax. At Prince Rupert, a mob of 200 youngsters assaulted the police station to rescue two pals. In Vancouver, window-smashing gangs battled police. In Toronto's east end, a gang built bonfires in the street with wooden fences and barricades, then raided gas stations and poured gasoline down the streetcar tracks and lit it. Teenagers met fire engines with a hail of two-by-fours and concrete blocks. Police marched 13 rioters to No. 10 Station, only to be followed by a mob of 7,000 intent on rescue. When the rioters smashed windows along the way and at the station, they were met by firehoses and most of the city's police force. Casualties for the night included six police, five firemen, and a couple of rioters clubbed hard enough to go to hospital. *Time* magazine claimed, with much exaggeration, it was "the worst riot in Toronto's history".

Most Canadians would have been content to hear Canada described as "a white man's country" in 1945. Asiatic immigration had been virtually banned since the early 1920s, and newcomers from Africa or the West Indies were virtually unheard of except as students. The vast majority of Jews fleeing Hitler in the 1930s had been turned away by the icy judgement of the federal official in charge of immigration, Frederick Blair, that "none is too many". As a younger man, Mackenzie King had negotiated Asiatic exclusion agreements; even if his Liberal Party commanded the support of most voting immigrants, nothing had yet persuaded the prime minister to broaden Canada's ethnic mix.

VJ Day found almost 22,000 Japanese Canadian men, women, and children still excluded from their west-coast homes. Some had found a grudging welcome on Alberta sugar-beet farms or Ontario building sites. A few had persuaded a school or university to accept them. As the war came to an end, federal officials got busy persuading Japanese Canadians to "go home". Reports that seven out of ten would go back to Japan delighted most British Columbians and dismayed *The New Canadian*, the Japanese Canadian newspaper. Since their property in British Columbia had been seized and auctioned off after Japan entered the war, there was little to draw Japanese Canadians back to that province—but they had found no warmer welcome elsewhere. In Ontario, the Lincoln County council raged at reports that twenty-three Japanese Canadians, assigned as farm labour, would be located near a camp of fifty "farmerettes". "I am absolutely opposed to Japs coming here," announced Ontario labour minister Charles Daly. "They wanted Kiska [an Aleutian island the Japanese had tried to capture] and tried hard to get it. Let's put them there now." Alberta had accepted 4,000 Japanese Canadians for hard agricultural labour, but its public works minister and acting premier, W.A. Fallow, had stipulated, "When the war is over, these birds will have to get out."

In the 1945 election, Liberal and Tory candidates competed in promising British Columbian voters that no Japanese would return. "If the Japs are in," pledged veterans affairs minister Ian Mackenzie, "I'm out." Victoria Cross winner and Tory candidate Lieutenant-Colonel C.C. Merritt told Vancouver voters, "A vote for Merritt is a vote

Japanese Canadians suffered more from wartime racism than any other Canadians. Some nonetheless joined the services, but all too often they suffered from discrimination there too.

against the Japs"—the Dieppe hero may not have known that a Montreal Nisei, David Tsubota, had also been a German prisoner after Dieppe. But there were other voices— many, but not all of them, associated with the CCF and the United Church. D.M. Lebourdais, better known as an Arctic explorer, found himself chair of the national Co-ordinating Committee on Japanese Canadians, and Toronto lawyer and CCFer Andrew Brewin was secretary. At last some white Canadians were making the unfashionable argument that people who had done no harm, but who had been confined and stripped of their property, should suffer no more. In July, the Ontario Command of the Legion was ready to echo the call for Japanese expulsion until an Ojibwa veteran from Cape Croker got the floor: "When it comes down to brass tacks, everybody here is a foreigner except me. The Legion must never associate itself with racial prejudice." Other delegates found the courage to condemn the expulsion as "unfair", "intolerant", and "undemocratic", and a majority conceded that at least the Canadian-born Japanese should stay in Canada.

The government would cheerfully have answered the public call for expulsion. Clause G of Bill 15, the National Emergency Powers Act, introduced on October 5 to replace the War Measures Act, gave the Cabinet absolute power over entry, exclusion, deportation, and revocation of nationality. Though no mention was made of the Japanese, the intent was obvious. When Paul Martin introduced the new citizenship bill, he assured British Columbia Tories Howard Green and Davie Fulton that it would not stand in the way of deporting the Japanese.

In fact, Clause G provoked an unexpected uproar. By the end of 1945, the wartime enthusiasm for sweeping government powers had eroded faster than politicians realized. *Maclean's* editor H. Napier Moore spoke for an unexpected number of influential Canadians: "Our whole war experience produced no such example of back door methods or of devious approach to dubious goals." Canadians born in Italy or Germany were not sent home, he added; "Japanese Canadians are singled out, not because they are enemies, but because they are Orientals."

Balked by the opposition and surprised by its influential critics, the government dropped Clause G. Instead, on December 17 it tabled three orders in council under the dying War Measures Act to do all that Clause G would have allowed. Humphrey Mitchell, the minister of labour, announced that 6,844 Japanese Canadians had signed requests for repatriation; counting their wives, parents, and children, 10,347 people, or half the total shipped inland in 1942, would be leaving.

Opponents were galvanized. Three-quarters of the proposed deportees were Canadian-born or naturalized British subjects, they argued. Had they signed freely or had they been coerced? A desperate Japanese-Canadian community and its allies raised cash and public consciousness. More and more people came to believe that a cruel and arbitrary deed was being rushed to completion.

While more than 800 people waited to board a ship in Vancouver harbour, the new Supreme Court building in Ottawa opened its doors for its first hearing. Andrew Brewin, who helped argue the case, felt that a few of the justices were sympathetic. When the verdict came down on February 20, 1946, Japanese Canadians were distraught but, as a lawyer and a political strategist, Brewin was delighted. The Supreme Court verdict upheld the government case, but four of the seven justices had reservations. That encouraged Brewin to appeal to the British Judicial Committee of the Privy Council, then Canada's ultimate judicial authority. There too the appeal failed, but it bought months of additional time for public opinion to shift. By the end of 1946, opponents of repatriation to Japan had won.

For 3,947 men, women, and children—including the family of at least one Canadian soldier and several First World War veterans—it was too late. Hundreds of children and elderly people had limited hope of survival in the devastation and starvation of postwar Japan. But the rest would stay in Canada. For all the prejudice and oppression they had experienced, the majority had refused to go for a simple reason: by naturalization or birth, they were Canadian. Strenuous lobbying by the members and organizations in the Co-operative Committee on Japanese Canadians, eventually

Waving the Flag

In 1945, the closest thing Canada had to a distinctive flag was the Red Ensign, with a Union Jack in the upper hoist and an emblematic shield in the lower fly. Originally the shield had been an untidy collection of all the provincial emblems, but a committee after the First World War had designed Canada's own coat of arms, and the king had approved it in 1921. The new shield included the symbols of England, Scotland, Ireland, and France over a sprig of three green maple leaves. Old or new, the Red Ensign affronted Canadian imperialists, who clung to the pure Union Jack, and French-Canadian nationalists, who objected to any inclusion of the British flag.

More than one person had attempted a unique Canadian design. Robert Benjamin, an enterprising seaman on the Canadian-owned *Westend Park*, made his own on a voyage from Panama to Newcastle-on-Tyne. When the ship's British master wasn't looking, he hoisted the flag—a white canvas maple leaf on a blue curtain—and promptly attracted the Newcastle police, who threatened a hundred-pound fine. Locals, Benjamin reported, were divided, but crews of other Canadian ships and some Canadian soldiers on leave were delighted. The flag disappeared when the ship finally returned to New Westminster. "The design wasn't beautiful," Benjamin acknowledged, "but to us it was a symbol we'd never had before—our own Canadian flag."

After the 1945 election, Parliament formed a committee and flag designs were collected. The predictable arguments ensued. Then Mackenzie King had his inspiration. On New Year's morning, 1946, the first words he heard on his bedside radio were "The maple leaf our emblem dear. . . ." Hitherto, King had been a proud promoter of the Red Ensign. He had ordered it raised over the Parliament Buildings for its first postwar session. But the patriotic song inspired a new thought. "A beautiful golden maple

Nationalist though they sometimes were, Canadians fought the war as British subjects, and patriotic occasions were still celebrated under the Union Jack. These schoolchildren, marking VE Day in Whitby, Ont., had been raised to sing "Rule Britannia" and would have to wait almost two decades before Canada had its own flag.

leaf with tinges of red, with other autumn shades, would look very well, on a red field." Canada House in London, King recalled, had a particularly lovely leaf as its emblem. The shield would vanish.

The Cabinet, of course, agreed. So did most of the flag committee, and even the Liberal caucus; but not all. The aesthetes had objections. So did King's Quebec followers. The Union Jack was unacceptable. To others, even King himself, it was indispensable. Hadn't it been the flag under which Quebec had gained religious freedom? "Spoke very firmly about the day of nationalism being passed (*sic*) and the need of all countries sharing common ideas of freedom, to keep as close together as they can."

Would Quebeckers be mollified if the field was white, not red? Or would they bolt the caucus and bring down the government on the flag issue? Absurd, but possible. King's timidity returned and somehow the moment passed. Canadians would wait until 1964 for their unmistakable red and white flag with its stylized maple leaf. Lester Pearson, not Mackenzie King, would be its sponsor.

including the Canadian Jewish Congress and the National Council of Women, plus the evidence of fortitude and patience by the Japanese Canadians themselves, derailed the Liberal government's plan for "repatriation".

The deportation of the Japanese Canadians was an act of official racism. The marvel was that, perhaps for the first time, millions of Canadians felt ashamed. Even in 1945, most people had yet to recognize how racism had lit the flames under Hitler's gas ovens or how racial discrimination stunted the lives of victims and perpetrators. At a mass rally at Jarvis Collegiate in Toronto at the end of 1945, Rabbi Abraham Feinberg forced his audience to make the connection: "I am here on behalf of six million Jews who were slaughtered . . . for no reason other than being Jews. . . . The ghost of Hitler still walks in Canada." Many church leaders belatedly mobilized official support for "relocated" Japanese Canadians, and after VJ Day many congregations protested officially against Ottawa's plan to deport them to Japan. However, when the Department of Labour answered the protest letters by requesting help from the congregations in resettling the Japanese Canadians, it got no replies. "In this and other instances," wrote Ken Adachi, "were revealed the conflict between creed and deed, between statements of piety and action."

———— •·•· ————

Discrimination was not, of course, restricted to Japanese Canadians. In May of

It took time and postwar prosperity to accustom Canadians to refugees and immigrants. These Jewish refugees, here at a Passover seder, were looked on with suspicion in 1944 Montreal.

clubs, university fraternities, and banking jobs. Real estate covenants "maintained property values" by barring sales to Jews. McGill University, he claimed, wanted 10 per cent higher marks from Jewish applicants than from Gentiles. At the University of Manitoba, 1,125 students had ranked "the Jewish problem" behind the French-Canadian problem but ahead of the Japanese.

In Quebec, Jehovah's Witnesses and their offensively anti-Catholic propaganda faced continuing persecution. Three times in the fall of 1945, Witnesses set up their stands in Châteauguay only to have mobs topple their tables, pelt them with rotting vegetables, and send them flying. At the climax, police arrested seventeen of the fleeing Witnesses for selling without a licence.

Were attitudes changing? The same year, in Quebec City, the Château Frontenac accepted a reservation from Dr. and Mrs. George D. Cannon but the hotel restaurant refused to serve them; the Cannons were black. The Cannons hired a local lawyer and got an injunction. French-Canadian opinion was sympathetic. *L'Action Catholique* urged the couple to take their case to the highest court in the land, while the hotel manager blamed protests from visiting white Americans. In Toronto, Harry Gairey and a Jewish chum were stopped at the door of the Icelandia skating rink: "Coloured people can't come in." Gairey's father, a First World War veteran, was in tears when he

Door-to-door canvassers from the Jehovah's Witnesses were persecuted during the war for their beliefs and for their anti-Catholic proselytizing. The religion was actually banned for several years.

1945, a plan to convert a house on Toronto's Huron Street into a Finnish Lutheran church generated a turmoil of neighbourhood hostility. "Do we have to put up with people like Finns?" a neighbourhood delegation demanded of aldermen. Rabbi Feinberg reminded *Maclean's* readers of what many of them must have known: Jews were still kept out of most ski

Immigrants were not always "grateful" for being admitted to Canada. These new arrivals staged a hunger strike at St Paul l'Ermite, Que. to protest separation from their families and the lack of work.

asked the Board of Control for justice. "If we are to be divided into racial and colour groups," claimed Gairey, "there is little left to live for." Mayor Saunders promised action, and Ontario's legislature, on its way to adopting a Human Rights Code, passed a law prohibiting "Gentiles Only" advertisements. The Workers' Education Association bought a lot in East York only to discover a clause that prevented the land being sold "to Jews or persons of objectionable nationality". When the case was taken to court, lawyers insisted that nothing in British or Canadian law allowed such covenants to be annulled. The Workers' Education Association resorted to the Atlantic Charter, the U.N. Charter, and even the Soviet constitution, and Mr. Justice J. Keiller MacKay, a Great

War veteran and future lieutenant-governor, promptly declared such clauses "offensive to the public policy" and henceforth void in Ontario.

Race and scarcity had shaped Canadian attitudes to immigration. From its earliest cap-in-hand lobbying sessions with the federal government in the 1880s, the Trades and Labor Congress had denounced immigration as a threat to jobs and living standards. Except for a brief tolerant interlude when it would have allowed one Asian per thousand immigrants, the TLC's "Platform of

Principles" demanded a ban on Asiatic immigration. Suddenly, in 1945, the TLC and its younger rival, the Canadian Congress of Labour, switched course. Astonished observers heard the TLC urge changes "with a view to accepting a greater number of immigrants to this country." The CCL agreed: newcomers would open up the country and create new industries. For the first time, the leaders of Canada's workers believed that there was enough work for their own members and, more important, that immigration could expand employment. That might be true. What was now unmistakable was the nightmare outcome of any form of racism.

It was an astonishing conversion. In the 1930s, few Canadians had asked whether their government's refusal to accept Jewish refugees condemned them to Nazi concentration camps; none could have anticipated the gas chambers of the "Final Solution". The Canadian National Committee on Refugees, launched by the League of Nations Society in 1938 and headed by Senator Cairine Wilson, had been neither popular nor very influential. Among its few beneficiaries was Thomas Bata, the Czech whose shoe business would become an international giant. The main influx of Jews before 1946 was as part of the 2,500 "enemy aliens" shipped from British internment camps in 1940. Most turned out to be Austrian and German refugees from

Canada's special relationship with The Netherlands, formed during the wartime liberation, was cemented by a postwar influx of immigrants. The Dutch ambassador and his wife greeted a shipload of immigrants dockside in Montreal in June 1947.

Mirror, Mirror, on the Wall

During the war, advertisers struggled to link even the most personal products to the war effort. It was implied, if not quite stated outright, that a woman who neglected her hair or skin was putting the nation at risk; beauty and hygiene were patriotic drills.

With the return of peace, such noble motives could be set aside. The men were back, and the magazines urged women to compete for them. "When that man's here again," warned *Chatelaine*'s beauty editor, Adele White, "he'll expect you to be the same sweet girl who waved him good-bye." It was time to pull out a mirror and some old photographs, and take stock: "Have you gone definitely in the red on the ledgerbook as far as beauty goes?" As for those militant habits of the manless years, they had to go; "there are more suitable ways of asserting yourself than by swinging down the street in a chest-out, forward-march swagger. The new posture is graceful and at ease, without slumping, and when you step out you should feel you're walking on air."

In "The New Hope Dawning Day", *Chatelaine* said, women would have to look "gay, feminine and very very sweet . . . to prevent our guys from going out in the evenings." Cartoon strips for Woodbury Facial Soap showed torrid scenes of women swept off their feet by handsome men in uniform—usually closing with a passionate kiss at the altar. "Soon now," DuBarry Beauty Preparations crooned, "we trust ALL the women of Canada will be back in the flowered hats and romantic, feminine clothes that go with a return to peace. For the women of this country have earned the right to indulge their love of beauty and to express their personal allure in the ways that women understand and instinctively desire." "Clothes Go Man Crazy" was *Chatelaine*'s fashion statement for October 1945: "We're dress-

ing for men, making ourselves easy on the eyes that have been gazing at mud and debris and drab colour for too many years."

But beauty was no frivolous concern; a woman had to attract a man if she was going to have a family. And without a husband and children, what would she do with her life? In 1945, few offered women a different choice.

Fashions were lean and mingy during the war, with stern rules controlling materials; in any case, it seemed disloyal and even unpatriotic to wear tantalizing clothes when your man was overseas. But with peace came a "New Look" of tiny waists, full bodices, and long, swirling skirts; Paris was back in action.

Postwar Canada was far from perfect, but these Polish women, brought from a Nazi forced labour camp to Calgary in 1946, found husbands and built new lives for themselves.

Nazism, among them scientists, theologians, writers, musicians, and teachers. Half of them went back to England in 1941; the rest were released under sponsorship. Eventually, 972 became Canadian citizens.

No arguments would easily convert Mackenzie King's government to favour expanded immigration. King's own political instincts had hardened with age. The depression of the 1930s was still too powerful a memory. Labour economists might argue that more people meant larger markets and economies of scale, but such experts were few in number. King knew that if immigration was increased, the Conservatives and

their allies would roar about threats to Canada's British character. Even organized labour's conversion was tentative; immigration policy, warned the CCL, must be planned. A draft statement by its research director, Eugene Forsey, repeated familiar arguments in more civilized terms: "We cannot afford to expose Canadian workers to the constant threat of having their standards undercut by immigrants who must take any kind of job at any wages and under any conditions to avoid sheer starvation."

The end of the war left millions of people far from their pre-war homes. "Displaced persons", or DPs, as they were quickly labelled, could not go home. Some were economic refugees, others faced death or prison at the hands of the Soviet army or the puppet regimes it was establishing over most of eastern Europe. Many had simply been expelled from their homes as first Hitler and then Stalin remade the map of Europe. *Saturday Night* editor B.K. Sandwell called them "prisoners in a great, dark, airless room which . . . had fifty different doors . . . but every door locked, barred and bolted." There was no unlimited obligation to grant sanctuary, Sandwell acknowledged to the Senate, "But the obligation to grant sanctuary still exists, the need for sanctuary is greater than ever before in history, and the nation which ignores this obligation will suffer as all nations ultimately do which ignore the fundamental moral obligation, the debt which man and nations owe to the human being at their gates simply because he is a human being."

Being lectured on immigration as a moral obligation was a relative novelty for Canadian politicians. In July 1946, Ottawa accepted a British appeal to take in up to 5,000 of the Polish soldiers who had fought as allies in Italy and North-West Europe. By November 1946, a year later than the Truman administration in Washington, Mackenzie King was prepared to accept European refugees and "DPs". In 1947, he even allowed that Asians might again come to Canada, though he insisted "the racial and national balance of immigration would be regulated to preserve the fundamental character of the Canadian population." Nothing less was imaginable.

If a war for freedom and democracy had made it easier to fight overt racial discrimination, it had also further embittered French–English relations. Once again, conscription crises had reminded French Canadians that they were a minority whenever English-speaking Canadians wanted to use their power. The despised zombie had been stereotyped as a French Canadian shirking his patriotic duty. Those francophones who had enlisted had found that French was the common language of only a few select units, mostly infantry, and that the use of French would sometimes be met by the derisive cry "Speak white." At the end of the war, not a single French Canadian over the rank of brigadier held an operational command.

Contempt for Canada's other language was not restricted to barrack rooms or bars. At the end of 1945, a Protestant committee demanded that Ontario wind up its French-language schools. When a delegate at the Tory provincial convention used French to introduce a candidate for party office, other delegates shouted him down. The success of Radio Ouest-Française in raising $50,000 to set up four small stations across the Prairies generated seething opposition in Manitoba and Saskatchewan, outcry in the Alberta legislature, and angry questions from the Tories' sole prairie MP, John Diefenbaker.

Nationalism and conservatism in Quebec had triumphed in 1944 with the return of Maurice Duplessis and the Union Nationale, seemingly annihilated in an election five years earlier. Wartime tensions and frustrations were the obvious explanation for Duplessis's renewed support. Liberal senator T.D. Bouchard, a former mayor of St. Hyacinthe, had ignited a furious Quebec reaction by publicly denouncing the Ordre Jacques Cartier, a secret nationalist society known to its critics as "La Patente". The speed and unanimity with which Bouchard was excoriated by editors, stripped of his public honours and offices, and treated as a

Eager to fit into their new homeland, two young women attend "English and Citizenship School" in 1952 Toronto.

pariah almost seemed to confirm his claim that "La Patente" controlled opinion in French Canada. Sensitive Quebeckers saw him differently. To journalist Roger Duhamel, Bouchard was "a spiteful and small-calibre politician"; the real pain came when "we find the Anglo-Canadians, whom we want to believe sincere, are unable to recognize our real interpreter." What was the order, after all, but a French-Canadian version of the Masonic Lodge, where "the

Anglo-Canadians develop their cohesion and wonderful 'team-play'"? Duhamel listed the grievances of French Canadians in 1945, from low incomes and meagre representation in the civil service, to English Canada's reluctance to cast off British loyalties and become fully sovereign:

We do not like having our democratic convictions questioned, even if we do not believe ourselves bound to consider Stalin as the defender of Christianity and Democracy. We do not enjoy having our political Parties accused of being Fascist because they hold that it is necessary to distinguish between liberty and licence.

"Can We Teach Love of Country?" Donalda Dickie asked *Chatelaine* readers in April 1945. A nation that could play a worthy role in the world needed a sense of nationality. Once children could say their names, she suggested, they could be taught to say, "I am a Canadian." Later they could sing songs like "O Canada", "Land of Hope and Glory", "The Maple Leaf Forever", or "Three Cheers for the Red, White, and Blue". They could have a flag. In practice, her suggestions raised difficulties. Was Canada even entitled to have its own citizenship and a distinctive flag, or did being a British subject and waving the Red Ensign suffice?

The answer, of course, was that Canadians could do what they wanted. It was not Britain but the premiers of Quebec and Ontario who had insisted that Canada's constitution still be amended by the Parliament at Westminster. It was Mackenzie King, not King George VI, who refused to proceed with Canadian military decorations for valour and special service. With the end of the war, a flag committee was hard at work, but it was Canadians, not the British, who subjected its task to ridicule (some of it doubtless deserved). While many Canadians rejoiced in being "British subjects", at least one Cabinet minister was determined that wartime pride and sacrifice would help him create a specific and explicit Canadian citizenship.

When the government had argued its right to deport Japanese Canadians, some Supreme Court justices had doubted that they could be forced to revoke their status as British subjects. No one had mentioned Canadian citizenship, because it did not exist. In 1945 it was still hardly more than one man's dream. Paul Martin, a Franco-Ontarian, had represented Essex East since 1935. In January 1945, he had visited the graves of more than a hundred Essex Scottish at Dieppe. The wooden crosses, with their miscellany of names—French, English, Ukrainian, German—gave him a burning conviction. Promotion to the minor Cabinet post of secretary of state gave him the opportunity to argue for a distinct Canadian citizenship. It was not Martin's goal alone. An Ottawa lawyer, T.S. Ewart, had fulminated for years against forcing Canadians to be designated as "British" when they were registered for births, marriages, deaths, or passports. Wartime propaganda

Peacetime texts began to discard the heavy pre-war emphasis on imperial rhetoric. In place of "Rule Britannia", children now memorized "There's a thing we love...our birthplace, Canada!"

THE PROVINCES

British Columbia

As usual in British Columbia, nature was news in 1945. Ripple Rock, the navigational menace up the Fraser River, was being prepared for yet another dynamiting attempt. Victoria's Consolidated Whaling Corporation announced that it would use former navy ASDIC (sonar) operators and their equipment to find whales in the Pacific. During the war, a good many of the mammals had been depth-charged before the navy realized that asdic pings from a whale were "mushier" than those from a U-boat.

That summer, the blackheaded budworm threatened the hemlocks of Vancouver Island's Quatsino Sound, and the budworms themselves had trouble: a "wilt disease" that turned their flesh to liquid. Already thinking about its need for post-war work, the RCAF offered a Canso flying boat to spray both problems into oblivion with DDT. Spared the bitter winter that had wiped out eastern apple growers, Okanagan Valley producers could expect an ideal harvest of 6 million boxes—big enough to fill the market, small enough to avoid the price-damaging glut they had suffered in 1944.

Forest companies reported a desperate shortage of loggers. Employers could have three hundred from Quebec, said National Selective Service, if they paid their fares. No, said the employers, such generosity would be a bad precedent. Conditions had improved enough during the war: cabins with bedrooms, not "loggers' barns", steel bed springs, not "jack-pine mattresses", even central heating. Only the old cookhouse was unchanged. Experts insisted that it could not be improved.

Like other provinces, British Columbia faced an election that year, and the possibility of a CCF victory. In 1901, B.C. had been the first part of the British Empire to elect a couple of out-and-out socialists, and the left had been strong ever since. Even its support of Asian-Canadian voting rights had not stopped the CCF from becoming the official opposition in 1935, and growing in 1940. John Hart's Liberals seemed to be in trouble. However, as elsewhere, it was not the CCF's year. On October 25, the lines in B.C.'s class-war politics were drawn just a little straighter. Harold Winch's CCF got only ten seats, but a Liberal-Tory coalition with thirty-seven seats would keep the province safe from the socialists. The pattern for the province's postwar politics was set.

had fostered a sense of distinct nationality.

The normally nervous Mackenzie King was converted by delicate flattery. A distinct citizenship, argued Martin, would let King reach Laurier's goal of a separate Canadian nation—though Martin reassured him that Canadians would continue to be British subjects. Martin's bill was introduced on October 22, 1945. It promised citizenship to anyone born in Canada or on a Canadian ship or to Canadian parents abroad, to any British subject who had lived for five years in Canada and cared to apply, and to any alien who met the general requirements of literacy and sanity. Much desk-pounding greeted Martin's promise that Canadians would remain British subjects. Although Martin had a well-managed press campaign, he saw the wisdom of deferring a vote until Parliament had exhausted itself in a typically furious flag debate. The Citizenship Act would have to wait for 1946.

With the war over, war correspondent Lionel Shapiro set out to tell Canadians what their returning servicemen and service-

The soldiers who had been fighting "for a new world" were eager to begin their civilian lives. Lt. A. L. Grosson of Montreal was greeted on his return by ecstatic friends.

women wanted. In one sense, it wasn't much. They didn't have to be persuaded that Canada was a great or powerful country, or even the most beautiful place on earth. They had been overseas and they knew that this was the country where they belonged. "We're not going around crowing that we did the fighting and therefore the country should pat us on the back and stick a cigar in our mouths the rest of our lives. All we want is a fair break." Veterans, Shapiro claimed, wanted the country they had left, but they wanted some changes too. Fighting men had lived in constant danger of death but they had also known economic security and community spirit. "Someone saw to it that they had no cares to distract them from doing the best possible job in their dangerous profession." In the ordeals of war they had escaped ruthless economic competition, the terror of losing a job, the shame and sadness of meeting as a family to discuss whether they

could afford hospital treatment for a mother's illness. The average serviceman, warned Shapiro, would not willingly return to that world:

He has been fighting for a new world, a better world, and in the process of fighting for it he has discovered the basis for that better world even in the midst of mud and slaughter. He has discovered that men can attain the hitherto impossible if they have the spirit and the motivation. He has discovered that the nation, united by necessity, can organize the machinery for secure living and carefree health. If the nation can do this to achieve success in war, why cannot it be done to achieve a more lasting and worth-while success in peace?

Postwar Canada had the answer to the question—it could be done.

CHAPTER EIGHT

THE FIRST OF THE MIDDLE POWERS

Canada came of age in the Second World War. It was a virtual colony in 1939, despite its formal autonomy, but by 1945 its politicians and officials bargained toughly with both Britain and the rest of the world, fighting for national advantage. As representatives of a strong middle power, they played a critical role in creating the United Nations and a host of postwar organizations.

President Franklin Roosevelt and Mackenzie King had a good relationship of long standing. At Ogdensburg, N.Y., the two signed the first-ever defence agreement between Canada and the U.S.

THE RUSSIAN OFFICER SAT IN THE OPEN JEEP beside his driver, his face reflecting his surprise and anger at the barrier across the road. It was May 2, 1945, and here were these Canadians at Wismar, the German town on the Baltic Sea that was the Soviet army's necessary objective as it sought to head north to liberate (and loot) Denmark.

The 1st Canadian Parachute Battalion, a crack formation, had dropped into Normandy in June 1944 before the assaulting troops hit the beaches. As part of the 6th British Airborne Division, it had landed east of the River Weser, right in Hitler's crumbling Reich, on March 24, 1945. The Canadian paras, under Lieutenant-Colonel G.F. Eadie, had taken part in the long dash to the Baltic, sometimes clinging desperately atop Churchill tanks of the Royal Scots Greys as they raced ahead at sixty miles an hour. Ronald Anderson, a paratrooper with the battalion, remembered years later "that we suddenly started passing through German regiments and battalions…. these exhausted troops were sitting in fields at the roadside, fully armed, but clearly wishing to surrender." The political intention behind the drive to the Baltic, probably never communicated to the soldiers, was to block the Russians off from the Danish peninsula, a task the battalion's capture of the historic port of Wismar successfully accomplished.

The Canadians' next job was to take a patrol into Soviet-controlled territory to make contact with an officer, and Anderson was one of four soldiers sent out in a jeep. There at the barrier, at the very end of the war, the Canadians and the startled Russians shook hands, meeting for the first time. There were already indications that the peace was to be every bit as difficult as the war had been. The angry Red Army officer would be obliged to tell his general that the route to Denmark was blocked, and over the next few days growing suspicion began to envelop relations at the official level. "The Russians wanted us to leave Wismar," Anderson recalled, "and they made life miserable for us."

But for most of the soldiers and junior officers in both armies, there was initially only relief that they had survived. The officers ate and drank together, the Canadians reporting that their new comrades were "the most persistent and thirsty drinkers we have ever met." The privates looked at each others' equipment, the Russians marvelling at the profusion of Canadian gear and eagerly trading loot and vodka for wristwatches. Most of the Soviets were hard, tough, simple soldiers, men who had suffered through the most terrible fighting of the war. They wanted revenge on the Germans, and to the Canadians they often seemed drunk and ill-disciplined, bent on pillage and rape. The Canadians, for their part, were children of the Depression, almost as inured to hardship and fighting. It was a meeting of equals, with both armies proud of their accomplishments, both happy the war was over, and both starting to think only of returning home.

In Europe, though, the end of the war marked a new stage in hardship. The devastation of six years' fighting had left economic ruin, while the killing and destruction had left a legacy of hatred. With

The 1st Canadian Parachute Battalion was the first Canadian unit to land on D-Day, and the unit that made the furthest penetration into Germany. Here a Canadian para shakes hands over the barrier at Wismar, Germany, with a Soviet officer. The smiles hide Russian anger that the Red Army's route to Denmark had been barred (see map p. 49).

the old balance of power overturned—with borders redrawn and populations displaced—an aftermath of suspicion, hostility, and political manoeuvring was inevitable. Many people felt that the only way they could secure a decent life, for themselves and their children, was to emigrate and seek a fresh start.

Canada was one of the countries they sought desperately to enter. Its cities and farms were untouched by destruction. Its people had no territorial demands, no claims for the rectification of borders, no age-old rivalries that could only be satisfied by military victory. Canada had gone into the war in

1939 because Britain had, not for national interests of its own, though many people believed firmly that Hitler had to be stopped before he devoured all of Europe. But while victory had been sweet, it had been costly, and most Canadians felt they had done enough. By 1945, they wanted to turn inward. Let the rest of the world solve its own problems, they seemed to say; let us now solve our own.

If only it could have been so simple. The world's problems still seemed almost insoluble, and because Canada had played its part well during the war, other states expected it to continue to do so. This was also the desire in Ottawa, where, perhaps to their surprise, politicians and officials had discovered that they could hold their own in negotiations with the Great Powers. There was absolutely no sense of national inferiority at the upper reaches of the public service—nor should there have been.

At the 1943 Quebec Conference, Mackenzie King was shut out from the main discussions between Roosevelt and Churchill. But there were important Anglo-Canadian meetings involving the two prime ministers, the Canadian Cabinet War Committee, and both nations' chiefs of staff.

During the war, Canada had been caught between Britain and the United States—the first a declining power despite its gallant struggles, the second a rising superpower. There was a natural desire to help the mother country in its hour of crisis, but it was also necessary to accept the reality that Canada was a North American nation, reliant on the U.S. for its defence. By the summer of 1940, when France had fallen to Hitler's legions and the British had barely escaped home from the evacuation at Dunkirk, Britain's chances of survival seemed slender indeed.

If Hitler triumphed over Britain, democracy elsewhere would soon be at risk. More immediately, much of Canada's trade would be lost, causing serious dislocation to agriculture and industry. The Canadian soldiers and airmen in Britain—two divisions of infantry and virtually all Canada's pilots—also would be sacrificed, eliminating most of the country's trained manpower. And, depending on the course of battle and the surrender terms the Nazis demanded, the British navy could fall into Hitler's hands, exposing North America to the threat of attack for the first time in the twentieth century. Canada itself could be subject to invasion.

Worried as he was about Britain's fate, Mackenzie King's first concern had to be Canada, and that meant that its defence was the top priority, however much military and economic aid might be sent overseas. One wholly new option was a military alliance with the United States. After-dinner speakers had long boasted of the "undefended border", but Canada's military co-operation with the U.S., except for a few months during the Great War, had been largely non-existent. The Canadian and American chiefs of

staff had met briefly in 1938 to talk about North American defence, but that had been the extent of the venture.

Now more was needed, and people in Canada had begun to meet, talk, and write about the new situation. The American minister to Canada quickly became aware of the trend in opinion, and he recommended that military staff talks be held at the first opportunity, a suggestion that was followed in July 1940. Meanwhile, officials in the Department of External Affairs pointed out that naturally the Americans "will expect, and if necessary, demand, Canadian assistance in the defence of this continent and this Hemisphere. . . . the negotiation of a specific offensive-defensive alliance is likely to become inevitable."

Roosevelt had reached the same conclusion. In mid-August, he called Mackenzie King and invited him to meet the next day at Ogdensburg, New York, a little town across the St. Lawrence River from Prescott, Ontario. In an almost casual discussion after dinner in the president's railroad car, the two leaders agreed to set up a Permanent Joint Board on Defence. Leaping at the opportunity to safeguard Canada against invasion, King did not even query Roosevelt's insistence that the board be permanent. What Roosevelt had meant, or so the president said, was "to help secure the continent for the future." That was fair enough, and King readily agreed.

But there was a hint of steel when Roosevelt talked about a deal then being negotiated between London and Washington, which would have the U.S. give Britain much-needed destroyers in exchange for the right to establish U.S. military bases on British soil, in the Caribbean and elsewhere. King said that his country had no intention of allowing U.S. bases on Canadian soil, and Roosevelt assured him that he only wanted to get troops into Canada quickly in case of invasion. That was "all right", King said, as were military exercises on each other's territory. But then Roosevelt added that he could not understand Britain's reluctance to lease West Indian bases to the U.S. because, as King noted in his diary, "if war developed with Germany and he [Roosevelt] felt it necessary to seize them to protect the United States, he would do that in any event. That it was much better to have a friendly agreement in advance." The implicit threat was clear.

When negotiations on a joint defence plan began in the autumn, the Americans sought strategic control of Canadian forces in the event of a British defeat. The Canadians agreed; after the summer of 1940, that made sense. But the next spring, with Britain still in the war after its victory in the Battle of Britain, the negotiations for a second defence scheme—designed to take effect when the U.S. joined the war—were much tougher. Again the Americans sought strategic and tactical control, and the integration of eastern Canada and British Columbia into their defences, in effect treating Canada as part of the U.S. for military purposes. But Ottawa resisted fiercely and all that was agreed on was "mutual co-operation".

Nor was it any easier dealing with Britain. After the Ogdensburg agreement, King had told Churchill what he believed to be self-evident: that with Canada's defences secured, the nation could now do more for Britain. But the imperialist Churchill, with his long view of events, believed that Canada had put itself into the American orbit, and he immediately fired off a wire to Ottawa:

I am deeply interested in the arrangements you are making for Canada and America's mutual defence. . . . there may be two opinions on some of the points mentioned. Supposing Mr Hitler cannot invade us and his Air Force begins to blench under the strain all these transactions will be judged in a mood different to that prevailing while the issue still hangs in the balance.

Churchill had come close to accusing Canada of scuttling for cover under the American defence umbrella. This blunt and angry message almost shattered Mackenzie King, who believed that he had done a good day's work for Britain by binding the still-neutral Americans closer to Canada.

In fact King was completely right in his actions; Britain's military weakness had forced Canada to look out for itself, and that meant an alliance with the United States. But Churchill was right about the long-term results. The Ogdensburg Agreement marked Canada's move from the British to the American sphere of influence. World power had shifted, and Canada had shifted with it.

This was soon evident in economic areas as well. Before the war, Canada had maintained a state of balance with its two main trading partners, holding a trade surplus with Britain and a deficit with the United States. The two were in rough balance, and surplus pounds could be easily converted into dollars. But the war obliged London to forbid the conversion of sterling into dollars, and as Canadian trade to Britain grew during the war, the money earned could not be transferred to Canada. Because the war increased critical imports from the United States, this produced a crisis. Every artillery piece or aircraft built in Canada required American parts, and the huge jump in imports began to erode Canadian holdings of

What Did the War Cost Canada?

Estimates of the Second World War's total direct cost to Canada put it at about $16 billion in 1945 dollars (or an estimated $150 billion in our present inflated currency)—though the total depends on what one counts as war expenditures. To that figure should be added, among other things, the costs of veterans' benefits and medical care, the perpetual maintenance of war cemeteries, support for war widows and orphans, and the interest costs of carrying the debt incurred during the conflict. The true cost, in other words, is still being paid. It is virtually incalculable.

In fiscal 1944–45, the government's figures (in millions) were as follows:

War expenditures

Army	$1,415
Navy	407
Air Force	1,325
Dept. of Munitions & Supply	215
Dept. of National War Services	26
Other Departments	414
United Nations financial assistance	815
Total war	**4,617**
Other government expenditures	815
Total expenditures	**$5,432**

In the last year of peace, government expenditures had been $550 million. During the war, in other words, the government spent ten times as much as it had in peace.

Such expenditures quickly ran the federal budget deficit sky-high. In 1939–40, the deficit had been $119 million; by 1942–43 it was $2,148 million, and by 1944–45 it was $2,734 million, with government revenues, despite very high taxation, producing only 50 per cent of the money needed to fight the war and run the government.

It may have cost only $114.82 to outfit a soldier, but Canada's army in 1944-45 spent $1.4 billion fighting the war. War swallowed billions of dollars, and without wise management it could bankrupt countries very fast.

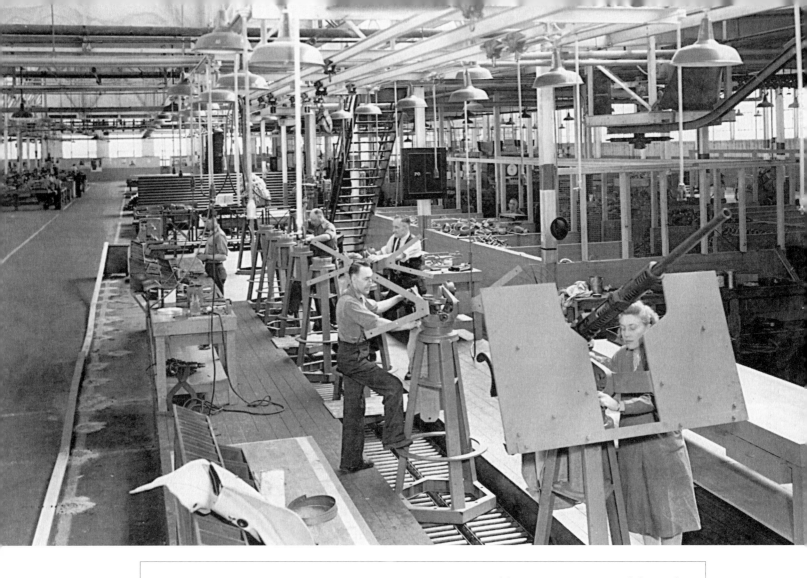

These light anti-aircraft guns being put together at Regina Industries Ltd. required specialty steels and parts from the United States. Importing them required U.S. dollars, and by early 1941 Canada was in crisis because of a dollar shortage.

American dollars. The government put controls on non-essential trade with the U.S., but such measures proved ineffective.

Was there an escape from this economic crisis that threatened Canadian war industry in the lend-lease bill then making its way through the United States Congress? The bill, a product of Roosevelt's fertile imagination, would let the United States lease or lend war equipment to Britain, itself desperately short of American dollars. But there was a problem for Canada in this "most unsordid" act, in Churchill's phrase. If Britain could secure war material from the U.S. free of charge, why would it pay for goods from Canada? Lend-lease, far from being Canada's salvation, threatened to destroy the Canadian economy.

The way out came when King met with Roosevelt at Hyde Park, New York, in April 1941. What King wanted was to get the benefits of lend-lease to meet Canada's shortage of American dollars while avoiding the sacrifice of the country's bargaining position with Washington. Lend-lease was generous indeed, but there was no desire to be beholden to Uncle Sam. Canada itself would never accept lend-lease.

The Prime Minister had the right approach. "Why not buy from Canada as much as Canada is buying from the U.S.,— just balance the accounts?" Roosevelt thought this idea was "swell", and the Hyde Park Declaration, issued on "a grand Sunday in April", stated that "in mobilizing the resources of this continent each country should provide the other with the defense articles which it is best able to produce. . . ." The declaration anticipated that Canada could provide up to $300 million of war material over the next year, "purchases that would materially assist Canada in meeting part of the cost of Canadian defense purchases in the United States." That was a great help to the dollar shortage. So too was the key clause: "In so far as Canadian defense purchases in the United States consist of component parts to be used in equipment and munitions which Canada is producing for Great Britain, it was also agreed that Great Britain will obtain these parts under the Lend-Lease Act and forward them to Canada for inclusion in the finished articles."

King and Roosevelt had resolved Canada's shortage of American exchange. At a stroke, the Hyde Park Declaration liberated Canada from fear of economic collapse and permitted the nation to do its utmost to produce munitions.

This was a major agreement whose wartime consequences were entirely beneficial. Canada soon built up large surpluses of American dollars as the U.S. made substantial and continuing purchases north of the border. But the country was in the American orbit economically as well as militarily. Canada would never be the same again.

———•◆•———

The U.S. entry into the war in December 1941 pushed Canada into the background even further, and there was an almost schizophrenic response in Ottawa as events developed. On the one hand, there was great satisfaction that Britain and the United States were now working hand in glove; on the other, Ottawa felt left out as a result of the new Anglo-American unity, which confirmed Canadian diplomats in their secondary status. After Churchill visited the United States in December 1941, the two Great Powers set out to co-ordinate their efforts. A Combined Chiefs of Staff Committee was to run the military side, while a series of combined boards tackled the economic struggle. No Canadian seriously sought a place with the Combined Chiefs of Staff—our military contribution, large though it was in Canadian terms, was merely a small part of a vast array. But Canada's economic war effort was a different matter, and Ottawa was shocked that its contribution was simply assumed. Canada produced great quantities of food and raw materials. Its factories were hitting their stride and products were moving across the Atlantic in a flood. So great was the flow that in 1942 the Canadian government gave Britain a gift of a billion dollars' worth of war supplies, a testimony to Canada's support for the war effort and to its recognition that England could not pay for all it needed. Yet Ottawa had now been shut out of the war's direction by an ungrateful London and Washington. Was its war production to be allocated by the new boards without so much as a by-your-leave?

It fell to Hume Wrong to draft the response to the Anglo-American affront to Canadian pride. The minister-counsellor at the Washington legation was the most clear-headed member of the Department of External Affairs, and he understood that Canada had been shut out because "the Government has hitherto adopted in these matters what may unkindly be called a semi-colonial position." In early 1942, Wrong found a way off the sidelines:

> The principle . . . is that each member of the grand alliance should have a voice in the conduct of the war proportionate to its contribution to the general war effort. A subsidiary principle is that the influence of the various countries should be greatest in connection with those matters with which they are most directly concerned.

This would come to be known as the "functional principle", and its formulation marked the beginning of the middle-power concept that Canada would champion during the rest of the war and into the postwar era. The first challenge came in July 1942, when Canada, the second most important Allied producer of foodstuffs, tried to secure a seat on the Combined Food Board, the agency designed to allocate food supplies. London replied with the infuriating argument that membership "would not make for technical efficiency", and would only support Canadian membership on the much less important Combined Production and Resources Board. The prime minister, showing what one disgruntled diplomat called "the strong glove over the velvet hand", accepted the offer; Canada became a member of the CPRB, a board without much of a role. But in March 1943 Canada renewed its claim for a seat on the Combined Food Board. Again the British were reluctant, now countering that if Canada got a seat Australia and Argentina would want one too. The exasperated Canadians responded that when those countries produced as much food as Canada, they too would be entitled to a place on the CFB. By October, after much hard bargaining, London and Washington finally conceded, and Canada gained membership on the board—the only junior ally to win such status.

But Canada's battles for recognition were not always succesful. The United Nations Relief and Rehabilitation Administration, created in 1942, was designed to distribute aid to liberated territories. Canada was expected to be one of the major contributors, but the Great Powers also assumed that it would not have a place on the senior

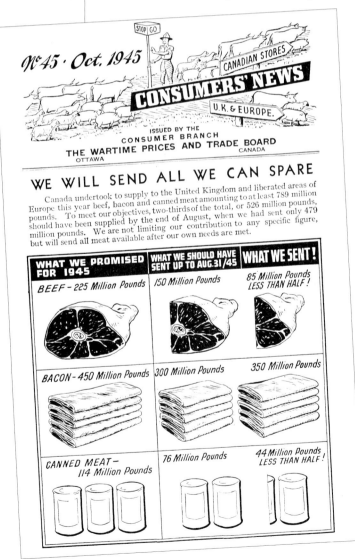

Canada was the Allies' second-largest food producer after the United States, though it often received scant notice for its contribution. This fall 1945 poster, exhorting Canadians to postwar sacrifice, gives some indication of the scope of food shipments—even as it complains that Canada is not meeting targets.

directing committee of UNRRA. The "Americans might not like the British side overweighed by Canadian representation," Whitehall officials said, as though the country were a mere British puppet. Such a response was guaranteed to get Ottawa riled. The manoeuvring went on for months, with the British, Americans, and Soviets stalling. Unfortunately, when the British pressed King to yield, offering a place on UNRRA's supplies committee and representation on the key policy committee when supplies were discussed, the prime minister agreed; he feared the ill will of the Great Powers and he had no stomach to try to bring UNRRA crashing down. Canada would give one per cent of its GNP to UNRRA in 1943 and a similar contribution in 1945, and Mike Pearson, the Canadian delegate to the relief organization, would play a major role in its deliberations.

In January 1944, Britain again displayed its disdain for Canadian autonomy, in proposing a great "imperial bloc". The British ambassador to the United States, Lord Halifax, advanced the idea in a speech in Toronto. Halifax foretold a postwar world where China, the Soviet Union, and the United States would be unquestioned Great Powers. Britain could not be a Great Power on her own, he said, so the dominions had to band with her to help keep her in the forefront.

Outraged by this speech, the prime minister squashed Halifax's request. In an address in the House of Commons, King asked how Canada, located as she was between the U.S. and the U.S.S.R. and at the same time a member of the Commonwealth, could support such an idea. The proposal, he said, "runs counter to the establishment of effective world security, and therefore is opposed to the true interests

Mackenzie King was not greatly admired by Canadians, not even by those who voted for him. But he won British regard for the way he created Canada's massive war effort, and when he went to Britain for a 1944 Prime Ministers' Meeting he had Canada's huge contribution to the war to bolster his arguments for more recognition.

of the Commonwealth itself." The only possible course for Canada was in a regional or global scheme of international security, a United Nations. The same points were made to Churchill and the dominion prime ministers at the Commonwealth Prime Ministers' Conference in London in May 1944. "We should not forget," said Mackenzie King, "that a major lesson of this war is the truth that the seas do not divide and that the peace and prosperity of the world are indivisible." Canada would not accept a plan that labelled

THE PROVINCES

The North

No region of Canada had been more transformed by the war than the North. Construction of the "Crimson Route" had spotted northern Quebec, Labrador, and the eastern Arctic with airfields used by newly built aircraft to fly from American factories to Allied users. In peacetime, linking Edmonton and Fairbanks, Alaska, by road would have remained a pipedream; but the war had brought thousands of U.S. army engineers and civilian contract labourers to northern Alberta, British Columbia, and the Yukon to build the Alaska Highway. Crude oil brought from Norman Wells by the Canol Pipeline would be refined at Whitehorse to fuel highway traffic.

Just how perilous the Alaska Highway actually was had to be hidden as a war secret. Ottawa later got the blame for letting it go to rack and ruin—but that was more or less how it had been when Canada inherited it in 1945. As for the Canol line, it was simply abandoned as an economic folly. Yet for all these assets, Ottawa grimly paid Washington's price. The U.S. had yet to recognize Canada's Arctic sovereignty; there must be no excuse for a lingering American presence.

The wartime highways and airfields that opened the North also revived old dreams of mineral wealth. As headquarters for the vast Alaska Highway enterprise, Whitehorse replaced Dawson as the administrative centre for the Yukon. Wartime experience inspired plans for further roads, from Dawson Creek to Prince George, for example, or from Grimshaw to Great Slave Lake.

Meanwhile, northern communities like Yellowknife would depend on tugs and barges in the summer and "Cat trains" in winter, with four or five sleigh "box-cars" and a caboose for the five-man crew hauled by a Caterpillar tractor. Supplies cost $10 a hundredweight by Cat, a dollar a pound by air, and $4 a hundredweight by barge.

With no u-boats to threaten them, ocean-going ships once again docked at Churchill in 1945. The Hudson's Bay Route Association renewed its efforts to get more substantial imports than Scotch whisky and English toffee on the inbound journey. If the government used patrol planes to spot ice, would marine insurers allow Churchill more than a two-month season?

Developing the North had always pitted dreamers against cost accountants. The war had given dreamers money for almost anything they could promise. An affluent postwar Canada could afford most of the consequences.

the Commonwealth a single power, with the dominions represented in the councils of the great by Britain. Such schemes, reeking of the days before the Great War, would only encourage American isolationism, and that had destroyed the League of Nations and led to war in 1939; the same mistake could not be made again. The Churchillian scheme was dead and buried.

The functional principle, not the imperial principle, was the Canadian way. The nation that had entered the war as an autonomous dominion that still thought and acted much like a colony had been turned into a middle power, and the leader in defining just what that term meant and might mean. The test would be to convert this new status into a proper place in the United Nations and the postwar world.

———

Canada had some cards to play. The war had ended the Depression and the country was rich with jobs for all who wanted to work.

The factories and farms had produced vast quantities of goods—Canadian war production had amounted to 10 per cent of British Commonwealth production. And with a million men and women under arms, Canada had done its share and more of fighting and winning the war. All this justified the claim to be a middle power. Unfortunately, as the long and difficult negotiations to create the new United Nations demonstrated, Canada's claims were not given much weight by the Great Powers. The United States, the Soviet Union, Britain, and China had their own interests to serve.

What Canada wanted was a new world body to replace the defunct League of Nations, but including the United States. Although it was a member of the British Commonwealth, Canada must have independent representation in its own right— and this time it would use it. Moreover, the functional principle demanded that Canada's special strengths be recognized by inclusion in any U.N. bodies designed to deal with subjects in which Canada had particular interest or involvement. No one was rash enough to suggest that Canada attempt to take the lead in postwar organization; that would have been far beyond Ottawa's capacity. On the other hand, Canada could no longer automatically accept whatever London or Washington wanted.

But the Great Powers still intended to shape the United Nations to suit their own concerns. At the Dumbarton Oaks meeting in September 1944, wholly unacceptable proposals emerged. The Security Council of the U.N. was to have all Great Powers represented—pleasing Ottawa, which desperately wanted the powerful states to be in the new U.N. from the outset. The difficulty was that non-permanent members were to be elected by the General Assembly, where Latin and South American states that had played little or no part in the war could form half the Assembly and possibly latch onto half the Security Council's non-permanent slots. Another problem was that the U.N. was intended to be a collective security organization, one that could wage war against aggressor states. "The central Canadian difficulty," one senior diplomat wrote, "will arise from the imposition of permanent and indefinite obligations which might, in the extreme case, require Canada by order of a Council on which Canada was not represented, to impose heavy burdens on the Canadian people." Sir Robert Borden in 1919 had fought against Article X of the League of Nations covenant, which imposed collective security obligations on Canada. The King government in the 1920s, like Sir Wilfrid Laurier's during the South African War, had resisted British efforts to commit Canada to action. Could the nation now allow a second world organization to bind the government's hands? Some Canadians even suggested organizing a boycott of the U.N. by secondary powers, an idea that went nowhere—as did Ottawa's efforts to find some way around the Dumbarton Oaks proposals.

The final attempt to win concessions from the Great Powers came at the United Nations Conference on International Organization, held at San Francisco in April 1945. The Americans, Russians, and British often seemed equally difficult, and Canada's eight pages of amendments to the Great Powers' proposals for the U.N. Charter met with heavy resistance. Still, there was some success. A clause (Article 44) was put into the Charter after strenuous Canadian efforts to ensure that non-members of the Security

The key Canadians at San Francisco were King and his justice minister and future successor, Louis St. Laurent. In the middle is CCF *leader M.J. Coldwell.*

Council would be invited to attend Council sessions discussing the use of those countries' forces. As one Canadian put it, "It is impossible for us to grant to a Council on which we may not be represented the right to order us about without our having participated in the decision." Moreover, the Canadians, their functional principle firmly in mind, had the charter drawn so that, in electing non-permanent Security Council members, "due regard" was to be paid to the "contribution of Members of the United Nations to the maintenance of international peace and security and to the other purposes of the Organization. . . ." That too seemed a victory, though Australia captured a seat in the first elections to the Security Council, not Canada. Perhaps Canada's consolation prize was that the U.N.'s International Civil Aviation Organization, which laid down the rules for international airlines, located its headquarters in Montreal.

Overall, Canada did not succeed in winning most of the points it had sought. Everyone wanted to keep the Soviet Union, still bleeding from its wartime wounds and paranoiacally suspicious about the intentions of the West, happy enough to join the U.N.— and that virtually demanded that the Great Powers' unity, hard-won at Dumbarton Oaks, not be challenged on important points.

The net effect of the long, acrimonious discussions at San Francisco was that any idealism that had survived the war was gone, at least among Canadian representatives. Great Power foreign ministers had already met to divide up Germany into occupation zones, and in their subsequent conferences they began to quarrel about everything, while lesser powers like Canada watched uneasily from outside the chamber. And always the Soviet Union seemed to take a harshly critical, deeply suspicious view of whatever the U.S. and Britain suggested.

———————

Canada had had no diplomatic relations with the Soviet Union before the Nazis invaded Russia in June 1941. Indeed, the British and their allies had all looked with extreme disfavour on Moscow, for its alliance with Germany, its share in the conquest of Poland in September 1939, and its aggressive war against Finland. But once Hitler attacked the Soviet Union, Moscow became an ally, and the democracies hastened to forge links with the Russian government and people. Canada offered such governmental aid as it could, and individuals and charities, stirred by the Russian people's vigorous resistance to the *Wehrmacht*, sent millions more dollars. Ottawa exchanged diplomatic representatives with the Soviet Union in late 1942, and Dana Wilgress, the Deputy Minister of Trade and Commerce and one who knew the U.S.S.R., became the first minister to Moscow, while the Russians sent a large team of diplomats and officials to Ottawa. In December 1943, the countries' legations were raised to the status of embassies.

Ambassador Wilgress proved a shrewd observer of the Russians. He noted the "desire of the Soviet Union for a long period of peace in order to recover from the ravages of the war," but he also understood clearly that the U.S.S.R. "will continue to represent a distinct social and economic system to that of the United States" which might "lead in the more distant future to a conflict of interests if the system of collective security does not function effectively." Those potential difficulties worried Ottawa, and studies there ranked the possibility of a Soviet–American war as unlikely but not something to be neglected. Moreover, in the event of any such war, geography left no doubt that Canada had to be on the American side from the outset. As the drafters of "Post War Defence Arrangements with the United States" noted,

> This closer tie-up with the United States need not conflict with the Canadian tradition of basing military policy and training upon British practice. However, if Canada and the United States are to be efficient in the defence of North America, common experience between the national forces will be desirable.

The Cabinet duly decided in July 1945 that defence ties with the United States had to be maintained in the peace.

The Soviet presence in Ottawa was centred on the embassy on Charlotte Street. The Soviets were allies and friends, and Canadians treated them as such. And when Moscow's ambassador said that only four countries had really fought the war—the U.S.S.R., the U.S., the U.K., and Canada—Canadians blushed prettily and agreed that it was so. For their part, the Russians threw parties where the vodka flowed freely, and occupied themselves with the usual work of diplomacy. Or so it seemed—until September 6, 1945, when Igor Gouzenko, an embassy cipher clerk, turned up at newspaper and government offices claiming to have documents proving that Soviet embassy officials were running spy rings in Canada. Poor, terrified Gouzenko was shunted from pillar to post, with no one taking his story, presented in broken English, very seriously. When word reached senior officials of this man's strange tale, the prime minister was consulted. He too wanted to do nothing, but Sir William Stephenson, the Canadian-born head of British Security Co-ordination (Britain's

Igor Gouzenko's defection with documents proving Soviet spying shook Canadians—and left Gouzenko, here with a book he later wrote, in constant fear for his life.

INDEX
Amusements—16-11 Radio—18
Births, Deaths—23 Sports—12-15
Comics—23 Want Ads—32-33
Markets—14 Women's—20-23

TORONTO DAILY STAR

54TH YEAR

Authorized as second class Mail, Post Office Department, Ottawa.

TORONTO, SATURDAY, FEBRUARY 16, 1946—34 PAGES

THE WEATHER
Toronto and vicinity: Military Sunday—Fresh northwest winds, cloudy, a little colder, snowflurries. Low tonight, 20; high tomorrow, 28.

3c PER COPY, 18c PER WEEK

40 TO 50 HELD IN SPY CASE
RUSSIA NAMED BY MINISTER

FEDERAL CIVIL SERVANTS RESEARCH MEN ACCUSED

Royal Commission Named by Premier King to Investigate and Prosecution Will Follow Where Warranted, He Says

HOME AND SPORT EDITION

PRIME MINISTER TOUCHES OFF SENSATIONAL INTRIGUE STORY

SPY HUNT MAY SPREAD TO WASHINGTON-REPORT

Hint Communist Organization May Be Involved—F.B.I. and R.C.M.P. Work Together in Round-Up of Accused

MOST SENSATIONAL story of espionage and intrigue since the end of war is touched off by Prime Minister King's announcement of the highly confidential state secrets have been disclosed to a foreign power. The prime minister, shown with Hon. George Zarubin, Soviet ambassador, and Mrs. Zarubin, consulted Truman and Bevin before making charge.

BEVIN CLASHES WITH VISHINSKY OVER LEVANT

Claims 1,700 Soviet Spies in Canada, U.S.
By DREW PEARSON
Copyright Bell Syndicate

POLISH THREAT TO YUGOSLAVIA SEEN BY RUSSIA

The heat of war had passed—but the Cold War was on.

intelligence operation in North America), was coincidentally in Ottawa on a visit, and he learned of Gouzenko. His advice was clear: "Take him." The next day, after security officials from the Soviet embassy broke into the Gouzenkos' apartment while the Gouzenkos hid themselves in a friendly neighbour's flat, the Canadians did take him. Gouzenko and his family were squirrelled away under protective custody at Camp X, a highly secret spy-training base near Oshawa, on Lake Ontario. Gouzenko's documents were translated in haste, and the prime minister learned "that everything was much worse than we would have believed. . . . They disclose an espionage system on a large scale . . . things came right into our country to a degree we could not have believed possible." There was a spy in the coding room at External Affairs, one at the British high commission, and another at the Montreal laboratory that had worked on the atomic bomb. The

Russians' espionage networks included military officers, civil servants, and a Montreal MP, Fred Rose of the Labour Progressive Party, the name adopted by the banned Communist Party during the war.

Mackenzie King was shattered by the revelations. "I think of the Russian Embassy being only a few doors away," he wrote in his diary, "and of there being there a centre of intrigue. During this period of war, while Canada has been helping Russia and doing all we can . . . there has been . . . spying. . . ." Canada had fought the war believing that its allies were united in the cause; now that was seen to be the most utter naivety. Moreover, the government had assumed that its own officials and officers were united by a shared belief in democracy, and that only the lightest internal security was therefore necessary.

Marxist ideology had been shown to be strong enough to divert Canadians from their loyalty to the state, and this realization soon led to a system of security checks, to the limiting of information to those with a "need to know", and to the strengthening of the RCMP's role in the protection of the state. The Examination Unit, the secret wireless interception team built up during the war to listen in on enemy communications, was to have been shut down before the end of 1945; instead it was strengthened and its targets became the U.S.S.R. and the countries within its sphere of influence, soon to be labelled "satellites".

King and Roosevelt

The two political leaders who led Canada and the United States were a study in contrasts. Mackenzie King was a short, stocky man with a boring speaking style and the charisma of a turnip. Franklin Roosevelt, though crippled by polio, was a big man with enough personal appeal to light up the entire United States with a single smile and a wave of his jaunty cigarette holder. Yet the two men were friendly, if not friends, and they had an evident respect for each other's skills as politicians. Just as dogs sniff each other out, so these two politicians had taken each other's measure and found much to admire.

Though they had met several times before 1939, it was the war that forced them together in their nations' self-interest. Roosevelt guaranteed Canada's safety in the face of Axis victories by proposing the Permanent Joint Board on Defence in August 1940, and he saved the dominion's economic bacon by accepting King's financial proposals at Hyde Park in April 1941. King yielded to Roosevelt's entreaties in early 1942 and allowed the U.S. to build the Alaska Highway through the Yukon and Northwest Territories so that Alaska could be defended more easily. All these measures increased the potential for American economic and military dominance over Canada, as King realized, and though the prime minister trusted Roosevelt, who could say how his successors might behave? At war's end, therefore, every U.S. installation in Canada was purchased at full value, to eliminate any lingering claims.

Still, when King was in trouble over conscription in November 1944, he sent General Maurice Pope to see the president, not to ask for anything directly, but simply to apprise the American of the situation. As Pope wrote to King, the president "would be glad to be of any possible help to you in the psychological field." Later Pope recollected that Roosevelt had muttered something inaudible when he delivered the message, but then "visibly drew back . . . and said aloud, 'But no, that's operational.'" There were limits, in other words: Roosevelt's desire to help his neighbour could not lead him to intervene in strictly military matters.

Roosevelt did not survive the war. When King heard of his death on April 12, 1945, his reaction was revealing: "I seemed too exhausted and fatigued to feel any strong emotion. It all seemed like part of the heavy day's work. Just one more fact." The effect of the war on the two leaders had been immense, a slow, grinding concern that had eroded their reserves of strength. That King, who was eight years older, survived until July 22, 1950, was a testament to his extraordinary constitution.

Cautious, shrewd, and prudent, Mackenzie King inspired little admiration in most of his countrymen. Canada's real war leaders, the press argued, were Franklin Roosevelt and Winston Churchill, here with King at Washington in 1942—sentiments that rightly infuriated King.

The Gouzenko affair led to widespread arrests, with prisoners held incommunicado, a royal commission investigation, and a series of widely publicized and sensational trials. It led to the sharing of information and the co-ordination of tactics with Britain and the United States; officials of both nations were named in Gouzenko's documents or in the course of his interrogation. Astonishingly, Moscow admitted that it had run spies from its embassy, though the Soviets said the information obtained "did not, however, present great interest for the Soviet organization . . . in view of the more advanced technical attainment in the U.S.S.R." Poor backward Canada apparently had few secrets that would interest a sophisticated state like the U.S.S.R.

The impact of the case was enormous. Public opinion became increasingly suspicious of domestic Communists. Fifty-two per cent of Canadians claimed to hold a dark view of the U.S.S.R. in early 1946, after the spy case hit the press, while only 17 per cent expressed any sympathy; a large majority supported the government's actions in handling the arrested and suspected spies. In London, where the Gouzenko revelations had been followed closely, they played a part in shaping one of the seminal addresses of the era, Winston Churchill's "Iron Curtain" speech in early 1946. Washington too was very nervous, because Alger Hiss, a senior State Department official, and Harry Dexter

The fear created by the awful power of nuclear weapons was profound. Warfare had been changed forever, but for the first time the prospects of survival for the civil population—in caves or out—seemed in jeopardy.

White, the key official in the Treasury Department, had been fingered by Gouzenko. Even if the Gouzenko case did not single-handedly start the Cold War, it undoubtedly helped create the conviction that the U.S.S.R. was transforming itself from wartime ally into postwar enemy. Hitler was gone, but Stalin remained.

For the Canadian government, the spy

case left only apprehension. An American embassy diplomat reported that "the Canadians are like the brave little boy who has talked back to the bully and is wondering what is going to happen to him." That was understandable.

The global stakes had been raised by the harnessing of nuclear power, and the devastation of Hiroshima and Nagasaki showed the overwhelming might of the new weapon. The Soviets, shut out of the huge Allied research effort to develop the atomic bomb, had used spies to speed up their own wartime research. Their espionage had included successful efforts to penetrate the subsidiary Canadian research program at McGill University, and purloined samples of bomb-making uranium had been smuggled to the U.S.S.R. The "secret" of the bomb and huge stocks of the uranium needed to build it were in Canadian hands.

Despite the insecurity of the times, however, the Canadian government resisted the temptation to arm itself with nuclear bombs; it would use its nuclear know-how for peaceful benefits instead. A reactor known as ZEEP (Zero Energy Experimental Pile) was up and running at Chalk River, Ontario, soon after the end of the war, and "the secret of the sun", as the newspapers called it, soon would be used to heat Canadian homes.

———— • ✦ • ————

The Canadian government had conducted the country's foreign policy with confidence. Did they have the support of their people for their actions that aimed at enhancing Canada's place in the grand

ZEEP was followed in 1947 by NRX—National Research Experimental—a versatile and sophisticated research reactor.

Code-Breakers

Canada was slow to get involved in the electronic spying that characterized the Second World War. There had been some amateurish efforts to follow German and Japanese communications from the outset of the war, but not until 1941 did Canada begin to play an important part. Then the Department of External Affairs created the ambiguously named Examination Unit, and carefully hid its budget in the estimates for the National Research Council. The unit worked on code-breaking, initially trying—successfully—to crack the coded messages sent from the Vichy France legation in Ottawa to Paris. The Vichy administration was too close to the Nazis, there were concerns its diplomats were stirring up trouble in Quebec, and the Vichy-controlled islands of St. Pierre and Miquelon, off Newfoundland, were perilously close to the North Atlantic convoy routes; in short, there was every reason to keep a sharp eye on the legation. The unit's efforts also focused on Japanese and German codes, in close co-operation with the British and Americans, and it operated a secret wireless system called "Hydra" from Camp X, a heavily secured base on Lake Ontario.

By VJ Day the unit was scheduled to be wound down, as its work was completed. But early in September Igor Gouzenko defected from the Russian embassy in Ottawa, carrying documents that proved the Soviet Union had spy rings in Canada. Gouzenko helped to change Canada's trusting attitudes to the Russians, and the Examination Unit continued and expanded its work, but with a new target.

---

alliance against Hitler? The only possible answer is yes and no.

The Canadian on the street was much less sure about the country's place in the world than were foreign observers and Canadian diplomats. Opinion polls demonstrated repeatedly that Quebeckers wanted Canada to have an independent, if very modest, policy in world affairs—much more so than English-speaking Canadians, who in large numbers still yearned for an imperial bloc as a counterpoise to Russia and the United States. Strongly anti-Communist, Quebec was always also much more suspicious of the Soviet Union and its intentions than was the rest of Canada, and was less enthusiastic about the prospects for the United Nations. In other words, Quebec remained almost as isolationist as it had ever been, a position that was regularly reflected in newspapers such as Montreal's nationalist *Le Devoir* and in the speeches of Bloc Populaire spokesmen like Maxime Raymond. Gouzenko's revelations of Moscow's espionage confirmed Quebec in its militant anti-Communism, and in its view that the only part of the world that mattered was Canada.

The Gouzenko case and the birth of the atomic age did not have immediate implications for Canadian defence. The pre-war military had been tiny—the permanent force in 1939 had consisted of just 450 officers and 4,000 men!—and the senior officers who had led the huge armed forces during the war had no intention of seeing Canada sink back into complete unpreparedness. Surely the war proved the folly of that? Surely the Soviet intransigence, espionage, and threat-making demonstrated that caution was required?

Perhaps. But the King government had no special admiration for senior officers and their views, and there was little sign that the public had much interest in anything other than the quickest possible return to a free and easy Civvy Street.

Moreover, the government's confidence in the military's good sense was badly shaken by the army's effort to secure peacetime conscription in late 1945, a move that demonstrated utter remoteness from political reality. Universal military service for men at eighteen was a European concept that had few supporters in Canada, and after

the troubles over wartime conscription in 1917, 1942, and 1944, no politician—and certainly not Mackenzie King—would touch it. The result was that demobilization proceeded at full speed, the great wartime army melting away, the air force shrinking, the navy selling off ships to the scrapyards much faster than it had ever been able to put them to sea. The army's peacetime regular-force component, now simply the "Canadian

The Alaska Highway—built by U.S. Army engineers at a crash pace in 1942, when a Japanese attack seemed likely—provided a secure land route between Alaska and North-West Canada. The Americans poured in men and machines and altered the landscape permanently. Canada took over the highway at war's end.

Army", was to have a strength of 25,000, with its sole operational element the Mobile Striking Force, a brigade group intended to be capable of reacting to enemy lodgements on Canadian territory. The reserve force optimistically was to number 180,000— enough for six divisions, four brigades, and enough supplementary units to provide an army of two corps, much as during the war. Unlike the wartime army, however, this was all paper. The air force's strength was fixed at 16,000 regulars and an auxiliary of 4,500, organized in fifteen auxiliary and eight regular squadrons. The navy's strength was set at 10,000, with two aircraft carriers, two cruisers, and ten or twelve destroyers. That was a virtual armada compared to the RCN of 1939, but it was a far cry from the peak wartime navy. Defence links with the United States were renewed in 1947, and there were pledges of standardization of arms and

As the Soviet nuclear threat increased, Canada and the U.S. co-operated in building the Distant Early Warning (DEW) line—a chain of twenty-two radar stations stretching across 5,000 miles of the Arctic.

equipment. There were even annual exercises in the Arctic to test equipment. "We all know," one Cabinet minister said in late 1945, "that invasion of North America, if and when, will come from the north. . . . We have to be ready . . . to be able to live, travel and fight in the cold."

Canada was not ready. With an authorized strength of approximately 50,000 for all three services—five times the pre-war strength—the military prepared desultorily for the Cold War. Training was rudimentary, wartime equipment was ageing, and morale was frail, as might have been expected of a force without a clear mission. There were strikes (ominously called mutinies by some alarmed admirals) on RCN ships, apparently a reaction to poor pay and to the dictatorial Royal Navy style affected by some officers; the army's training had not progressed much beyond company level; and the RCAF was slow to move into the jet age. (Its fighter squadrons flew wartime Mustangs—on weekends—until December 1948, when regular-force pilots began training on Vampire jet fighters.) Canada's entry into the North Atlantic Treaty Organization (an alliance for the mutual defence of Western Europe and North America that Canadian diplomats had played a major role in creating) in April 1949 was one sure sign that rearmament was coming.

The real spur to the postwar military was the outbreak of war in Korea on June 25, 1950. Canada sent destroyers, air transport squadrons, and a brigade of infantry to Korea, and—for fear that Korea presaged a Soviet attack on Europe—an air division of interceptors and a strong infantry brigade group went to Europe, beginning in 1951. The Cold War had finally hit home, and expenditures and personnel strength rose dramatically. The defence budget in 1949, $361 million, escalated to $1.9 billion in 1953, 7.6 per cent of the GNP; over the same period, the strength of the forces increased from 41,676 in 1949 (significantly under the authorized ceiling) to 104,400 in 1953.

Barely five years after the end of the Second World War, Canadian troops were in action again, though the Korean War was much different from the earlier conflict. This was a war nominally run by the United Nations, and one with strictly limited aims. The Canadian commitment was also less than whole-hearted, and Ottawa fretted about the United States' impatience with the conflict and sought to work at the U.N. for a negotiated settlement. Washington was not always

The Korean War, which began in June 1950, was the first United Nations war. Even so, a reluctant Canada participated primarily because the United States wanted it to do so.

happy with the tactics of its Canadian friends.

Meanwhile, Canadian foreign policy was undergoing change. In September 1946, Mackenzie King gave up the post of Secretary of State for External Affairs, which he had held for all the years he had been prime minister. To take his place King chose Louis St. Laurent, a Quebec City corporation lawyer who had entered the government as Minister of Justice and as Ernest Lapointe's replacement at the end of 1941. Fluently bilingual, intelligent, decisive, and a man of principle, St. Laurent had intended to leave politics soon after the end of the war, but King persuaded him to remain with the offer of External Affairs and an implicit suggestion that even higher office might follow. At the same time, Lester Pearson, the ambassador in Washington, became under-secretary, the senior official post in the department. Pearson was enormously affable, a charming man who let his persuasive talents camouflage his intelligence and his innate understanding of just how far his country's limited resources could be committed to costly courses of action.

The two new men were very different from Mackenzie King. Both wanted Canada to play an important role in the world and not retreat into its pre-war isolationism. Pearson was adventurous, sometimes almost rashly so; St. Laurent was calm and collected, but also capable of erupting in anger. Unlike most of his compatriots in Quebec, he understood that Canada could not retreat out of world affairs—the atomic bomb, the development of long-range aircraft, and the Soviet Union's efforts at subversion made that impossible. For the next two years, he and Pearson worked together closely, and significantly changed Canada's foreign policy. And when St. Laurent succeeded King as prime minister in late 1948, Pearson replaced him as Minister of External Affairs.

Mackenzie King remained fundamentally suspicious of the world, always wary of foreign entanglements that could divide Canadians, but St. Laurent and Pearson had few such worries. The Second World War had proved that Canada could play its role with great effect, and they wanted it to continue to do so. As St. Laurent phrased it in a lecture he delivered in 1947 at the University of Toronto, the growth of the foreign service during the war had been "a natural development. We are preparing ourselves to fulfil the growing responsibilities in world affairs which we have accepted as a modern state."

He carefully added that he was not proposing to have Canada turn its back on Britain and the Commonwealth. Nonetheless, the country was also committed to the United Nations for "constructive purpose[s]", and as a middle power Canada had to associate with others to be able to exercise any influence. Moreover, Canada had to work with the United States in this new postwar world, and he left the clear implication that this was now Canada's single most important relationship. As he put it, carefully but correctly, "There is little point in a country of our stature recommending international action, if those who must carry the major burden of whatever action is taken are not in sympathy."

St. Laurent's lecture was a clarion call for Canada to accept international commitments and seize the opportunity to play its proper role in the world. As John Holmes, a senior diplomat and distinguished academic, would later put it, the war had changed Canada from a timid, isolationist state into a "moderate mediatory middle power". For those who remembered the Canada of the low-spirited and mean-minded pre-war days, this was a major advance.

CHAPTER NINE

THE WAR THAT CHANGED EVERYTHING

Canadians must be one of the few peoples in the world who have a benign memory of the Second World War. A conflict that devastated two continents and killed 30 million left Canada and its neighbour the two richest countries in the world. That wealth and how Canadians used it transformed their lives and their country.

A S THEIR MEMORIES OF THE hostilities and sacrifices faded, Canadians came to have almost a trivial memory of a war in which most of them had gained more than they had lost. In 1919 it had been different. Apart from Newfoundland, which had commemorated the Great War by giving itself a university, most communities built themselves conventional war memorials, sometimes purchased from catalogues furnished by American travelling salesmen, and often with a German war trophy stationed in front. The ultimate war monument, the national cenotaph in Ottawa, had been unveiled by the king and queen in 1939, months before the outbreak of a second and even greater war. Perhaps it was symbolic—certainly it was realistic—that municipal councils moved their post-1945 memorializing in more practical directions. The Depression and the war had left communities with obvious needs and a deep sense that money was not to be wasted on artistic frills. Almost always there was some way of adding "1939–1945" to the existing cross of sacrifice or plinth at minimum cost; then the community could benefit from anything from a new hockey arena to a new hospital. The tiny Toronto suburb of Mimico immediately began planning the swimming pool that would launch a number of world champions. Prairie communities started erecting the curling rinks where they would store their wheat in times of glut. In British Columbia, Victoria announced that its memorial would be a $215,000 arena, while Vancouver would have a civic auditorium neatly combined with a rehabilitation centre and suburban Kitsilano would have a $25,000 combination swimming pool, library, recreation room, and gymnasium. It seemed that postwar Canada wanted no new monuments to heroic sacrifice.

It had been a good war for the world because, on the whole, good had triumphed over evil. No one could argue that Stalin was a defender of freedom, democracy, and the rights of small nations. But the struggle between democracy and fascism was, quite literally, a struggle between light and darkness. Hitler's Third Reich had invaded Austria, Czechoslovakia, Poland, Denmark, Norway, The Netherlands, Belgium, France, Yugoslavia, Greece, and the Soviet Union. Had Britain not kept its fleet intact and its air force battling in the skies, Hitler's armies would have invaded England. North America could eventually have been next. Mussolini had supported Hitler's conquests and tried for his own, though with less success. Japan's corporate and military elite had given Hitler his greatest ally in world conquest. Its powerful army, navy, and air force had ravaged China and seized every British, French, Dutch, and American colony it could reach.

For centuries, nations had invaded their neighbours with cruelty and without provocation, but behind Hitler's steel-helmeted legions rode an army of bureaucrats with plans to exploit the conquered people for Germany's Nazi elite. Close behind the soldiers came the Gestapo and the ss extermination squads, with orders to rid Europe of those whom the Nazis decreed to be *Untermenschen*—Jews, gypsies, Slavs, homosexuals, the disabled, the mentally disturbed. Initially, the squads merely shot their victims. When that proved inefficient, Nazi officials ordered more concentration camps, and gas chambers. Men, women, and children were crammed in until the weak vanished under foot, only to be asphyxiated by poison gas. Giant gas ovens destroyed the corpses. Engineers devised ways to collect gold fillings from calcified corpses, and to keep molten grease from the bodies from dousing the burners. Was this a regime with which Britain and Canada could have made peace? Or was peace possible with Imperial Japan? After its troops had destroyed their enemies and imprisoned the survivors (including 1,500 Canadians) in bestial conditions, the killing went on. For its "Greater East Asia Co-Prosperity Sphere", Japan slaughtered millions of Chinese, Filipinos, and other Asians. This was no war of liberation, but an imperial conquest as cruel and arrogant as any in recorded history.

For all their faults, Canada and its allies had no real alternative to fighting the Axis. Their shame was that it took them so long to draw a line and defend it. Perhaps it was the

VE Day found Mackenzie King and Louis St. Laurent at the San Francisco Conference that was creating the United Nations. The two broadcast home to Canadians, praising their efforts in the field and at home. The terrible irony—that a new "cold" war was already taking shape as Hitlerism crumbled into dust—had just begun to dawn on Canada's leaders.

wrong line in the wrong place, but the alternatives remain almost unthinkable. No one, winner or loser, fights a war with clean hands, perfect foresight, and a balanced sense of justice. Even a good war has terrible moments, such as the firestorms of Hamburg, Dresden, Tokyo, and Nagoya, and the nuclear devastation of Hiroshima and Nagasaki, with the unexpected collateral horror of radiation sickness.

If ever a war had to be won, it was the Second World War. Had the Allies lost the war, the world would not look the way it does today. The revisionists would not have had to wait fifty years to revive the nightmare of Hitlerism.

———————

And it was, on the whole, a good war for Canada. The country emerged richer, more powerful, more outward-looking, than anyone could have imagined in 1939. Wartime taught most Canadians what they could accomplish when they worked together as a people, and memories of that lesson would last for at least another decade.

It was not good for everyone, of course. A wiser people would have found better ways to spend $13 billion than on tanks and bombers and artillery shells, and on putting a million people into uniform and sending them to die. One of them, a brilliant student killed over Germany in 1942, inspired his professor, Lorne Morgan, to write his passionate essay, "Homo the Sap". What else could you call people, Morgan asked, who failed to find peacetime work for a fine young man but created the finest aeronautical technology to send him to kill and be killed? In all, 42,042 Canadians died on active service, sometimes in terrible deaths. Another 54,414 suffered wounds or injuries. Many lost limbs, suffered hideous disfigurement, or came home hopelessly damaged in mind or body.

The war was, on the whole, a tragic period for almost 22,000 Japanese Canadians, though their dispersion across Canada enriched the country and conveyed the most effective lesson other Canadians ever received on their old and besetting sin of racism.

In law, the country that went to war in 1939 was a fully sovereign nation, an autonomous member of the British Commonwealth. In fact, Canadians remained psychological colonials. Emotional ties to Britain, not hatred of Hitler, drew Canada into the war. Those who blame the war on appeasement should know that Canada was an eager, if silent, appeaser. Its reward for the 60,000 dead of the Great War had been membership in the League of Nations and its agencies, but Canada had played a meagre role. Its League delegate in 1923, Raoul Dandurand, had proclaimed that Canada was "a fire-proof house, far from inflammable materials". From 1919, Canadian politicians and officials had resisted any commitment to collective security under the League's Covenant. Whatever feeble pressure Canada exerted in the late 1930s had favoured appeasement of the European dictators.

Here too the war changed everything. Canada's astonishing war effort laid the groundwork for a new identity. A country of 11,507,000 people became a major military power, with the world's third-largest navy and fourth-largest air force, and an overseas field army of five divisions and two armoured brigades, with the reserve manpower to keep them in action. In view of this, and the country's immense industrial and agricultural contribution to the Allied war effort, the Great Powers had to listen when Canada spoke. And Canada, at last, had something to say.

The war cost Canada the off-shore power and influence of Britain. It left Canadians themselves to preserve the frail distinctions that set them apart from the behemoth to the south. Could Canada keep its sovereignty if its territory was an outwork of Fortress America? By 1948, the country that feared commitments and condemned collective security was pressing the nations of the North Atlantic for a treaty to link them in a common system of defence. When the North Atlantic Treaty Organization was formed, one of its Canadian architects, Escott Reid, called it "our providential solution". When North Korea hurled its forces against South Korea in 1950, Canada was among the first to respond to a U.N. call for help; its warships, aircraft, and a brigade of troops served under United Nations command. In 1951, another brigade and the first of twelve fighter squadrons went to Europe as part of a promise to NATO's new commander, General Dwight Eisenhower. Such bold commitments would have been inconceivable to Canadians fifteen years before. Seemingly, the war had taught them a lesson: unpreparedness and weak resolve benefit none but aggressor states and unprincipled dictators.

The heritage of the war, mixed with postwar prosperity made Canada very different from what it had been before. After 1945, it was a land of both opportunity and security. Steady growth in output, productivity, and purchasing power seemed to promise that there would always be more. There was also unprecedented protection from the economic catastrophes of life: poverty, sickness, unemployment. The combination made people both more optimistic and compassionate than they had ever been. It was harder to believe that there were too many spoons for the soup.

Until the 1940s, Canada had been a poor country, with much of the meanness poverty tends to induce. Pre-war Canadians often knew little beyond their own districts and neighbourhoods, which were small, largely homogeneous, and exclusive. There was usually no room in them for Japanese or Chinese Canadians, and scant tolerance for Jews or blacks or those with "different" attitudes or beliefs. Minorities did not have to be visible to suffer the lash of discrimination: French Canadians, Catholics, and Ukrainians felt it whenever they ventured beyond the regions and social classes where circumstances or history had made them a majority. So did English Canadians, though usually more discreetly. Immigrants, whatever their origins, often ran into barriers of contempt and hatred. Even the wealthy, living in the midst of poverty, were more timid, more afraid of change, and socially conservative than their affluent descendants would be.

The war softened such attitudes. Human rights legislation, a response to the Holocaust, originally targeted anti-Semitism, but inevitably it broadened to fight all forms of discrimination. The undermining of grosser forms of prejudice benefited the flood of postwar immigrants who reached Canada's shores from Europe. Eventually even the old barriers to immigration from Asia, the West Indies, and Africa collapsed.

Affluence offered Canadians and immigrants alike a new social and physical mobility, as homes and cars became attainable. An automotive industry that had mechanized most of the British army could put almost every Canadian family behind the wheel and send them, if they wanted, from inner-city slums to the new suburbs of Scarborough, the South Shore, or Burnaby, where home ownership and a new middle class and consumer-driven conformity awaited. Canada loosened up, lightened up, and became a kinder, gentler place.

For some Canadians, of course, the war made almost everything worse. Who can ever assess the loss? Someone who failed to return might have found a cure for cancer, written the great Canadian novel, or led us all to a better life. Children grew up without fathers; adults suffered losses they would bear for the rest of their lives. Men and women, not frozen statistics, paid a terrible price for a better Canada. Canadians must never forget those who paid in full for all we gained. It makes those gains even more worth defending.

To the Next of Kin of:
B/11210 Private Norman Clifford Jenner

This commemorates the gratitude of the Government and people of Canada for the life of a brave man freely given in the service of his Country. His name will ever be held in proud remembrance.

July 20th 1944   Minister of National Defence.

Private Norman Jenner of the Toronto Scottish was born in 1920, married in 1941, and had a son soon after. He was killed in action near Caen on July 20, 1944, one of more than 42,000 Canadians who died to defeat Nazism.

FURTHER READING

THIS BRIEF LISTING IS BY NO means comprehensive, and is intended only to point readers towards some readily accessible literature. The volume of writing on Canada's role in the Second World War has grown substantially in the last few years, thanks in large part to the spurt in interest caused by the fiftieth-anniversary commemorations gracing the years from 1989 to 1995, and to the furor caused by the television series "The Valour and the Horror".

For broad overviews of the war and immediate postwar years and of Canadian military history, readers should use Robert Bothwell *et al.*, *Canada, 1900–1945* and *Canada since 1945* (Toronto: University of Toronto Press, 1987, 1989), and Desmond Morton, *A Military History of Canada* (Toronto: McClelland & Stewart, 1992).

On the wartime armed forces, there is a substantial body of work. Even so, there is no complete modern history of the Royal Canadian Navy's role in the war. The best study is Marc Milner, *North Atlantic Run: The Royal Canadian Navy and the Battle for the Convoys* (Toronto: University of Toronto Press, 1985), a thorough look at the problems that beset the senior service. Also very helpful are two books of papers on RCN history: J.A. Boutilier, ed., *The RCN in Retrospect, 1910–1968* (Vancouver: University of British Columbia Press, 1982), and W.A.B. Douglas, ed., *The RCN in Transition, 1910–1985* (Vancouver: University of British Columbia Press, 1988).

Two volumes in the Royal Canadian Air Force's official history cover the war. W.A.B. Douglas, *The Creation of a National Air Force* (Toronto: University of Toronto Press, 1968), treats the RCAF role at home and the British Commonwealth Air Training Plan. Brereton Greenhous *et al.*, *The Crucible of War, 1939–1945* (Toronto: University of Toronto Press, 1994), examines the air force's role abroad, focusing on policy, the bomber offensive, fighters, air transport, and maritime air activities. Less argumentative about the RCAF role in bombing Germany is Spencer Dunmore and William Carter, *Reap the Whirlwind* (Toronto: McClelland & Stewart, 1991), a study of the RCAF's No. 6 Group.

The Official History of the Canadian Army in the Second World War (Ottawa: Queen's Printer, 1955–1960) is a model of what history can and should be—judicious, balanced, honest. There are three volumes: C.P. Stacey, *Six Years of War*, which considers the home front, the Dieppe raid, and Hong Kong;

G.W.L. Nicholson, *The Canadians in Italy, 1943–1945*; and Stacey, *The Victory Campaign*, an examination of operations in North-West Europe. Stacey also wrote *Arms, Men and Governments: The War Policies of Canada, 1939–1945* (Ottawa: Queen's Printer, 1970), arguably the best single volume on Canada's war.

There are too many books on aspects of army operations and personnel for this brief note to cover them all. Meriting notice are Terry Copp and Bill McAndrew, *Battle Exhaustion: Soldiers and Psychiatrists in the Canadian Army, 1939–1945* (Montreal: McGill-Queen's University Press, 1990), and Daniel Dancocks, *The D-Day Dodgers: The Canadians in Italy, 1943–1945* (Toronto: McClelland & Stewart, 1991). Copp also wrote *The Brigade* (Stoney Creek, Ont.: Fortress, 1992), a study of the Fifth Canadian Infantry Brigade of the 2nd Division from its formation through to its disbandment after much fighting in North-West Europe. Brigadier-General W. Denis Whitaker and Shelagh Whitaker published the impressive *Rhineland* (Toronto: Stoddart, 1989), on the First Canadian Army's battle to end the war, while another wartime officer, Jeffery Williams, treated the whole Canadian effort after Normandy in *The Long Left Flank: The Hard Fought Way to the Reich, 1944–1945* (Toronto: Stoddart, 1988). A useful memoir of the Italian campaign is Fred Cederberg, *The Long Road Home* (Toronto: General, 1985).

There are countless biographies and autobiographies of soldiers, sailors, and airmen, far too many to list here. Readers should be aware that there are biographies of Generals A.G.L. McNaughton, Guy Simonds, Harry Foster, F.F. Worthington, and George Pearkes, memoirs by Generals E.L.M. Burns, Maurice Pope, George Kitching, and Chris Vokes, and a collective biography of Canadian senior officers—J.L. Granatstein, *The Generals* (Don Mills, Ont.: Stoddart, 1993). Strangely, there are no memoirs or biographies by or about wartime senior air or naval officers. One RCAF memoir regrettably remains one of the great unknown books on the war and must be noted. Murray Peden, *A Thousand Shall Fall* (Stittsville, Ont.: Canada's Wings, 1979), is a superb and moving account of one pilot's wartime experiences.

A basic source in four volumes for all aspects of the war and postwar years is J.W. Pickersgill, *The Mackenzie King Record* (Toronto: University of Toronto Press, 1960–70), an edited version of Mackenzie King's extraordinary and voluminous diary. There are histories of the CCF aplenty, but only one study of the Liberal Party—Reg Whitaker, *The Government Party* (Toronto: University of Toronto Press, 1977)—and only one on the Conservatives—Granatstein, *The Politics of Survival* (Toronto: University of Toronto Press, 1967). There are many widely available biographies and memoirs of key political figures, including Cabinet ministers C.D. Howe, Chubby Power, Louis St. Laurent, Jimmy Gardiner, Brooke Claxton, Paul Martin, sometime Tory leader Arthur Meighen, and premiers such as Maurice Duplessis and Tommy Douglas. The federal bureaucracy is also well served, with books by and/or about Lester Pearson, Norman Robertson, Hugh Keenleyside, Escott Reid, and Charles Ritchie. One study that treats all the wartime civil service mandarins is J.L. Granatstein, *The Ottawa Men* (Toronto: Oxford University Press, 1982). These biographies are a good way into the complex subject of wartime federal-provincial relations.

The coming of the welfare state has been covered in special issues of *The Journal of Canadian Studies* (1979, 1986); in Malcolm Taylor, *Health Insurance and Canadian Public Policy* (Montreal: McGill-Queen's University Press, 1978); and in J.L. Granatstein, *Canada's War* (Toronto: Oxford University Press, 1974). The best study of women's expanded role during the conflict is Ruth Pierson, *"They're Still Women After All": The Second World War and Canadian Womanhood* (Toronto: McClelland & Stewart, 1986). On organized labour's rise and conflicts, the starting point is Irving Abella, *Nationalism, Communism and Canadian Labour* (Toronto: University of Toronto Press, 1973). For conscription, see J.L. Granatstein and J.M. Hitsman, *Broken Promises: A History of Conscription in Canada* (Toronto: Copp Clark, 1985). The expansion of industry and Canadian economic relations with the Allies are covered well in Robert Bothwell and W. Kilbourn's biography of the "minister of everything", *C.D. Howe* (Toronto: McClelland & Stewart, 1979). Canadian wartime foreign policy is treated in detail in John English's fine biography, *Shadow of Heaven: The Life of Lester Pearson*, Vol. 1 (Toronto: Lester & Orpen Dennys, 1989). Also very useful is C.P. Stacey, *Canada and the Age of Conflict*, Vol. 2 (Toronto: University of Toronto Press, 1984). For veterans' legislation and the reintegration of veterans into Canadian society, the best studies remain Walter Woods, *Rehabilitation (A Combined Operation)* (Ottawa: Queen's Printer, 1953), and Robert England, *Discharged* (Toronto: Macmillan, 1943). Barry Broadfoot collected veterans' memories in *The Veterans' Years* (Toronto: Douglas & McIntyre, 1985).

The demobilization of the military is only now beginning to be studied in doctoral dissertations. Similarly, there is as yet no good published study of life in wartime Canada, or of the struggle of families to survive war and separation intact. For such areas, only recourse to the newspapers and magazines like *Chatelaine, Maclean's, Saturday Night*, and *The Canadian Forum* can fill the gap.

There are many studies of civil liberties during wartime. The evacuation of Japanese Canadians from the coast has received substantial attention, with Ken Adachi, *The Enemy That Never Was* (Toronto: McClelland & Stewart, 1976), and Ann Gomer Sunahara, *The Politics of Racism* (Toronto: Lorimer, 1981), being the best-researched examples. Only one book has tried to suggest that the government had some valid reasons for its actions: Patricia Roy *et al.*, *Mutual Hostages: Canadians and Japanese During the Second World War* (Toronto: University of Toronto Press, 1990). A good collection of essays on the experience of ethnic groups during the war is Norman Hillmer *et al.*, eds., *On Guard for Thee: War, Ethnicity and the Canadian State, 1939–1945* (Ottawa: Canadian Committee for the History of the Second World War, 1988). For the Jehovah's Witnesses, see William Kaplan, *State and Salvation* (Toronto: University of Toronto Press, 1989); for the government's hostile attitude to the admission of Jewish refugees from Hitler, before, during, and after the war, the best source remains Irving Abella and H. Troper, *None Is Too Many* (Toronto: Lester & Orpen Dennys, 1982).

Finally, a number of fictional accounts are well worth reading. Bruce Hutchison, *The Hollow Men* (Toronto: Longman's, 1944), follows a journalist to Ottawa and war; Ralph Allen, *The High White Forest* (Garden City, New York: Doubleday, 1964)—initially published as *Home Made Banners*—is the best treatment, fiction or fact, of the strains conscription imposed on soldiers. Colin McDougall, *Execution* (New York: St. Martin's Press, 1958), is a sensitive study of the Canadians in Italy, and Earle Birney, *Turvey* (Toronto: McClelland & Stewart, 1949), remains the great humorous novel of the Canadian army.

PICTURE CREDITS

Every reasonable effort has been made to trace the ownership of copyrighted materials. Information enabling the Publisher to rectify any reference or credit in future printings will be welcomed. For reasons of space the following abbreviations have been used:

ALB: Provincial Archives of Alberta
AO: Archives of Ontario
BC: British Columbia Archives
CBC: Canadian Broadcasting Corporation
CJC: Canadian Jewish Congress National Archives
CN: Canadian National
CT/GM: City of Toronto Archives, *Globe and Mail* Collection
CT/SC: City of Toronto Archives, Special Collection
CV: City of Vancouver Archives
CWM: Canadian War Museum
DM: Collection of Desmond Morton
GB: Glenbow Archives
JLG: Collection of J.L. Granatstein
MAN: Manitoba Provincial Archives
MTRL/BR: Metro Toronto Reference Library, Baldwin Room
MTRL/CHJ: Metro Toronto Reference Library, *Canadian Home Journal*
MTRL/PD: Metro Toronto Reference Library, Picture Dept.
NAC: National Archives of Canada
NFB: National Film Board
SASK: Saskatchewan Archives Board, University of Regina
SN: Saturday Night

Endpapers: CN (44476-1); Page 1: CV/James Crookall (260-1455); 2: CN (X-18402); 3: ALB (B1529/4); 5: courtesy Harry Tate; 6: NAC (C-87139); 8: Town of Whitby Archives (29-003-008); 8-9: NAC (C-79574); 10 (top): GB (NA-4123-1), (bottom): The Toronto Star Syndicate; 11: courtesy Mrs. W.I. Giguere; 12-13: JLG; 14: JLG; 15: MAN/Foote Coll. (N-3000); 16 (top): CV/James Crookall (260-1458), (bottom): Saint John *Telegraph Journal*, May 8, 1945; 17: NAC; 19: Dept. of Veterans' Affairs 76-35; 20: GB (NA-2574-5); 24-25: AO-2397, by permission of T. Eaton Co.; 26: NAC (C-79573); 27: AO-2398, by permission of T. Eaton Co.; 30-31: CN (X-9750); 31: NAC (PA-167205); 32: NAC (PA-107907); 33 (top): NAC (PA-108268), (bottom): NAC (PA-137795); 34: NAC (C-1700); 35 (left): NAC (PA-132779), (right): NAC (PA-132878); 36: NAC (PA-135902); 37: NAC; 38-39: NAC; 40: courtesy Canada Communication Group; 41: NAC (C-44062); 42: NAC (PL-42740); 43 (top): DM, (bottom): NAC (PL-61240); 44: NAC (PA-132720); 45: NAC (PA-140683); 47: NAC (PA-115188); 50: John Collins/*Gazette* (Montreal); 51: NAC (PA-132907); 53: MAN/Cdn. Army Photo Coll. (N-10857); 56-57: NAC; 58: MTRL/BR; 61 (top): NAC (C-24354), (bottom): *Toronto Telegram* Collection, York University Archives; 64: NAC (PA-34170); 65: DM; 66: NAC (PA-113908); 68-69: NAC (PA-108015); 70: NAC (PA-138429); 71: NAC (PA-138047); 72: NAC; 74-75: DM; 75: NAC (PA-116154); 76: MTRL/CHJ Oct. 1945, by permission of Heinz Canada Ltd.; 77: NAC (PA-108300); 78: GB (NA-4072-61); 79 (left): SASK (R-B11611), (right): MTRL/CHJ May 1943, by permission of the Sanforized Co., a Division of Cluett, Peabody & Co. Inc.; 81: GB (NA-4028-3); 82-83: SASK (R-B9393); 84: GB (NA-5104-11); 85: GB (NA-3596-172); 86: SASK (R-B12707); 88: CT/GM (66374); 89: MAN (Cdn. Army Photo Coll. 293); 90: NAC (C-29458); 91: MTRL/PD, by permission of *Maclean's* and Neil Shakery; 92: AO-2389, by permission of T. Eaton Co.; 93: MAN (N-5210); 94 (top): courtesy Leonard Staite; 95:

NAC (C-116076); 96: BC (H-5793); 97: MTRL/BR; 98-99: BC (H-5794); 100: MAN (Cdn. Army Photo Coll. 143); 101: CT/SC 488; 102: SASK (R-A21099-1); 103: courtesy Syd Charendoff; 104: NAC (C-29464); 106: GB (NA-5009-12); 107: NAC (PA-107909); 108: SN; 109: NAC (PA-107943); 112-113: NAC (PA-115236); 113: NAC (C-68676); 114: MAN (Cdn. Army Photo Coll. 207); 115: SASK (R-A7917[1]), West's Studio, Regina; 116: DM; 118: NAC (PA-128782); 119: BC (H-5795); 120: MAN/Foote Coll. (N-3010); 123: SASK (R-B2895); 124: NAC (PA-121703); 126-127: NAC (C-26110); 129: Centre de recherche Lionel-Groulx (P2/B302); 131: CT/GM (99281); 132: SN, courtesy Canada Communication Group; 134: courtesy Canada Communication Group; 135: MAN (Cdn. Army Photo Coll. 131); 138-139: GB (NA-3770-6); 139: University of Toronto Archives (A74-0008P/011(03)0008); 141: NAC (C-22715); 142: The Toronto Star Syndicate; 143: ALB (G.1293); 144: NAC (PA-114810); 145 (top): BC (H-5790), (bottom): MAN (Cdn. Army Photo Coll. 27); 147: NAC (145983); 148: NAC (PA-114811); 149: Sunnybrook Health Science Centre, courtesy Marian Lorenz; 151: NAC (PA-112367); 152: MAN (Cdn. Army Photo Coll. 212); 153: GB (NA-4987-9); 154: CN (44850); 157: NAC (PA-116096); 158-159: CT/GM (100525); 161: NAC (C-49434); 162: SN; 163: CN (X18402); 164 (top): NAC, courtesy War Amps Canada, (bottom): NAC, courtesy War Amps Canada; 165: CT/GM (102055); 166: courtesy C.A. Krause; 168: NAC (PA-112901); 169: NAC (PA-115257); 170: University of British Columbia Archives (2601); 172: NAC (C-19380); 172-173: DM; 174: MAN/Foote Coll. (N3765); 176: CT/GM (98410); 177: NAC (PA-115255); 178: DM; 179: DM; 180: SN; 183: CT/GM 100941; 184: Archives of Labor and Urban Affairs, Wayne State University; 185: Archives of Labor and Urban Affairs, Wayne State University; 186-187: NAC (PA-93845); 188: NAC; 190: DM; 191: NAC (C-53642); 192: MTRL/PD; 192-193: CJC; 194: MTRL/CHJ Dec. 1945, by permission of The Singer Company; 195 (top): CBC, (bottom): SN; 197: NAC (C-128080); 198: CWM (11356); 199: CT/GM 104294; 200: NAC (PA-115260); 201: courtesy Jack Muir; 203: NAC (C-53648); 204 (top): SN, (bottom): MTRL/CHJ Oct. 1945, by permission of Heinz Canada Ltd.; 205: NAC (PA-128763); 209: GB (NA-3369-2); 211: Town of Whitby Archives (29-003-009); 212-213: CJC (PC1-1-20B.22); 214: NAC (PA-115256); 215: NAC (C-53624); 216: NAC (PA-123476); 217: AO-2396; 218: GB (NA-3091-47); 220: CT/GM (148335); 223: NAC (PA-115243); 224-225: CT/GM (68142); 227: NAC (PA-150930); 228: NFB (C-156); 231: MTRL/BR; 232: SASK (R-B9523); 234: MTRL/BR; 235: NAC (PA-132769); 238: NAC (C-23261); 239: JLG; 240: The Toronto Star Syndicate; 241: NAC (C-16670); 242: John Collins/*Gazette* (Montreal); 243: AECL Research (13052-3); 245 (top): Yukon Archives (5675), (bottom): Yukon Archives (1498); 246: Busse/NWT Archives (N79-052:0771); 247: NAC (PA-128804); 249: MAN (Cdn. Army Photo Coll. 203); 251: NAC (C-22716); 253: courtesy Mrs. Betty Reynolds; 254: NAC (PA-129380)

Colour inserts: MTRL/BR; MTRL/BR; MTRL/BR; MTRL/BR; MTRL/CHJ (Aug. 1944); MTRL/BR; MTRL/BR; MTRL/BR; MTRL/BR; CWM (56-05-12-258); courtesy Andrew Smith; CWM (72073); CWM (11373); CWM (10160); CWM (12282); MTRL/CHJ (Dec. 1943), by permission of GSW Inc.